D1559975

I Fear I Shall Never Leave This Island

UNIVERSITY PRESS OF FLORIDA

Florida A&M University, Tallahassee
Florida Atlantic University, Boca Raton
Florida Gulf Coast University, Ft. Myers
Florida International University, Miami
Florida State University, Tallahassee
New College of Florida, Sarasota
University of Central Florida, Orlando
University of Florida, Gainesville
University of North Florida, Jacksonville
University of South Florida, Tampa
University of West Florida, Pensacola

Johnsons Island Ohio
Dec 11th/64

Dear Kate

I expect you have been disappointed about
getting your things, and have been disappointed myself
about sending them. I had expected to have sent them
some time ago, but the weather has been so bad that
we have had no express here for several days untill yesterday, and I hope I may get them started in the morning.
You will find a small box for Miss A. Stewart with
two rings and a pin in it, sent by Lt Knisely, and
another small one, sent by E. M. Stone for Mrs M. E. French
there are two crosses and a ring in it. The other two larger
boxes are yours. The box with your name on it has the things
in it I intended for Lill and you. I send you two rings a
piece, though one of yours was spoiled, and a cross for each
of you. I had the pin with the acorns on it fixed so that
you might use it to fasten your watch chain to.
The other pin, cuff buttons, and ear bobs are for you also,
though if you want any of the things in the box for
your friends you may let them have them, and if you
want any more made like any of the things I
send you, let me know and I will have them made
for you. I had the pin with the long white oval set in
it made for your lady friend you speak of. If you think
it will suit her have another pin put to it and give
it to her. Kate you still seem to be very confident about
my getting a special exchange. I hope you may not be disappointed, though I am very fearfull you will be. If I could
have been sent through to make the exchange I have no doubt
but what I could have succeeded, but have very little confidence
in what I think has been done, Give my love to all.
Yours affectionately, M. Malle

I Fear I Shall Never Leave This Island

Life in a Civil War Prison

David R. Bush

UNIVERSITY PRESS OF FLORIDA

Gainesville · Tallahassee · Tampa · Boca Raton

Pensacola · Orlando · Miami · Jacksonville · Ft. Myers · Sarasota

Frontispiece. Letter from Wesley Makely to his wife Catherine (Kate), Johnson's
Island, December 11, 1864. Courtesy of The Library of Virginia.

16   15   14   13   12   11   6   5   4   3   2   1

Library of Congress Cataloging-in-Publication Data
Makely, Wesley.
I fear I shall never leave this island : life in a Civil War prison / [edited and
annotated by] David R. Bush.
    p. cm.
Includes bibliographical references and index.
ISBN 978-0-8130-3744-8 (acid-free paper)
1. Makely, Wesley—Correspondence. 2. Johnson Island Prison. 3. Prisoners of
war—Ohio—Johnson Island—Correspondence. 4. Prisoners of war—Confederate
States of America—Correspondence. 5. United States—History—Civil War,
1861–1865—Personal narratives, Confederate. 6. Confederate States of America.
Army. Virginia Cavalry Regiment, 18th. 7. Makely, Kate—Correspondence. I. Bush,
David R. II. Title.
E616.J7M35   2011
973.7'71—dc23
2011018991

The University Press of Florida is the scholarly publishing agency for the State
University System of Florida, comprising Florida A&M University, Florida Atlantic
University, Florida Gulf Coast University, Florida International University, Florida
State University, New College of Florida, University of Central Florida, University of
Florida, University of North Florida, University of South Florida, and University of
West Florida.

University Press of Florida
15 Northwest 15th Street
Gainesville, FL 32611-2079
http://www.upf.com

To Sue, Jake, and Adam for decades of support.

Contents

Illustrations

Figures

Table

Map

Preface

I cannot imagine examining one of the carved hard rubber rings from the Johnson's Island Civil War Military Prison site without thinking about Lieutenants Robert Smith or William Peel. I also cannot imagine looking at such a ring without wondering what this piece of jewelry meant to the prisoner who last handled it on this small island just off the shores of Sandusky, Ohio, in Lake Erie. I study the photographs taken by Lieutenant Robert Smith of the 61st Tennessee Infantry and see myself looking up into what used to be the garret of Block 4, admiring how he managed to take so many photographs of fellow prisoners without notice of the guard. As Peel, Smith, and others write about failed escape attempts, I ponder how they found the necessary courage to dig tunnels from the depths of the latrines in the hopes of once again reaching the South.

The site of the Johnson's Island Civil War Military Prison is inextricably tied to the writings of those imprisoned there as well as to the artifacts we have painstakingly recovered. One cannot fully appreciate the writings, the artifacts left behind, or the site without knowledge of all three. Walking on the site brings the memories of the prisoners' and guards' writings into my consciousness. As artifacts are uncovered, their association with those who described prison experiences in letters and diaries written long ago seems evident. I am not sure one can truly experience Johnson's Island, or any other moment in history, without in some fashion transporting oneself to that location via the words and materials surrounding them.

I remember my first introduction to the Johnson's Island Prison site as an unremarkable experience. I had no great revelations, no immediate sense of stepping back in time, no context within which to process the imagery. The perimeter of the island had been developed from a 1950s land deal, which resulted in a smorgasbord of homes constructed along the lake side of the road. As I drove around the outer limits of the island, I was struck by the isolation. Perhaps it was the oversized "No

Trespassing" sign at the causeway entrance to the island, or the Confederate Cemetery tucked away behind the twentieth-century architecture, that created the sense of loneliness. Each home seemed disconnected from the next. As summer vacation homes, most were empty of family life. Possibly the sense of isolation was a result of the interior of the island appearing to consist of abandoned woods. No matter what I felt on my first visit, it was certainly not remotely comparable to the experience all prisoners had as they either got off the boat or walked across the ice and had their first view of the prison. How different the island looked back in 1862.

I think back to 1988, my first year of study of the history and archaeological record of Johnson's Island. Although I was not a prisoner, I do at times feel captured by the multiplicity of human experiences the island holds. Johnson's Island is made up of thousands of stories "told" by multitudes of prisoners and guards who resided there. This is what keeps me trapped at this site: the expectation that each trowel of soil unturned will reveal a new story about the prison experience. With each new historical document that comes to light, a new voice is offered.

How is it that the first book this archaeologist chooses to write after excavating the site for more than two decades is not solely about the archaeological record but about the human experience between a man and his wife? What is the bridge connecting the artifact that has been in the ground for almost 150 years to a prisoner forced to spend months or years far from home?

As an archaeologist I attempt to get my students to realize that each artifact excavated represents a brief moment of the entire human experience. Over the years, literally hundreds of thousands of artifacts have been excavated, and each one can be tied to one or more human activities that took place there.

The human experience can be told through artifacts, letters, pictures, and even unspoken encounters. I encourage people to come to Johnson's Island and experience for themselves the connection between the land, the artifacts, and the written word, gaining through their own contact a sense of what this place offers. Through years of excavating and researching the experiences of prisoners and guards, it occurred to me the best way to share my understanding of the Johnson's Island

Prison was to begin by sharing one of its stories. It is not the story of the most famous. It is not a story of one of the generals imprisoned on the island. It is the story of one of the thousands of officers captured in battle, coping with the stress and isolation of imprisonment.

As I contemplated which diary or set of letters to publish first, it became evident that all had their own stories to tell, although incomplete. Obviously some individuals wrote more fluently, some wrote more prolifically, some were bitter, and some found solace in their beliefs. In each document is a slice of the truth of the Johnson's Island experience. It is as true today as it was in the 1860s; people experience Johnson's Island differently.

I chose to annotate the letters of Wesley Makely and his wife Catherine (Kate) with historical and archaeological data. For me, nothing is more important than understanding the context of these letters related to Johnson's Island. Although the written record can be a powerful tool, articulation of the physical remains with the written word results in an even greater appreciation for both. In the end, the stories from Johnson's Island all speak to humanity's struggles with the treatment of prisoners-of-war.

I hope students of archaeology and history, Civil War enthusiasts, descendants of prisoners or guards, and others with a general interest in these topics can all find points of engagement in these letters. In coupling the perspectives of Wesley and Catherine Makely with the anthropological interpretation of the historic and archaeological records, the result is the telling of one of the many Johnson's Island stories. I hope this connection will drive you to experience more.

I Fear I Shall Never Leave This Island

Introduction

It has been nearly two years since I have seen you, and I suppose
you have changed considerable since then. time makes a great many
changes, and I hope it may not be long before I will be with you again.

Wesley Makely to his daughter Lillie, December 27, 1864

Time does have a way of allowing for change. Captain Makely's last note from prison to his little girl represented not only renewing the relationship with his daughter but also recognition that he too had been changed by the experiences of the past two years.[1] Captain Wesley Makely, Company D, 18th Virginia Cavalry, arrived at Johnson's Island Military Prison Depot days after being captured on July 8, 1863, near Hancock and Clear Spring, Maryland. On July 3 the 18th Virginia Cavalry, acting as rearguard for the Confederate Army, had retreated from Gettysburg to guard the wagon train into Virginia. They reached Williamsport, Maryland, on July 5, but weather stalled their attempts to cross the Potomac River. On the day of their capture Captain Makely and Company D of the 18th Virginia Cavalry were seeking provisions for their horses (Delauter 1985:8–10). This was the last time Captain Makely would be anywhere close to his home town or his military unit until after the war.

Wesley Makely, described as six feet, one inch tall, fair-complexioned, with dark hair and gray eyes, was twenty-eight when he was captured (Delauter 1985). He had married Catherine ("Kate") Appich and their first child, Mary Louise ("Lillie") was two years old. As Wesley approached Block 1, his quarters on Johnson's Island, on Saturday, July 18, 1863, he must have been worried for his wife, Kate, and young daughter, Lillie. Ten days following his capture, he was transformed from a leader defending his ideals and homeland to the ambiguous role of prisoner-of-war hundreds of miles away from his family. He was among six hundred other officers captured during the fighting around Gettysburg who found themselves prisoners of the Union held at Johnson's Island (Official Records, Armies, ser. 2, 8:991; hereafter cited as ORA). Wesley faced what all new prisoners-of-war faced, an unfamiliar role in an unfamiliar place. What was it going to be like to be a prisoner-of-war? What was life like on Johnson's Island, in the North? How long until he would be exchanged? Would his family be able to communicate with him?

Being a prisoner-of-war during the American Civil War was a plight full of unknowns. Both the Union and the Confederacy had to manage increasing numbers of captured soldiers. Many had served together before the war but now found themselves on opposite sides. A prisoner exchange system was developed early in the war to return prisoners to their homeland. Unfortunately, by May of 1863, exchange was no longer assured (Hesseltine 1930:96). In fact, few exchanges took place, and the prospect of being exchanged was slight. Thus prisoners like Captain Makely faced the reality of being a prisoner for an indefinite period of time unless they attempted to escape.

The story of Kate's and Wesley's reactions to his imprisonment unfolds through their correspondence. Their frustration, pain, despair, suffering, struggle, and at times even their happiness are manifest in their letters. These are a firsthand account of life on the island, offering a picture of how lives are affected by war and by imprisonment. The prisoners at Johnson's Island expressed a continual desire to hear from family and friends. The question of their return to the South through exchange was a constant source of frustration. This set of letters provides insight into the day-to-day struggle of imprisonment, a situation not unique to the American Civil War.

Being institutionalized, and more specifically prisoners-of-war, forced those incarcerated to adapt to a restrictive way of life. The prisoners at Johnson's Island must have felt the loss of all their freedoms. They were controlled in movement, limited in possessions, constrained in how they communicated with others (especially those outside the prison), and stripped of their military trappings. On the outside they would have felt in control of their destiny; inside, their fate was in the hands of their professed enemy. The goal of a prison depot like Johnson's Island was to confine ambiguously defined noncitizens (Casella 2007:5). There was no attempt to convert them, to rehabilitate them, or to cure them. In other words, the depot's sole purpose was to keep the captured officers from future military action.

The American Civil War was the first time large-scale confinement of citizens was sanctioned. It was also the first time government policy authorized less than humane treatment of its citizenry. Both the guards and the prisoners faced moral and ethical dilemmas posed by broad public attitudes of the time. The Union and Confederate governments struggled with these conflicts in the question of how to treat the prisoners-of-war (Hesseltine 1930:175–76). Unfortunately, these questions still haunt us today.

The correspondence between Captain Makely and his family gives insight into the underlying mood of the country. There were times when he questioned the motives of his captors. Kate struggled with the bureaucracy in her efforts to arrange for her husband's release. The letters between Wesley and Kate demonstrate how institutionalization affects all involved. Inclusion of the archaeological record recovered from the site and the broader historical accounts alongside these letters provides a fuller context in the exploration of the impacts of institutionalization.

Today Johnson's Island presents little to remind us of its role during the American Civil War. There is the Confederate Cemetery, located at the northern end, just as one enters the island over the causeway. There are remains of two earthen fortifications constructed in late 1864 to protect the island from invasion by water-borne Confederates attempting to free the prisoners. One, Fort Hill, has been all but destroyed from quarrying that took place in the late 1890s and a housing development of the late 1990s. The other, Fort Johnson, is a fully intact lunette hidden by secondary forest in the interior of the island.[2]

Unseen by the casual visitor is the wealth of archaeological remains below the land's surface. Years of prisoner-of-war struggles are buried within these soils, revealing the connection between the human experience and its manifestation within the physical world. Just as the letters of Wesley and Catherine reveal part of the story, the archaeological remains overlap and further our awareness of how the prisoners at Johnson's Island coped with their institutionalization.

This book is structured to facilitate a context upon which the reader appreciates the bridge between the historic and archaeological records relating to the treatment of prisoners-of-war. Wesley Makely's experiences were not unlike those of many other men confined at Johnson's Island. To understand fully the correspondence Wesley had with his wife, and more broadly, to comprehend how people survived the prisoner-of-war experience, some background and guidance are provided. Chapter 2 sets the stage for the letters and this contextual framework.

Chapters 3 through 7 present the letters, almost entirely written by Wesley and Catherine Makely.[3] Included are a few written to or by others. The letters are arranged chronologically according to how Wesley would have encountered them. Each chapter begins with a discussion of a topic related to coping with prison life. Chapter 3 suggests in its title an absence of letters. The desire for more contact with those at home or those in prison was a common theme in almost all letters related to the prisoner-of-war experience. Wanting contact was probably never more intense than when a battle was over and the family was unclear on the status of their loved one in the military. Reading through all the letters provides a sense of those times when an absence of contact with those so central to one's life invoked fear, depression, and despair.

After capture, prisoners-of-war faced imprisonment until an exchange could be arranged. Ideally an exchange of equivalents—that is, a private for a private, lieutenant for lieutenant—would take place within ten days of capture. Chapter 4 highlights the common theme of exchange, which many letters throughout the series mention. Exchange was on the minds of all prisoners-of-war. After all, exchange would give back to Captain Wesley Makely the sense of freedom (power, prestige, and property) he lost when captured (Van der Elst 1999:138–39). Although he attempts to recapture some of this loss, only freedom to rejoin his family and military unit could alleviate the anguish and depression he struggled with throughout imprisonment.

In the other diaries and letters specifically related to Johnson's Island, the topic of sending and receiving personal images was well illustrated, as it was in Wesley and Kate's letters. Sending an image of themselves to the family must have been a way to assure the family all was right with the imprisoned. The more debonair and handsome the image could be, the more assurance it bestowed. Chapter 5 delineates the ways in which these desires were achieved by the prisoners at Johnson's Island.

One of the most distinctive aspects of the Johnson's Island prison site is the abundance of archaeological remains related to the prisoners' production of jewelry (Bush 1992). From 1862 through the mass exodus of prisoners leaving the island in June and July 1865, fine pieces of "gutta-percha" jewelry were created by prisoners to send or take home. Mourning jewelry was fashionable in affluent southern circles.[4] The hard rubber jewelry from Johnson's Island was not only styled in this mode but carried with it the additional quality of being associated with prisoners-of-war.[5] Chapter 6 utilizes the archaeological record to go into specific detail on how prisoners fashioned this jewelry and the significance it held. Many prisoner letters refer to various types of jewelry being sent, and Kate and Wesley's are no exception. This craft industry gets interwoven into the story of how these prisoners maintained their southern heritage.

The last of the letters, in chapter 7, reflect Wesley's trials and tribulations with the Confederacy's defeat and his return home. Transferred from Johnson's Island, Wesley still did not know when he might finally be released. Prisoners were faced with the adjustment of having to take the Oath of Allegiance—to "swallow the eagle"—and then find their way home. Most knew that going home meant facing yet more challenges. Homes had been ransacked, family members were lost, lands had been destroyed, and a way of life was altered forever.

Even greater implications existed for how governments could rationalize their inhumane treatment of prisoners. During the American Civil War the two governments at times intentionally sanctioned the mistreatment of United States citizens. Did this behavior set the stage for the governmental policies of prisoner-of-war treatment in future wars? Chapter 8 provides some of the main concepts to consider for an exploration of this question.

Johnson's Island Civil War Prison was unique in the Union's prison system because of its design. This facility was the only one dedicated strictly to housing Confederate officers, although prisons like Fort Warren and Fort Delaware held officers along with enlisted men. The type and condition of the archaeological resources available for study are rare among the prisons, North or South. Finally, the historical record available for Johnson's Island is vast. This combination of factors cannot be found at any other Civil War prison site. At times, it seems the possibilities for study are endless.

Attempts at understanding something as complex as a government's policy toward the treatment of prisoners-of-war should include an exploration of past human experiences. This book is such an attempt. What happened at Johnson's Island, and at the many other prisoner-of-war facilities during the American Civil War, is inextricably tied to our modern approach to this sensitive issue. The choices available to Wesley Makely during his imprisonment are presented in a context of evolving governmental policies and personal preferences. Insight into Wesley's daily fight with marginalization and feelings of abandonment begins with examining the site and experiencing the artifactual voices from his past.

Two

Johnson's Island Prison

The list is called, and one by one
The anxious crowd now melts away,
I linger still and wonder why
No letter comes for me today.
Are all my friends in Dixie dead?
Or would they all forgotten be?
What have I done, what have I said:
That no one writes to me?

Asa Hartz (pen name of George McKnight, prisoner at Johnson's Island)

After his capture Captain Wesley Makely was temporarily housed at Camp Chase, Columbus, Ohio, for a few days before the train brought him to Johnson's Island. His mid-July arrival at this isolated Lake Erie island was the beginning of a nineteen-month stay. However new this prison was to Wesley, the Johnson's Island Military Depot had already been holding Confederate officers for fifteen months. The treatment he was going to face had already been forged through government actions, guards' restrictions, and fellow prisoners' responses. A few thousand had already passed through the gate, and many thousands more were to follow.

The imposing physical facility set on this desolate island was the prisoner's first encounter with Johnson's Island prison. In the spring, summer, and fall months prisoners would be herded onto one of the steam ships operating within Lake Erie for the trip from Sandusky to Johnson's Island. Those unfortunate enough to arrive in the winter most likely walked over the frozen lake to the island. Incoming prisoners may not have realized the prison was built on a small three-hundred-acre island, since the docks and the prison compound were on its southeastern shore. The higher elevation of the center of the island and the fifteen-foot fence would have obscured any view the prisoners would have had of the north side of the island.

The growing numbers of captured Confederate soldiers and the realization that the war was going to be a long commitment forced the Union to consider options for incarceration of prisoners. Reasons for the selection of Johnson's Island in the fall of 1861 as the Union's first self-contained prisoner-of-war facility were readily apparent to arriving prisoners. Three miles off the coast of Sandusky, Ohio, in Sandusky Bay on Lake Erie, the island was barren of any other human activity. Necessary provisions were easily obtained from Sandusky. Being located so far north, there was little hope the Confederate army would attempt to free these prisoners.

The military prison was completed in early 1862. The first prisoners arrived on April 10, 1862, from Camp Chase. Three days later, on April 13, 1862, orders from Washington, D.C., determined use of Johnson's Island solely for Confederate officers (ORA, ser. 2, 3:448). Although originally designed to house both enlisted men and officers, its facilities were dedicated for officers only. At the time Captain Wesley Makely arrived, there were fewer than one thousand Confederate officers as unwilling guests of the Union (ORA, ser. 2, 8:987–1004).

The original 14.5-acre prison compound contained thirteen prisoner housing barracks known as blocks, twelve as barracks and one as a hospital; latrines known as sinks behind each block; a sutler's stand; three wells; and two condemned prisoner huts and a pest house.[1] Two large mess halls were added in August 1864 after the prison was expanded an average of ninety-five feet to the west on July 12, 1864. The blocks were two stories high and ranged in dimensions. The four blocks built for officers were 117 feet long by 29 feet wide. These blocks, numbered 1, 2, 3, and 4, contained twenty-two rooms each, with two mess facilities. Wesley was placed into Block 1. The other eight blocks, originally built for the enlisted, were slightly longer (130 by 24 feet), with each floor divided into three large rooms. Six of the other blocks had their mess facilities built on the ends as single-story additions. Blocks 12 and 13 did not have these additions. Block 6, measuring 126 by 30 feet, was used as the prison hospital (Frohman 1965:4–5).

Fig. 1. "Depot Prisoners of War on Johnson's Island," by Edward Gould. (By permission of the Friends and Descendants of Johnson's Island Civil War Prison.)

There were more than forty buildings outside the stockade: barns, stables, a lime kiln, forts, barracks for the Union officers and guard, a powder magazine, etc. These structures were used by the 128th Ohio Volunteer Infantry (OVI), originally known as Hoffman's Battalion. As the number of prisoners increased, the Union pulled the messes out of the blocks and constructed the two large mess halls mentioned, to the east of the odd-numbered blocks. Forts Johnson and Hill, the two major fortifications protecting Johnson's Island, were constructed over the winter of 1864–65 and were operational by March 1865.

The Hoffman Battalion, with other companies, formed the 128th Ohio Volunteer Infantry, the official guard of the prison, under Major William S. Pierson, former mayor of Sandusky. His cruelty to prisoners and inability to handle problems and keep the prison in good order resulted in his replacement. On January 18, 1864, Brigadier General Henry D. Terry replaced Pierson. A few months later, on May 9, 1864, Colonel

Charles W. Hill took command at Johnson's Island, remaining until the end of the war.

The Johnson's Island prison was unique within the Union prison system. It was the only facility built solely as a stand-alone prison by the Union to house Confederate officers. There are immense historical and archaeological resources, which remain to this day, directly associated with the prison (Bush 2000). These exceptional features allow study of prison life in a way not otherwise available.

Johnson's Island was the backdrop for Wesley's experiences. The prison population was made up of elite southern prisoners-of-war and inexperienced northern Ohio young men as the guard. Wesley did not realize upon his arrival on July 18 the adjustment to prisoner-of-war life that was already cast for him. "Prisonization" is a term used to represent the enculturation of an individual to prison life (Bukstel and Kilmann 1980). A prison consists of the multitude of experiences of the guard and prisoners. The guard posts rules on the bulletin board, but their impact goes well beyond the rules. Various guards develop relationships with the prisoners, and the prisoners learn which guards can provide items or services, at a cost. Some guards may be more likely to enforce the regulations strictly, while others are more indulgent. The guards and prisoners quickly create a relationship that achieves a momentum in itself. Incoming Johnson's Island prisoners would not only be instructed about the rules of the camp but would be guided through actual prison operations by benevolent prisoners. Prisoners and guards came and went, but the prison operations, with all their nuances, continued.

Captain Littleburg W. Allen, 49th Alabama Infantry, wrote of how these prisoner-guard relationships were beneficial after he was initially refused a pair of pants that had been sent to him.

> Major Scoville [128th OVI] was very kind in bringing me my pants, which were said to be contraband. He said he *stole* them for me. I have always found him very respectful indeed we are *cosy* and I find the benefit of keeping in good terms with him and with the rest of the officers. This I find can be done, by being frank, independent & candid, but at the same time respectful, courteous and kind. (Allen 1863–64, entry for December 4, 1863)

To illustrate further this concept of prisonization, the following was written by Captain John H. Guy of Virginia's Goochland Light Artillery. He arrived at Johnson's Island on April 24, 1862, after two months at Camp Chase. He wrote in his diary about the activities a prisoner could expect to be exposed to at Johnson's Island.

> Ring making rules the hour. Among over a thousand prisoners, more than half have employed most of their time making rings out of gutton percha buttons. Many of the rings made are plain, others have gold, silver or pieces of shell inlaid. Some of them are very neat, ingenious and tasty. Besides rings they make breast pins, watch chain ornaments and other such things. I have seen also several sets of chess men cut out of wood, with great pains and patience and very well done. In all this work the knife is the principal tool. But mastery of the workmen are provided with files and little chisels and small saws—the latter are generally made by themselves out of case-knife. Thus many hundreds of prisoners employ themselves. A smaller number, but still reckoned by hundreds pass their time in card playing, with some little chess, draughts and back-gammon playing. Of the small remainder some few—perhaps a dozen in all—pursue trades, such as shoe making, and repairing and tailoring; others read and the rest do nothing. Not one in ten in all the prisoners ever reads; and it is not for want of books, for there are some in the prison and the demand for them is so small that any one who wishes to read can always get a book. (Guy 1862, entry for July 28, 1862)

Guy's account could easily have been written a year later, when Wesley Makely arrived at Johnson's Island. Anthropologically, this sense of backdrop can be equated to context. The context used to interpret Makely's letters has been developed in over two decades of investigating Johnson's Island. In that time thousands of pages of primary documents and hundreds of thousands of provenienced pieces of cultural materials have been discovered, catalogued, and studied. Collectively, these cultural artifacts provide a broad comprehension of how the prisoners reacted to imprisonment. Their day-to-day existence is reflected both in the archaeological materials uncovered and in the various primary documents still available. No single set of letters or diary can capture all experiences or tell the entire story. At times, Wesley seemed unwilling to write frankly about his daily experiences. Why Wesley writes or omits what he does can only be understood within a broader context. There were events going on in prison that he chose never to mention or of which he was unaware.

Interspersed among his letters, significant incidents are highlighted to provide additional context. Wesley did not relate his hardships to his wife to the same extent others did in their letters or diaries. This may be due to his purposely disregarding topics because he realized the letters would be read by the postal inspectors. The guard inspected all outgoing letters for contraband topics. He also knew other members of his family read his letters. He may have been reluctant to share close, personal thoughts and feelings with others besides his wife. He may have censored his own mail to be protective of Kate.

Johnson's Island provides a multivocal approach to its past through the many primary accounts. Every prisoner-of-war had a slightly different perception; cumulatively, they supply a clearer picture of the experience. Wesley expressed his own interpretation of prison life and cannot be faulted for what he relates. The letters written by Wesley and Kate are moments in the long continuum of their experiences. They are artifacts of the Johnson's Island prison site just as much as are the slivers of hard rubber found beneath the floor of Block 4.

I use the phrase "artifactual voices" because each artifact has a portion of the story to tell. An in-depth knowledge of an artifact's context enables one to hear the portion of the human experience that the artifact represents. For instance, finding the rim fragment of a crystal glass tumbler in the soil beneath Block 4 indicates that at least one prisoner attempted to recapture some of the lost mannerisms of dining. Having fine crystal glass and china setting the table would be preferable to a tin cup and plate for a gentleman of the South. The past owner of the tumbler must have obtained this piece intentionally. He either traded items he had with the guard or paid the sutler to gain access to the crystal glass and, no doubt, other wanted items. Prisoners occupying the compound for months or years had ample opportunities to gain and accidentally lose or break articles sought to improve their condition.

Fig. 2. Photograph taken by Lieutenant Robert Smith of Lieutenant Colonel Nathan Gregg, 60th Tennessee Mounted Infantry (2.5 × 2 inches). (By permission of Nancy Feazell, granddaughter of Robert Smith, and Geoffrey Feazell, grandson of Nancy Feazell.)

Photographs are another kind of artifactual voice expressing the historic record. Lieutenant Robert Smith, who is discussed in some detail later, created a photographic studio and took pictures of prisoners at Johnson's Island. When we view a photograph of Lieutenant Colonel Nathan Gregg, 60th Tennessee Infantry, as an artifact of Johnson's Island, its story begins to be unraveled. This artifact would not exist except for the resourceful work of Robert Smith. This picture represents not only a production process but also a service Smith cleverly fulfilled. The incarcerated at Johnson's Island, like Nathan Gregg, were so eager to be photographed that Robert Smith performed this service in direct violation of the Union's rules. Smith and other prisoners risked discovery and potential punishment to procure self-imagery. Smith profited in this endeavor, and prisoners like Gregg obtained a portrait they could send to their loved one. This artifact thus has three voices it represents; Smith (its maker), Gregg (the subject), and the recipient. Nathan Gregg probably wanted this image to send to his wife, reassuring her of his health and well-being. Thus her interaction with this artifact is also one of the voices it represents.

In each case the artifact, whether derived through careful archaeological recovery or discovered in the vaults of a southern library, has a voice to be heard through a contextual relationship with all the historic and archaeological materials associated with Johnson's Island. Each letter written by Wesley or Kate represents a moment in their interactions with Johnson's Island. The letters need to be understood in the same way the cultural material from the soil needs interpreting. Contextual issues are presented when deemed necessary. The background provided is influenced by interactions with the historic and archaeological records of Johnson's Island, much like those of Wesley and Kate.

Artifactual materials need to be handled carefully to facilitate their interpretation. For the materials archaeologically recovered, recording their exact provenience assures that their associations and relationships to other artifacts and cultural features are maintained. Functional analyses and rates of recurrence provide more substantive clues about the lives these artifacts represent.[2] Throughout the presentation of the letters, the archaeological voice is interjected.

The next five chapters provide the letters between Wesley and his wife Catherine. As you begin to read these letters, you will note that Catherine calls Wesley "Nessa," and Wesley addresses his wife as Kate. Their daughter is referred to as Lill or Lillie, but her given name is Mary Louise Makely. At the top of Kate's letters she typically provides an abbreviation of her location. The vast majority of her letters were written from Alexandria, Virginia, but a few came from other locations. Wesley's letters are almost all from Johnson's Island, except at the end when he is taken to other prisons.

The original letters were transcribed, facilitating interpretation and allowing an easier read. Transcription may seem to be a fairly straightforward task, but it can be challenging. There are words that were written more phonetically than with regard to proper spelling. This is typical of many of the writings from Johnson's Island. No attempts were made to indicate each misspelling. The use of "*sic*" indicates a place where words were mistakenly repeated. From time to time minor inserts in brackets were added in order to help the reader interpret what was written. The overall intent is to appreciate what was being said and not the grammatical accuracy of how it was said. Making each letter grammatically correct would detract from appreciating the content. Although numerous people were involved in the initial transcription of the letters, each transcription was revisited by the author multiple times. Errors of transcription that may still be present are solely the author's responsibility.

Interpretation of the letters is facilitated through endnotes and periodic summaries. The endnotes are provided to give specific information about subjects mentioned in the letter. The periodic summaries are injected into the flow of the letters to provide the background or context necessary to appreciate more fully Wesley's changing approach to imprisonment as well as his struggle with isolation.

"Fresh Fish" would be the call for the newly arrived prisoners at Johnson's Island. Unknown to Wesley at the time, he was fortunate on that Saturday in July 1863 to be placed in Room 6 of Block 1. This was one of four barracks built for officers, so the rooms were smaller. He would have only six to eight roommates, as opposed to the prisoners in the other eight barracks built for enlisted men, where rooms contained forty to sixty prisoners. Although he never says so, he probably had only five roommates in Block 1. At this time Block 1 did not have any distinction from the other blocks beyond being one of four for officers.[3] From the beginning of the prison's use, Confederate officers were indignant at being housed in quarters outfitted for enlisted men, especially since they were not permitted to have their servants.

Wesley's veteran roommates probably informed the new arrival how things worked at Johnson's Island. This would include the all-important mail call, the intense craft industry, avenues for intellectual stimulation, indoor and outdoor gaming of every kind, the sutler (Mr. Johnson), and prayer meetings every Sunday. After some time, prisoners would have learned "through the grapevine" about other things, such as daring options available for regaining their liberty.

There is no information on Wesley's introduction to life at Johnson's Island, but an account by Virgil Murphy may shed some light on this experience.

Cries of "fresh fish" reached me from the dark buildings and many inquiries of where are you from etc. Through the kindness of Capt Sanford USA I was permitted to spend the night with Col Woods.[4] I was soon saluted by many friends and acquaintances who crowded around inquiring after their loved ones at home. I was literally besieged with questions and would have capitulated unconditionally but for the timely and opportune appearance of some good food which sustained me under the assault. I sat there and answered inquiries until 3 o clock notwithstanding my weariness and lassitude, and desire for repose. I cheered many desponding hearts and thank God I had no message of grief and woe for any of almost forsaken prisoners at Johnsons Island. (Virgil Murphy 1865:83–84, entry for December 6, 1864)

Prisoners-of-war had basically three choices to guide their prison ordeal during the American Civil War. They could choose to try to regain their liberty through escape; they could decide to survive as a captive for as long as was necessary; or they could assimilate to their captors, meaning taking the Oath of Allegiance to the Union and forsaking their southern heritage (Doyle 1994:3). Imagine being a captive, taken hundreds of miles away from home, placed with fellow officers but strangers, and having not only the amenities of life restricted but also your right to liberty. In the land of the free, you were its captive. These were the realities most prisoners-of-war faced, and Wesley was no exception. As Wesley walked through the gates of Johnson's Island for the first time, he began his journey of coping with his new identity as a prisoner-of-war. His first letters reflect the urgent need to establish communications with his family.

Three

Where Is Your Letter?

(August 16–December 13, 1863)

*The Col. wrote to me telling me that you were not wounded but nobody knew
where you were so you may know what a relief it was to get your letter.*

Catherine Makely to Wesley, August 18, 1863

Not knowing the fate of loved ones enlisted in the military during the
Civil War must have been unbearable. Were they sick, dead, wounded,
suffering? How was one to find out? Information in local newspapers
was always a few days behind what was actually happening, and certainly the specific individuals of interest would not be covered. Those at
home depended on letters from anyone remotely connected to a loved
one's military unit. In the army, letters from anyone in a family's county
or region might shed light on how parents, wife, or children were faring.
Nothing better illustrates this point than Kate's letter written to Wesley
on August 18, 1863. In it she states, "I received your letter of the 22 of
July you cannot imagin[e] the pleasure it gave me. The Col. wrote to me
telling me that you were not wounded but nobody knew where you were
so you may know what a relief it was to get your letter." He was captured
on July 8, ended up at Johnson's Island on July 18, wrote his first letter
to Kate on July 22, and she finally received the news on or just before
August 18, a total of six weeks after he was captured.

How unsettled thousands of families must have felt after the carnage
of Gettysburg. Thousands died, thousands were injured, and thousands
more were taken prisoner. As the papers reported on the immense battles, families must have been stricken with fear that loved ones were
lost. How would they ever know? Some never did learn exactly what had
happened. Many others did not find out the fate of a father, brother, or

son for weeks or months. Hospitalization or travel between temporary prison sites may have prevented a letter being sent immediately. Compounding the uncertainties, once a letter was received, it was usually short and gave only the barest of facts. If the writer was sick, the recipients were left wondering how sick. How long had he been sick? Was he getting better? Should they go to visit him? Getting answers to such questions would require even greater lengths of time.

Prisoners at Johnson's Island had several means of receiving news from the home front. A rush took place every time new prisoners arrived, inmates seeking news from their hometowns or recent battle updates. Newspapers were provided daily to paying prisoners, but they were northern papers. Prisoners suspected the northern newspapers were biased and wished to hear firsthand how things fared for the Confederacy. Newly arrived prisoners might also be able to provide more personal information about someone's relatives. The most treasured means of receiving news from family and friends was to receive it by mail.

For a prisoner to send mail back to his family in the South, the letter had to have Union as well as Confederate postage, or a due bill for the postage. Letters coming to the prison had to have the 3-cent 1861 U.S. stamp. Letters traveling between the Union and the Confederacy typically went by flag of truce to Old Point Comfort, Virginia (Fortress Monroe), at which point they would be transferred by flag of truce boats to the Confederate postal system in Richmond, Virginia (Walske and Trepel 2008:70–73). Letters were limited in size to one page and required the full signature of the writer. Postage to Richmond would require an additional 5-cent Confederate stamp, and beyond Richmond another 5 cents. One prisoner's description to his wife of how to send a letter back to him clearly explains the procedure:

> Ellen write your letter and put the United State Stamp on the envelop and then put a Confederate Stamp on another envelope put the United States envelope inside of the confederate envelope direct your confederate envelop to Hon. Robt. Ould Commissioner of Exchange Richmond Va. and on the United States envelope direct to M. C. Ready Prisoner of war Johnson's Island, Ohio. Put

this envelope in the Confederate one write one page only. (Ready 1864, letter of November 6, 1864)

All letters written by prisoners at Johnson's Island had to go through a mail inspector. With large numbers of letters being written, restrictions were placed on the length of letters. By June 1864 regulations required that letters written or received by prisoners could be no longer than one page of letter paper. This was later revised to no more than twenty-eight lines. Letters were also restricted to information of a personal nature. Inspectors either stamped or initialed the envelope once its contents had been inspected.

Prisoners discovered ways to circumvent these restrictions. Prisoners leaving the island on exchange were given letters written by other prisoners to take South. This method was unreliable, for inspections just prior to a prisoner's departure often revealed uninspected, potentially contraband mail. Some of the guard who functioned as mail inspectors accepted extra money from prisoners to pass along lengthy letters. Other prisoners found a fellow prisoner not writing letters and used his name when signing some letters. This devious method was not practiced by Wesley Makely, but a collection of letters by Thomas Wallace of the 6th Kentucky Cavalry demonstrates the use of other prisoners' names for his signature (James A. McLennan, 65th Alabama Infantry and Joel C. Archer, 16th Alabama Infantry; Wallace's letters are in the Filson Club Library in Louisville, Kentucky).

The envelope pictured in figure 3 was sent by Wesley Makely to his wife, Kate. It shows the 3-cent U.S. stamp and is postmarked "Sandusky, O, Sep 20, 64," with the concentric "killer" mark (Dietz 1929). In the bottom left-hand corner is the note "care of Mr. G. Appich." This refers to Kate's father, Gottlieb Appich, with whom she often stayed. Above the cancellation stamps are the initials GSB, which stand for George S. Brown, a postal inspector with the 128th Ohio Voluntary Infantry. The letter "E" underneath the postmark indicates that the letter was examined.

The letters in this collection are arranged chronologically as Wesley Makely would have received or written them. There were times when letters would arrive within a week, but normally they took at least two

Fig. 3. September 20, 1864, envelope to Kate Makely from Wesley. (By permission of The Library of Virginia, Makely Family Papers.)

weeks or longer. There were several periods when no letters made it through. Lapses in the delivery of mail were most often due to conflict in southern and border states or to weather.

With the many methods of instant communication of our times, it is almost unimaginable to write a letter with questions, concerns, or just wanting to share a moment and not to expect to hear back on any particular subject for a month. The contents of the Makely letters are sometimes redundant, but the need to restate information or questions in subsequent letters is understandable when we realize that the writers never knew for up to a month whether the initial letter had been received.

The first letter in the collection from Wesley Makely was written to his brother on August 16, 1863. In this letter he notes that he had written to Kate upon his arrival at Johnson's Island. That letter of July 22, 1863, is not part of the surviving collection. Kate responded to his letter on August 18. It is unclear when she received his letter of July 22, but it was six weeks from the battle of Gettysburg to her writing to Wesley. She writes on September 21 about having received only one letter from Wesley. Her letter of October 27 notes that she finally received two letters from Wesley, written on September 27 and October 1. As can be inferred from the dates of these letters, mail took from three to four weeks to reach Alexandria, Virginia. These first letters are very focused on relating information about family and friends.

The importance of communicating with family, especially a prisoner's wife and children, is readily apparent in Wesley's letters. In fact, he indicates that due to restrictions on the number of letters he can write, he must forgo writing others to ensure that Kate and Lillie hear from him. The greater percentage of all letters from Johnson's Island begin with some variation of "You don't know how much pleasure it gave me to receive your letter." Letters from home were the only source of comfort prisoners had to assure them all was well. The same was true for those waiting at home.

> Johnsons Island
> August 16th/63
>
> Dear Brother,
> I have just received your leter of the 13th I was very glad to hear from you. I wrote to you yesterday and directed to Washington Tell Mother if she writes to Kate not to let her know that I am sick as it would only make her uneasy for nothing. I wrote to her when I first got to the Island and intend to write again in a few days. Tell Mother that I am something beter to day.
> Yours & C.
> W. Makely

By the time Wesley Makely arrived at Johnson's Island, there were approximately one thousand prisoners being held there (ORA, ser. 2, 8:991). By the end of July 1863 the influx of prisoners from Gettysburg and related battles raised the number of prisoners to seventeen hundred. As we have seen, he was captured at Hancock, Maryland, on July 8 and arrived at Johnson's Island on July 18, 1863. He was briefly at Camp Chase prior to arriving at Johnson's Island, but he does not indicate this in his letters. Camp Chase, at Columbus, Ohio, was not preferred to Johnson's Island by those who experienced both. Arriving by train at Sandusky, Ohio, he probably stayed one night at a hotel (under guard) before being transported to the island on the *Island Queen*. Most prisoners noted the large fifteen-foot-high stockade wall they passed through when entering the prison. They were searched, all money was confiscated and recorded with the commander, and then they faced negotiating their new surroundings. Here they saw for the first time the 14.5-acre compound with thirteen blocks for housing. Of the thirteen, Block 6 was used for very sick prisoners. The blocks were arranged in two rows with the even numbered on the west side and the odd numbered on the east. Wesley Makely resided in Block 1, Mess 6.

Many of his fellow officers from the 18th Virginia Cavalry also captured were imprisoned on Johnson's Island. Captain William Ervin, Captain Mathias Ginevan, 2nd Lieutenant Henry Knicely, 1st Lieutenant Jacob Rosenberger, and 2nd Lieutenant William Triplett were all members of the 18th Virginia Cavalry captured at or just after Gettysburg and imprisoned on Johnson's Island. More detail about them is given later as they are mentioned in the letters.

Stribling Aug 18th/63

Dear Nessa

I received your letter of the 22 of July you cannot imagin the pleasure it gave me. The Col. wrote to me telling me that you were not wounded but nobody knew where you were so you may know what a releif it was to get your letter. Mr. K. was so ansious to here from you and said he know there could be no secrets in the letter that he took the liberty of reading it. I wrote to James L. the next day after getting your letter about your things and he had them sent up in two or three days after paid your trust was at Mr. Thomas Bosenbarg. Have you ever written home since you have been away if not do we are all well at present and my daily prayer is that you are the same Lillie cannot believe that Papa cannot come home when he wants to. Mr. and Mrs. H. send there respects to you. I want you to take care of yourself you wrote that you were well treated. I am ever thankful for that. Nessa put your trust in Jesus and all will be well! Write to me again the first opportunity you have. My prayer is that you are well and that we may meet again soon. Good bye. Yours most affectionately.

Katie

At the start of this letter Kate indicates her location as Stribling. This was Stribling Springs, Virginia, the location she refers to when she talks about going to the country.

There was no explanation of why Catherine, signing her name as Katie, calls Wesley "Nessa." This continued throughout all of the letters. Only once did Wesley sign his name Nessa.

Often the full name of someone mentioned in a letter was omitted, with only an initial used. This might have been an effort to save letter space or to keep the identity of friends limited to just the recipient.

> Johnsons Island Sept 1st/63
>
> Dear Father,
>
> Since I wrote to you last I have goten well and am now as well as a prisoner could expect. I received a package from some lady friends in Philladelphia. they also want to know how much money they would be allowed to send me and what I needed as they said they were anxious to supply my wants. Mr. Goldsbourough also wrote to know what he could do for me. But there is but little they can do for me unless they could get me out of prison I got a leter from Jack a few days ago he seames to think there will soon be an exchange I would like very much to get to se you all before I am exchanged I think perhaps McKensy and Masey might get me a parole for a few days to come home to see you all I suppose mother has not gon[e] after Kate yet if there is any chance for an exchange soon I think she had better let me try and get her home.
>
> Yours & W. Makely

Wesley was writing to Kate's father, Gottlieb Appich. In this letter he refers to Jack. Jack is his older brother, Metrah. The lady friends in Philadelphia were women sympathetic to the South. Many prisoners had correspondence with women in Philadelphia and Baltimore assisting them in their needs.

Prisoners originally expected to be exchanged within ten days of being captured. This was established in a cartel reached between the United States and the Confederate States in July 1862 (Hesseltine

1930:68–113). As soon as the exchange of equivalents was established, problems arose. The exchange of prisoners continued until May 1863, when the agreement broke down. After this there was no understanding of when or where exchanges might occur or who might be exchanged. Prisoners expecting to be exchanged quickly realized they might never get exchanged.

near Stribling. Sept 11th/63

Dear Nessa

It has has [sic] been ~~two~~ three weeks since I wrote my last let-ter to you whether you received it or not I do not know as I have not heard from you since. After I received your letter and found out where you were and that I could write to you I intended writ-ing every week. And would have done so but I have been sick. I am well again now and going all about again.

Nessa please try to take care of *your self* and keep well. I beleiv I told you before that J. L. had sent your valise and things up how are you off for cloths pretty bad I expect do try to get some warm clothing if possible and put them on. I believe I have writ-ten about as much as I can write except that we are all well Lillie often talks about you and send you a kiss.

Nessa I think that I will sell the poney say in your next if I must I can get 375 for her write soon as possible I very very anx-ious to hear from you I dream nearly every night that you have come and by day I trust in and pray to the all wise providence that it may be so soon. Nessa do you do the same I know you do. Keep up your spirits all will be well. Mr and Mrs. H. send there respects to you.

From your affectionate wife
Katie

Near Stribling Sept 21st/63

Dear! Dear Nessa.

Am I never to here from you again.[1] I have received but one letter from you since you were taken prisoner since then I have written three do you write or not, perhaps it it [sic] is the same with you that you do not receive mine. I received a letter from Mr. Rice he told me to write to you every week that was what I intended to and have done except two ever since I found out where you were I received a letter from Cousin Hollie A. for you he did not know that you were a prisoner he had seen a gentleman from home just a week before he write said all were well. I am thinking a great deal about going home, if I thought that I could see you I would certainly go. But will do nothing untill I here from you what to do. Lillie and I are both well and I hartely Wish and hope that you are the same. Nessa you must keep up your spirits and take good care of yourself. I thrust in and pray to God that we may meet soon

    Nessa please write soon and often as possible

    Good bye. Yours most affectionately

    Katie

    Nessa do keep up your spirits for my sake for I can but think that we will meet soon.

    K

Wesley never let Kate know what they received in rations. At this time prisoners were given baker's bread, either bacon or beef, coffee made of chicory, rice or hominy, and sugar (Stockdale 2010:55). Those with money supplemented their diet with cabbage, Irish potatoes, onions, beets, lettuce, snap beans, butter, eggs, molasses, pickle, mustard, sauces, dried fruit, cheese, crackers, and other items purchased from the sutler (Stockdale 2010:50). For much of the time Mr. L. B. Johnson, the landowner, functioned as the sutler (Frohman 1965:16). The amount of additional items depended upon the generosity of the members of the mess (those who dined together).

Stribling Springs Sept 28/63

    Dear Dear Nessa

    This bright and beautiful morning to others seems dark and dull to me. I heard this morning that you were sick. Oh Nessa how sick nor how long you have been sick. I cannot bear. I knew that some thing was the matter by your not writing. Surely you have a friend there that might write me a line or two if you are not able, but God forbid that you should be so sick as that and me not able to come to you.[2] Oh that I could know this moment how you are, I would give worlds to be with you. Nessa try try! To keep up your spirits and take care of your self. Lillie and myself are both well and my prayer to our Heavenly Father is that you be the same in a few days, Good bye till you hear again. Most Devotedly yours.

Kate

If W Makely is too sick to write will some one be kind enough to write me how he is and what his complaint is; am very very much oblige.

Mrs. K.M.

Stribling Oct 27th/63

Dear Nessa

You cannot immagin[e] the pleasure and gratification it gave me to receive your letter's of 27th of Sept and 7th Oct I received them both together last Friday[3] I had givin up all hope of getting another letter from you until I saw you again I have written every week untill the past two and never received but the first letter you wrote, from you I had heard that you were sick was it so you may know how I felt and could not hear from you

Mrs. Smith wrote me that Mrs. Fountain had received a letter from Mr F. and stated there in that you were sick.[4] You said somethin[g] about my going home I assure you I was in for going but for one thing I might pass you, I spend last night with Mrs K she told me that the Gen would be there I though[t] I had better consult him on the subject he advised me not to go. I have sold my poney and will sell your horse the first opportunity Lillie and I am very well. L send a kiss to Papa and says that she want to see him, I received a letter from cousin Hal A. last night he is well, say I must send his respets to you. Mr and Mrs H send there respets also to you, now so write again soon, I have written home this evening from your affectionate wife Kate

Kate certainly had cause to be concerned about Wesley's health, whether she had knowledge of the details or not. Eleven prisoners died in the month of October 1863 at Johnson's Island. Two died on October 26, 1863, from smallpox. They were Private John J. Bevins and Lieutenant Nathan F. McLeroy (National Archives, General Registry of Prisoners 1865; hereafter cited as NAGRP). More prisoners died from dysentery and diarrhea than any other cause at Johnson's Island. Additionally, one Union soldier was executed on October 23, 1863. He was private Reuben Stout, 60th Indiana Infantry, executed for desertion and murder (Frohman 1965:59).

Baltimore Dec 1st/63

My Dear Dear Nessa

Just to think I will get home tomorrow. I reached this place this evening. Mr & Mrs Abe M. have just left. I had good company nearly all the way. Have had no trouble so far. Mr. M is going to telegraph to Pa to meet me tomorrow. All I want now is to have you with me. Then I could be happy. Nessa you have been wondering why I have not written to you lately you will know now.[5] I can assure you that you have never been out of my mind. Do you want for any thing? If you do let me know immediately. Nessa why did you not let me know about your being sick. I want you to write me a long letter and tell me all about your self and what was the matter with you when you were sick. Let me know if there is any possible chance of my seeing you if I were to come on. Tell Capt. F that his wife sent a letter through for him his wife is looking very well all other family are well except Mrs. W tell him his little Mary is walking all about and Kate says he must bring baby a blue mouslin dress when he comes back

Nessa poor Tom Marshall's dead. Mr. John S. met with a misfortune lately. Mr. H's family were all well when I left poor little Lillie I wish you could hear her talk she has a great deal to say about her Papa she and I are both well and hope you are enjoying the same blessing. Oh Nessa my prayer is that this war may soon be over and we all may once again enjoy peace and quietude.

Do write immediately you must take good care of yourself

and keep in good spirits you must excuse me from writing more of present as it is quite late and I am very tired. God bless and protect you. Your affectionate wife,

Kate

Johnsons Island Dec. 6th 1863

Dear Kate

You cannot imagine how glad I was to heare from you. And to heare that in a very short time you would be safely at home. I had just started to write a letter to your Father to inquire if he had heard anything from you lately but got your letter just in time to save me the trouble and to write to you. Kate you wanted to know if you would be allowed to se me if you were to come heare. I do not think there would be any objections made. But you would first have to get permission from Washington. Although I am very anxious to see you but still I think you had beter not come for the present I would much rather se you at home than any ware els. Kate you thought strange that I did not let you know that I was sick. If you had been at home instead of Dixie I should not have hesitated in letting you know. I did not want to let you know anything that would trouble you when there was no chance of you doing any good. I am now enjoyin tolerable good health or at least as good as I expect whilest I am a prisoner. Prison life dos not agree with me. Kate I cannot write you a long letter now but will write to you again in a few days again. I have a great many things to ask you but cannot now as I am anxious send it by this mornings mail[6] Give my love Father and Mother. Hoping soon to se you

I remaine yours Truly

W Makley

Obtaining permission to visit a prisoner was not easy to do. Usually a prisoner needed to be either deathly ill or condemned to death for someone to see him (ORA, ser. 2, 4:151–53). In such cases permission would usually be granted only to close relatives. Many tried to visit prisoners at Johnson's Island, but at best could only view them from outside

the prison walls. The visitor also needed permission from the commandant to go to the island. This policy was instituted to keep the curious
from making a trip to the island.

Johnson's Island Dec 10th 1863

Dear Kate

I am glad to have the pleasure of writing to you at Alexandria
and hope it may not be long before I may be there with you. I saw
Capt Fountain this morning. He says he has not received the letter from my wife you spoke of and wished me to ask you ware it
was mailed at. Kate I will send you a ring.[7] It was made by one of
the prisoners hear. I sent you a very nice one some two months
ago, but suppose you did not get it. Tell Lill I have not forgotten
her. I will send her one the next time I write.

Kate when you write again direct your leters to Block 1 Room
6,[8] and tell Jack to do the same. You must excuse this short leter.
Capt. Fountain was anxious for me to write this morning and
as the the [sic] mail leaves early this morning I have not time to
write more. Give my love to Father and Mother.

Yours Truly W Makely

Johnsons Island Dec 13th 1863

My Dear Kate,

I received your and Jacks leter of the 10th, and also the leter
you wrote me from Baltimore. Since then this makes the third
letter I have written you. I am sorry to heare that Lill is sick, but
hope it may not be any thing more than a bad cold. Tell Mother
I am not in want of anything at presant, and am very much
obliged to her, and hope that before this will reach you she may
be enjoying good health again. I was somewhat surprised to
receive so short a letter from you for I thought after an absance
of nearly three years from home, you would find a great deal
to write about. The last leter I wrote you, I sent you a ring and
promised to send Lill one this time. Tell her it is the only thing
I can get heare to send her. My health is not very good, nor do I

think it will be as long as I remain heare. Give my love to Father and Mother

Hoping that I may be with you soon again, and with my best wishes for your happiness, believe me my dearest Kate, your affectionate

Wes

The ring Wesley mentioned was made from hard rubber. Hard rubber finger rings were mostly carved from buttons or hard rubber rules. The prisoners were restricted to a pocket knife or a hand carving set for their tools. The skill of the jewelry makers varied. Wesley and Kate periodically discussed jewelry in later letters, and detailed information on the production of hard rubber items is presented in chapter 6. The jewelry and traces of jewelry making in the Johnson's Island archaeological record provide a poignant artifactual voice: through the jewelry, men who could otherwise support their families only with letters found a second way to express their love and role as provider.

Fig. 4. Hard rubber finger ring carved from a button (FS1843, dia. 15.5 mm). FS signifies field specimen number from the archaeological catalogue; all items pictured with FS accession numbers are the property of the Friends and Descendants of Johnson's Island Civil War Prison and curated at the Center for Historic and Military Archaeology (CHMA), Heidelberg University, Tiffin, Ohio. (Photograph by author.)

Thoughts of Exchange

(December 24, 1863–May 8, 1864)

I am glad to heare that there is a probability of an exchange. I realy
think humanity demands that something should be don[e] to release
the prisoners on both sides.

Wesley Makely to Kate, December 24, 1863

One of the recurring topics brought up by both Wesley and Kate was
his being exchanged. Prisoners on both sides had expectations of exchange back to their military units or home. At times throughout his
imprisonment, the idea of exchange almost consumed Wesley; for short
of escape, this was the only hope he had for getting back to his family.
Exchange was his means to freedom.

During the American Civil War, captivity resulted in two general
fates—either parole or indefinite confinement (Hesseltine 1962). Parole meant the captive could no longer bear arms against his captor,
could not visit proscribed areas, and could not perform any duty typically associated with the military. Once captured, the prisoner expected
to be paroled within ten days, with exchange to occur within a reason-
able amount of time (ORA, ser. 2, 4:265–68). With the large numbers
of troops being captured, many parolees ended up going home until officially exchanged.

Confinement meant total loss of liberty, removal from familiar lands,
placement in a prison under military guard, and other restrictions
and impositions dictated by social mores and political sentiment. The
American Civil War resulted in confinement of more than four hundred
thousand prisoners-of-war, almost evenly divided between Union and

Confederate forces (Hesseltine 1962:256). Early in the conflict almost all prisoners taken were paroled and/or exchanged. Although the official Union policy was to confine prisoners, stating that the Union did not recognize the South as anything other than traitors, unofficial exchanges, or paroles were ordered. The South had a policy of parole and exchange, for it allowed their troops to rejoin the fighting army. The South was forced to change its official position in response to the North's attitude. No matter what officials in charge were stating, those in command at the front, faced with the potential need for managing hundreds or thousands of prisoners, often engaged in paroles and exchanges immediately after a conflict.

Once the reality of a long-term war set in, negotiations for a formal exchange and/or parole policy were initiated. Both sides aimed for a cartel similar to that established in the War of 1812 between the United States and Great Britain. With accusations from both sides about inequalities in exchanges, and stories of mistreatment from both camps, conditions were ripe by July 1862 for a cartel to be signed. On July 22, 1862, the Dix-Hill cartel was ratified between the United States and the Confederate States (ORA, ser. 2, 4: 265–68). In essence the cartel established an exchange by equivalents, with both sides monitoring the numbers and ranks of various prisoners captured and exchanged. Within ten days of capture, captives were to be exchanged (if opposing forces had equivalent prisoners for the exchange) or paroled until such time as exchange of an equivalent prisoner or prisoners could take place.

Almost from the day the cartel was signed and in effect, problems arose. Soldiers were accused of wanting vacations from the war and of allowing themselves to be captured, paroled, and returned home until such time as their exchange was official. Accusations of misrepresentations in rank abounded. Parole violations were paramount—some prisoners, having been captured and paroled, were later captured again. But these problems did not keep both sides from attempting to institute the cartel, because they were not well equipped to incarcerate thousands of prisoners.

The realization of a protracted war resulted in the Union creating a more formal prison system, with Johnson's Island as its first standalone facility. After September 1862 the number of prisoners kept at

Johnson's Island remained well below two thousand and was not above five hundred between December 1862 and May 1863, evidence that the exchange system was working (ORA, ser 2, 8:991). Regrettably, in May 1863 the exchange system was formally suspended for officers by the Union's General Henry Halleck (ORA, ser. 2, 5:701). Many issues affected how exchange would take place and who would be exchanged. The North wished to retain captured officers to ensure that their own captured officers would be treated fairly. There continued to be problems with the South's treatment of captured Negro troops and the officers who commanded them.

Although some exchanges occurred after this date, they were never part of an overall policy agreement between the Union and Confederacy. The number of prisoners at Johnson's Island rose from fewer than one hundred in May to just over eight hundred in June 1863. It doubled again by July and never went below two thousand after August 1863 until July 1865 (ORA, ser. 2, 8:991). Those captured at Gettysburg and imprisoned at Johnson's Island, like Wesley Makely, did not realize that their chances of exchange were slim. As it turned out, except for a handful of special exchanges, only the very sick were exchanged until after the war.

Wesley Makely suffered from an inability to control the most important aspect of his freedom, his release. He tried to regain aspects of his pre-prison life through interactions with fellow prisoners and communicating beyond the walls, but he was unable to gain any headway on exchange. Expectations of an early exchange were replaced with despair. The officers' frustration was expressed in their letters.

The struggle over exchange forced the imprisoned to look constantly at other choices available—escape, assimilation, and survival. Escape was viewed as an all or nothing proposition. Accepted military code understood that prisoners had the right to attempt escape, but at the price of being shot by the guards, whose duty it was to prevent such escapes (Eversman 1865; Frohman 1965:50). Prisoners attempting escape through tunnels or by scaling the stockade wall were most vulnerable to a deadly end. Several prisoners were shot while attempting escape in these ways, and at least two were killed (NAGRP 1865). At least one prisoner escaped in a tunnel and three escaped by climbing the wall.

Probably the most common form of escape attempt was masquerading as a Union soldier and walking out of the gate with work or roll call parties. Scores attempted this ruse, a few were successful, and none were shot or killed when discovered. Lieutenant James Murphy epitomized this approach by dressing the part of a Union soldier and gaining transport across the bay on a steamer to Sandusky. From Toronto, Canada, he wrote to Major Scovill, 128th Ohio Volunteer Infantry, shortly after his escape: "It was on Sunday the 6th [August, 1864] and you were aboard the boat when I crossed, but seeing that you did not recognize me I thought I would not introduce myself to you" (James Murphy 1864). Murphy went on to acknowledge Major Scovill's kindness toward him.

Escape gave the successful prisoner his liberty. With liberty came access to those aspects of life which had abruptly been denied. More than ten thousand Confederates were imprisoned at Johnson's Island, and there are records of only twenty escapes. Several men escaped while being transferred to Point Lookout (NAGRP 1865). From the number of tunnels discussed in diaries and the official records of the Union, and revealed by archaeological study, many more prisoners were engaged in this activity than were actually successful.

The choice to assimilate was not attractive to most prisoners. It is best summed up by Virgil Murphy's account of how oath takers were viewed.

> When a craven white livered man applies for permission to take the oath and pleads his sincere repentance for his past errors, invokes forgiveness for his political sins and concludes with denouncing his country kindred and Jeff Davis, and the pen can discover him, he is immediately ejected from his block avoided shunned and scorned by the entire mass.[1] Yankee bayonets alone saves him from hanging to the nearest joist amid the acclamations of all. (Virgil Murphy 1865, entry for December 6, 1864)

Other prisoners made very clear to Virgil Murphy during his first day in prison the fate of anyone taking or considering the Oath of Allegiance. He arrived on December 6, and he was immediately able to articulate the fortune of any "razor back."[2] It was no wonder Wesley's discussion of taking the oath did not appear in any real form until after he left

Johnson's Island, although his letter to Kate on January 10, 1865, alludes to being agreeable to taking the oath.[3] He does not mention the oath until April 27, 1865, at Fort Delaware, needing to take the oath to be released. By this time, with the Confederacy defeated, there was no stigma associated with the oath.

The threat of being shot during an escape and the reality of permanent ridicule in taking the oath left Wesley with only one viable choice. The choice was to survive imprisonment, for as long as it took. Wesley assumed exchange would be a part of his future and chose survival until released.

Johnson's Island Dec 24th 1863

Dear Kate

I received your letter of the 17th. I was supprised to heare that you have not received my leters from me, Since you have been home. This makes the fourth letter, I have writen you since you got home. I thought very strange that you did not write oftener. This is the first time I have heard from you since you got home, with the acception of the few lins I got from you on the 10th. I got the letter you write to me from Baltimore and answered it at once. Tell Jack I got the money he sent me, and will write to him in a few days. I am glad to heare that there is a probability of an exchange. I realy think humanity demands that something should be don to release the prisoners on both sides. If I should be exchange I want you to remain at home, and hope it will not be long before I will be there with you.[4] You spoke of Shofs wanting Jack to pay him a bill that Florence was owing him. Tell him not to pay it. Tell mother we are allowed to receive things from near relations. Kate if she has not sent the box when you get this, I wish you would send me some blackberry wine, or something that will be good for the disentary.[5] I have suffered a great deal with it since I have been here, and cannot get any thing that dos me any good. Also send me a pair of good heavy shoes, such as those Jack sent Lt. Knicely.[6] I am sorry to heare that Lill is sick. Also to heare that Father and Mother are still complaining. I hope they may all be well in time to enjoy a pleasant Chrismas.

Give my love to them all, and tell Mother she is not more anxious for me to be at home, than I am to be there. Kate write often if only to let me know how you all are.

Hoping this may reach you safely, and with my best wishes for your happiness, believe me, my dearest, Kate, your affectionate

Wes

After November 12, 1863, the sutler was removed from the prison until the end of March 1864. The first sutler, Mr. Johnson, had been sent to Washington, D.C., to face charges related to mismanagement. During this period of late 1863 and early 1864 several cuts in rations were imposed on the prisoners, as was curtailment of their ability to receive items from the outside. Wesley never mentioned any hardship directly except for his ill health. His receipt of money from his brother Jack assured that he would address some needs, even with the restrictions imposed.

Alex Dec 21st 1863

My Dear Nessa

Ma has sent off with this letter a Christmas box for you. And we all hope that you will enjoy the contence Ma says make haste and eat all up before you are exchanged which you know will be very soon. Lillie wants to know if Papa is coming home when he gets this box, says she would like to see him and wants you to come home. There is some talk of an exchange soon I believe. I hope so anyhow. I suppose you have received the money that Jack sent you before this. $25.00 for your self also 10 for Luet Nicely. I send you one pair of socks if you have not been wearing yours yet put them on and buy more. I supose you can get them out there. I want you to write once every week here after to me, you have never written to me since I have been home. Your Ma has been down and stade a few days with me.[7] All send there best love to you. Ma & Pa are still complaining rest all well.[8] Remember and write every week. Good bye from your Affectionate

Wife

[On the back of the letter] Things sent to you this day in a box. 1 fruite cake, 1 plain cake 3 pies, 2 beef tongue's 2 bolonies 1 can peaches 1 can pickled oysters, 1 pair sock, almonds, 8 lemons, candy

The letter was signed as Wife instead of Kate, or Katie. She signed most of her letters from this point on as Kate. She began her letter with Alex, an abbreviation for Alexandria, Virginia.

> Johnsons Island, Jan 6th 1864

Dear Kate

I received your letter of the 21st of last month. Since then I have not heard from you. I also received the box mother sent me, and have been livin high ever since. Kate I drank your health on new years day, and for the want of something stronger, I drank it with coald water. The oald year has now gone and we are now broching a new one. I hope it may be a much plasanter one to us than the oald one has been. Tell Jack to write to me. I wrote to him about two weeks ago, but have not heard from him since.

Kate I sent you some rings + c [etc.], by express, several days ago, and directed them to your Father. If you have not received them yet, you had better send to the express office for them. Write often. Give my love to Father, and Mother.

Hoping I may soon be with you all again, and with my best wishes for your hapiness, believe me my dearest Kate, your affectionate

Wes

The large hard rubber button pictured in figure 5 was being carved by a prisoner at Block 4 of Johnson's Island with designs of making a finger ring. One of the flat surfaces for sets for a ring was cut too deep. Etched on the surface is the interior circumference of the ring. Many prisoners tried their hand at carving rings; some with little success. Archaeologically, we have discovered many aborted examples of hard rubber buttons and chart rules that were intended to be rings but ended up tossed onto the ground. Chapter 6 presents many examples of these recovered materials.

Fig. 5. Hard rubber button abandoned after an attempt to carve it into a finger ring (FS0026, dia. 25.6 mm). (CHMA. Photograph by author.)

Alex Jan 2nd/64

Dear Nessa

Your letter of the 25th was brought to me this morning by Doc. I was glad to rec it for it seemed like a long time since I heard from you last. Nessa it has been a whole week and more since I wrote to you last and I am almost ashamed now to write but I know that you will forgive me for I have been going backwards and forwards to Washington and from office to office doing all I can for you. I would have written before but have been waiting for something more definate before I wrote and you will think more definate did not Stanton promise my exchange. So he did Nessa but it seems they all make promises to day to be broken tomorrow though I have not given up all hope yet. I went up to see Col Hoofman [probably Col. Hoffman] on Wednesday he and Gen Wessel say that your name has never been sent out the next day.[9] Myself and the friend who interseeded for you and who Stanton told that he had sent the name's she mentioned out. And she saw him with your and Capt Shell's name and send it out of the room[10] anyway we went the next day to see Gen Hitchcock[11] he said your name had never been sent there and then went to see Stanton who we could not see then but saw his son who said there was a mistake that your name certainly had been sent out that he would see his father about it again. My friend would have gone up to see him Saturday but for the weather tomorrow she will go. I supose Jack told you what Underwood said, I went to see him myself he will do nothing for you unless you take the oath[12] if that no thanks to him, all well and send love Good buy, affectionately

    Kate

                                      Alex Jan. 7th/64

    Dear Nessa.

    Ma has sent by express this day a box for you containing blackberry wine. lofe sugar. candy. Cakes. 1 can peaches. 1 tin cup. 1 pair shoes. 1 paper farina, 2 boxes sardines.[13] The farina prepare by the first direction on package and get milk and eat with it as much if you can it will be very good for you. We have never heard if you received your Christmas box or not I hope that you will receive this safe. I hope the wine will be of benefit to you it is very good and good for desentary. The shoes are the strongest Pa could get, you spoke of my writing so short a letter after getting home. I thought that more than one page was not allowed to pass and another thing I could tell you a heap more than I could write. I asked Lillie what I must tell Papa for her. She says tell him she is a good girl says she has her purse full and is going to give it to Papa when he comes home. We are all well at presant except Ma she has a very bad cold and cough. All send there love to you and hope that this will find you a great deal better. Write soon and often. Lillie send a kiss to Papa. Good bye. Yours most affectionately.

    Katie

There was some confusion among commanders at the various prisons over allowing prisoners to receive packages containing food and clothing from relatives and friends. Some commanders were stricter than others about prisoners receiving such items. At Johnson's Island, enforcement of any prohibitions on the receipt of food and clothing were not adhered to except for contraband items (Union uniform–colored clothing and liquor).

Johnson Island Jan 20th 1864

Dear Kate

I received your leter of the 18th. Also the box you sent me on the 7th. All came threw in good order. The wine is very nice, and I hope it may do me some good. My health is still very bad, and seames to be slowly declining. For the past few days I have scarcely been able to get out of my room at all. I think I would soon get well if I could be at home. You wanted to know how much you would be allowed to write to me, we are not restricted in writing or receiving leters.

Kate you must excuse my short leters for I don't feel like writing or anything els. Tel Jack to write to me Give my love to Father, and Mother With hope that I may soon be with you

I am truly your affectionate,

Wes

At several times throughout the war, restrictions were imposed on prisoners' ability to communicate with the outside world. In July 1862 Colonel Hoffman, commissary-general of prisoners, issued regulations that all commanders of prison depots were expected to follow. Item 10 of this set of regulations notes that letters written by prisoners could not be more than one page in length (ORA, ser. 2, 4:151–53). There was no specific indication of how long letters to prisoners could be, but many assumed incoming letters were limited to the same length. The number of letters per week was not officially restricted until September 1864.

Johnsons Island Feby 13th 1864

Dear Kate

I have been looking for a leter from you for some time, and have delaid writing to you on that account. I am glad to say that my health is much beter than it was when I wrote to you last. I am now enjoying tolerably good health and in fine spirits. We are all expecting to be sent away soon. About five hundred have been sent off allready. how soon the rest of us will be sent, or ware we will be sent, I do not know. I would rather have remained heare, but still if I am to be kept in prison it dos not make much difference ware I am at, so that I can keep my health.[14] I was sorry to heare that Fathers and Mothers health was bad, though I hope they may soon be enjoying good health again. Give my love to them. Kate write often. If I am sent away I will write to you and let you know.

Your anxious, and affectionate

Wes

Just over 370 prisoners were exchanged in the month of February 1864 (ORA, ser. 2, 8:987–1004). Major General N. P. Banks (U.S. Army) and Major General R. Taylor (C. S. Army) were arranging several cartels during this period. General Terry, commander at Johnson's Island, requested of Colonel Hoffman the removal of the Confederate officers to

Fig. 6. Amber-colored wine bottle recovered from an 1864 Block 1 latrine (FS1071, height 28.5 cm). (CHMA. Photograph by author.)

allow substantial improvements to the prison. Hoffman acknowledged this request on February 6, 1864 (ORA, ser. 2, 6:922–23). Thus there was some justification for the rumors of exchanging all or most of the prisoners. Unfortunately for Wesley, no further exchanges were undertaken from Johnson's Island at this time.

Johnson's Island Feby 16th 1864

Dear Kate

I received your letter of the 6th to day. I had not heard from you befor for upwards of two weaks. When I wrote to you last I was in very bad health, but am much better now. You say you had not received my leters from me for several weaks. I have written you two leters since I received your of the 26th of last month. You wanted to know if we are to be sent to Point Lookout or not. I don't think there is any doubt but what we will be sent away from heare soon. About six hundred have been sent off allready. But still there may not be any more sent away at all. As for my part I don't care how soon they send me, or ware they send me. As long as I am a prisoner it dos not make any difference to me ware I am at. I do not know wether you had beter write to me any more untile I can ascertain for certain wether we will be sent away or not, and ware we are going to. I will write to you again in a few days and perhaps in that time we may know wether we will be sent from heare or not. When you do write again I want you to send me some postage stamps.

Give my love to Father and Mother with my best wishes for your happiness I remain your affectionate

Wes

The number of prisoners Wesley claimed had left had increased since his previous letter, but there was only one major exodus of prisoners during February 1864. These prisoners were transferred to Point Lookout. The guard was anxious to have the prisoners leave, making their work much easier. From his letter it appears that Wesley realized exchanges were not going to take place. The exchange system was complicated, and in early 1864 the Confederacy was not inclined to cooperate with the

Union because General Benjamin F. Butler was an agent of exchange for the Union. Butler had been proclaimed an outlaw by President Davis in his General Order No. 111, where it was further stated that "no commissioned officer of the United States taken captive shall be released on parole before exchange until the said Butler shall have met with due punishment for his crimes" (ORA, ser. 2, 5:795–97). This created a continuing controversy between the Union and Confederacy, and that one exchange would be the last one sanctioned by either side.

Johnsons Island Feby 23rd 1864

Dear Kate

I received your leter of the 19th to day. I was glad to heare that mothers health is beter. You want to know if we will be sent away before you could come to see me. I do not think there will be any more of us sent off for some time, at any rate not before you would have time to come and se me, and as you have permission to come I think you had beter come at once, as we may be moved soon.

Give my best respects to Miss Mary Entarsel. Tell her that I think it is very cruel in her to keep poor Phill waiting so long. I heare of a great many of my acquantaines that have married since I was there but Miss Stile remains single I would like very much to get back to se some of my oald acquaintances, but as it is I can only send them my best wishes and content myself to remain in prison. I wrote to Dock some six or eight weaks ago but have not heard from him yet. Is he still at New Bloomfield Pa or not. He was speaking of leavin there on account of his health when I heard from him last. Give my love to Father and Mother and if you do not come write soon.

Your anxious and affectionate

Wes

No information exists on how Catherine Makely received permission to visit Wesley. With all the accounts of mistreatment claimed by the belligerents, hope of humane treatment for either side was waning. Throughout the fall of 1863 there were reports from citizenry and military alike of the poor treatment of prisoners from both sides. Disease seemed rampant as the numbers of prisoners kept increasing. Wesley did not mention that rations continued to be short or that the weather had been variable, at times extremely cold, and exacerbated by the Union restricting how much wood was given to the prisoners for heating and cooking.

Between February 23 and March 12 Catherine Makely visited Wesley at Johnson's Island. She saw him on March 8, but the circumstances of the visit are not well documented. Typically, visitors could only peer through the walls, and close contact was not permitted. Colonel Hoffman had been strict about these rules with Colonel Pierson, the former commandant of Johnson's Island, reprimanding him on several occasions for lax implementation of these regulations. On July 7, 1862, Hoffman sent out regulations for prisons, which stated:

> 9. Visitors to these stations out of mere curiosity will in no case be permitted. Persons having business with the commanding officer or quartermaster may with the permission of the commanding officer enter the camp to remain only long enough to transact their business. When prisoners are seriously ill their nearest relatives, parents, wives, brothers or sisters if they are loyal people may be permitted to make them short visits; but under no other circumstances will visitors be allowed to see them without the approval of the commissary-general of prisoners. (ORA, ser. 2, 4:151–53)

There is no indication that these regulations had changed by 1864. Early 1864 saw the Union trying to contend with growing dissent by treating the captured Confederates humanely. Continued reports of atrocities at southern prisons pushed the North into responding. Interestingly enough, in early March the North lessened restrictions on what the sutler could sell to prisoners, hoping to influence policy at southern prisons. Here is Hoffman's order:

> March 3, 1864
> Respectfully submitted for the approval of the Secretary of War, and approved. Tobacco, cigars, pipes, snuff, steel pens, paper, envelopes, lead pencils, pen knives, postage stamps, buttons,

tape, thread, sewing cotton, pins and needles, handkerchiefs, suspenders, socks, underclothes, caps, shoes, towels, looking glasses, brushes, combs, clothes brooms, pocket knives, scissors. Groceries: Crushed sugar, sirup, family soap, butter, lard, smoked beef, beef tongues, bologna sausage, corn-meal, nutmegs, pepper, mustard, table salt, salt fish, crackers, cheese, pickles, sauces, meats and fish in cans, vegetables, dried fruits, sirups, lemons, nuts, apples, matches, yeast powders. Table furniture: Crockery, glassware, tinware.

W. Hoffman,

Colonel Third Infantry and Commissary-General of Prisoners. (ORA, ser. 2, 6:1014–15)

Johnsons Island March 12th 1864

Dear Kate

I am sorry that I could not se you again before you went home. I felt very confident that you would get permission to come over again, or in case you could not, that you would write to me from Sandusky. I have been watching the boat, and the male [mail] every day since you left, but could not even get a letter from you. I have no doubt but what you wrote to me from Sandusky; but the leter must have been over looked in some way. I have had the blues ever since you left. I try every way to pass of time but it hangs on very heavily in spite of all I can do. I try to read, but my mind seams to be on anything, and everything but what I am reading. I walk about and try to drive dull thoughts away. Kate we can only hope that there is a brighter and beter day not far off.

Take the bright shell from its home in the lea,
Warever it goes twill sing of the sea;
So take the fond heart from its home and its hearth,
Twill sing of its loved to the ends of the earth,

I would have given anything if I could have been at liberty and to have gon home with you. I have been moping about like some one that had lost their last friend they had in the world, ever since you left I will try and content myself, for I cannot help but think that we will se each other again soon; and that I will find you in good health and in much beter spirits than you were when I saw you last. Kate enclose you will find your cross an ring. I think they are very pretty and hope they will pleas you. Kate I will write to you by male in a day or to. I hope you had a plesant trip home. Give my love to Father and Mother, and with my best wishes for your happiness I remane your anxious and affectionate

Wes

P.S. Write often

Actual hard rubber items that Wesley sent to Kate have not been located, but archaeological investigations have produced examples of the kind of jewelry Wesley provided. Figure 7 depicts a cross and finger ring discovered at Johnson's Island. The cross is shell set in a hard rubber rectangle; the ring is a solid hard rubber band.

(a)

(b)

Fig. 7. Hard rubber jewelry from Johnson's Island:
(a) small hard rubber and shell cross (FS0490, length
13.1 mm); (b) hard rubber finger ring (FS5973, dia. 16.7
mm). (CHMA. Photographs by author.)

Sandusky City March 8th/64

My Dear Dear Nessa

You will know with what pain and sorrow it gives me to have to record to you that we will not be permitted to see each other again this time. I might possibly see you again by pressing the matter but I do not feel that it would be right. It might be the cause of debassing others from seeing there friends. Then you know the Officers have been very kind to me. I may want and *will!* try to come to see you again some time so it wont do to ask too much.

Nessa I have bought you a very nice ham weighing 37 lbs also a paper sack of flour 49 lbs the Major told me not to get more. I do not know if you will get them or not I tried to get them sent by express but they would take nothin[g] from here to the Island by express. The Merchant Robertson & Son who I bought them of promised to send them over so you can get the Major to do you the favor of seeing that you get them let me know if you ever do.[15] Remember what I told you about excersizing and take good care of yourself. I am afraid as this is such a large sheet I will have to close though I could keep on all night. I will send you're a box from home soon must I Oh Nessa must bid you good night. I do May God be with and ever remain with you now and forever.

Yours most Truly

Kate

The pass granting Kate permission to go to the island on March 8, 1864, mentions her brother M. Makely. Wesley's brother Metrah Makely had probably accompanied Kate to Ohio. This was her only "visit" with her husband. The permission slip was signed by Brigadier General H. D. Terry, who replaced William Pierson as commander of this post on January 14, 1864 (ORA, 841).

Johnsons Island March 13th/64

Dear Kate

Your leter of the 8th has just come to hand; and you cannot imageon how gladley it was received I had been looking for it for some time, and had almost give out geting it at all. I have had the blews the worst sort ever since you left, though I have gotten pretty well over them since I got your leter. Kate I am under many obligations to you for the things you sent me. The ham and flower I have not got yet, but have no doubt but what I will get them. You need not send my anything more at presant. When you send another box dont forget to send me some Hosteters biters or some other good biters. Capt Winser says his Sister wrote to him to be certain to se you so that you might tele her how he was looking.[16] You can tele her I say he is looking very well. All your other acquaintances from Alexandria we are anxious to se you also. They all send there best respects to you. Kate I have sent your cross and ring by express, and hope they will reach you safely. He had (The cross is my anchor) ingrave on it. I wanted him to fix it so that you could wear it as a brestpin but he says you can have it fixed much nicer there than he could fix it so if you want a pin put on it you can have it done there. Give my love to Father and Mother, also to Jack and with my best wishes for you all

I remain your affectionate,

Wes

Fig. 8. Side panel fragment from a bottle of Dr. J. Hostetter's Stomach Bitters (FS5348, length 79.2 mm). (CHMA. Photograph by author.)

Hostetter's Bitters was a popular "cure" legitimized through the Union's approval as an accepted medicine. Although liquors were considered contraband, bitters were classified as medicinal. The specific contents of Hostetter's Bitters were a guarded secret, but it is well known that it consisted of water, 47 percent alcohol, and various herbs (Fike 1987:36). Many prisoners requested bitters from family and friends.

Alex March 12th/64

Dear Nessa

We arrived at home yesterday afternoon and I intended to write as soon as I got here but I was so tired and felt so badly I could not. So it is the first thing I do this morning. Jack wrote this morning to Gen. Terey about what you requsted him.[17] There has been arrangements made and all look forward to an early exchange. Butler has taken as Ma says a partner in and the exchange I believe is to go on through him.[18] Did you get the meat and flour I sent you let me know if you did or not. I send you a couple of gazettet papers and will send them often I do not know if Jack has written about the paper you wanted or not. All are well. Lillie sends a kiss for her ring. I could write an hour longer but you remember what about the one page. I will write in a day or two. Write soon and often. All send there love to. Yours most affectionately.

Kate

Alex March 14th/64

Dear Nessa

You said that I must write or that is I might write you a letter twice a week, and I think so too for there no telling how long I can write. The exchange is so uncertain. About last Friday I thought by this time you would all most be in Richmond but it seems the exchange has stopped again. Nessa how are you. How do you feel now. I hope no worse than when I was there. Lillie says tell poor Papa she is a good girl and send a kiss to you. Tell Capt Ginevan I have written to Mrs. C. Ginevan respecting the sending of those rings.[19] Jack and Will Ford have just come from

Washington. I supose you heard of Antonia Fords marrige with Major Williard of Washington what do you think of it. Mosby overhauled them on the way. All are well and send there love to you. Write very soon. Good bye. Your affectionate wife

Kate

Do you get the papers I send you or not.

K

The activity of writing letters required pen, paper, and ink. These supplies were available from the sutler when permitted. The archaeological discoveries include several different types of glass and ceramic ink wells and pen nibs. Some prisoners had fancy ink wells that they filled with ink purchased from the sutler.

Fig. 9. Umbrella-style glass ink well (FS6928, dia. 6 cm, height 6 cm). (CHMA. Photograph by author.)

Dear Nessa.

Ere this reaches you I expect you will have another Rebel amoung you in the form of Lieut Triplett a very nice young man the son of Mrs. William T. of near this place.[20] She wants you to seek him out an make his acquatence he has been confined some time in the Capitol. Tell Capt Winsor I saw his Pa yesterday and delivered your message his family are all well. Nessa I received your letter of the 13. But not the ring & cross yet. Jack has written to the man about your ham & flour. Also about the paper you wanted do you get the paper I send you. In your letter you said don't send anything just now so you can write when you want anything. I hope you are well. We are all well expect colds. Lillie sends her love and say she is a good girl. Now write soon all send there love to you Good bye

Yours ever affectionately Kate

Kate's March 18 letter to Wesley is an excellent example of how letters served the whole community in relating news and also in taking care of friends. In just a short line or two, Kate has relayed the wishes of her neighbors and friends to Wesley. This is common in many letters written to or from Johnson's Island.

Lieutenant William Triplett was among the few who found a covert means of getting off the island early. As earlier noted, the most common means of escape or attempted escape was to dress as a Union soldier and go out with work or roll call parties. Many tried to tunnel out of the prison from the blocks or latrines, but there was only one instance when escape was successful. The prisoners used table knives, large bones, or iron bars to excavate the path to freedom (Bush 2000). There is no information available on how Lieutenant Triplett escaped from the island. The official rolls state that he was recaptured on October 31, 1864, and sent to another prison (NAGRP 1865).

Alex March 25/64

Dear Nessa.

I have received your letter of the 16th. You spoke about Jack's writing to Gen Terry. I thought that I explained to you in my letter from Sandusky why he wrote. It was late before we got over that evening it was after dark then we went to see about your ham & flour. By the way have you never received them yet or heard anything of them. Then when we got through it was too late to see the Gen. Jack was up home yesterday for the first time for I don't know when. he went up with Purdy , Al and your Ma have been very much complaining Ma with her feet.[21] She wants to come down and I have been looking for her for some time. Al complains of his head ever since he had the fevor a year or more ago. I have written to you before since I received the ring & cross you sent me. Do you get the papers sent you or not you seem to think you will never be exchanged. Hope for the best it will come after awhile. Write and let us know when you want a box and if you want clothing. All well and send there love to you Good bye

    Yours ever affectionately Kate

Fragments of newspaper have been recovered from most of the latrines (sinks) excavated. The discovery of newsprint in the latrines was quite surprising. Newspaper reacts with lime and the print is preserved, although often there are just a few legible letters or words. Occasionally larger amounts of text are recovered, allowing the newspaper's name or publication date to be ascertained. This information is used with other data to help establish the chronological placement of the latrine, a major research question needing to be answered (Bush 2000).

Alex March 28th/64

    Dear Nessa

    I have just read a letter from Cousin Hallie A. to his sister Emnia. he is at Kingston NC. He writes a very good letter full of hopes and in fine spirits says he and all the Alexandrian's are well sends his love to you and myself and says that he is watching out for Capt M. by every Flag of Truce boat and supposes that Kate will accompany him when he does come. Nessa tell Capt Ginevan that I send the rings he sent by me to his sister to day by express not knowing that they could be send out there by exp I wrote to her to know how. I was to send them and never received an answar until last Saturday so they go today tell him they are all well and that he certainly has a set of affectionate sister. Pa, Lillie and I walked out to the buriel ground yesterday evening. Oh how I did wish that you could be here to walk with me. Nessa Pa has just brought me a letter from you dated 21st I tell you I was glad to get it and to hear that you had gotten your flour and ham. Nessa about the exchange I shall hardly dare to hope any thing more. Pa has just gotten a letter from Thomas B. Cochran of Salem he is a prisoner at the Old Capitol and want clothes and something to eat, and if there is anything peticular you want let us know as we are going to send you a box soon.[22] How are you off for shirts. Nessa write to me oftener will you. I write every Monday and Friday we are all well and hope you are the same all send there love to you, Good bye

From your ever affectionate Kate

Johnsons Island April 2nd 1864

Dear Kate

I received your letter of the 25th some two or three days ago. I almost feel ashamed to acknowledge, but I expect I might as well out with it. I have also received your letter of the 28th. I expect you will give me a scolding, but I will not mind that if you will only continue writing as you have don[e].

If you only knew how gladley your letters are received, I think you would write almost every day. You spoke of the pleasant walks you had, and how much you wished I was there, to enjoy them with you. Nothing could give me more plasure than to be there with you. But however I have some long walks myself, or at least what we call long walks, though I cannot say much for the plesantness of them. Nor I cannot say that I ever wished you to be heare to enjoy them with me, in fact I don't think there is any enjoyment in prison. And then you know when they get any one inside of this pen they generaly keep them, or at least that has been my experience. Tell Jack I have not forgoten him although

I have not writin to him since he was heare.[23] Tell him I would write to him but I know you want all the letters I write sent to you, and I was about to say that I wanted all the letters you write sent to me, but I believ I ought to be satisfide with what I get. You say you want to send me a box, and wanted to know what I wanted. I am not in want of any clothing, except some good co-ton socks, and a few shirt collars, and also send me those gloves I spoke to you about No.7.[24] As for the balance I will leave it all with you and mother, as I know you know beter what to send me than I can tell you. Give my love to Father and Mother and with hopes that I may be with you soon and my best wishes for your happiness I remain your affectionate,

Wes

The prisoners used walks for exercise while in prison. Many prisoners complained of not getting enough exercise earlier in their captivity and actually gained weight. However, as rations were cut and conditions got worse, their complaints switched to losing weight from not getting enough to eat.

This letter, written on April 2, 1864, was one day after April fool's day. The pranks that go along with this date were practiced on John-son's Island. Wesley does not note this, but other prisoners discussed the various jokes played on fellow prisoners (Wilds 2005:149). William Peel, quartered in Block 8, received an express package on April 1, 1864, with several smaller packages for other prisoners. He could not get them to respond to his postings on the bulletin board until the next day, for fear that they would fall prey to an April fool's joke.

Major Edward Thomas Stakes wrote in his diary: "My room mates are trying to catch each other with April fools. I salted a cup of coffee and gave it to Lieut. L. M. Wood who tasted coffee and finding a joke played on him, he set it down amid a roar of laughter from his room mates" (Stakes 1864:52, entry for April 1, 1864).

Kate wrote to Wesley on April 1, 1864, that she pulled one over on his brother Jack; she never explained what the joke was.

Alex April 1st/64

Dear Nessa

One of your ever welcome letters was received this morning.
Lillie and her Grand Pa went to the office and brought it. Nessa
I am afraid that you are getting low spirited and impatient out
there now don't just please for mysake keep up your spirites will
you. You think you would like to be transferred to Point Lookout or the Capitol.[25] Nessa you would be nearer to us and we
might be able to see you oftener but just think you would not be
allowed to go out of your room now what kind of change of air
would you call that. Ma thinks you had better be satisfied to remain where you are and so do I then another thing I do not know
that such a thing would be done but you could find out by asking
some of the Officers out there then if it can and you still wish
it we will do all we can for you. Nessa the letter I received from
you this morning had never been sealed what does that mean I
think that one out of the family is enough to read the letters.[26]
Lillie has just come in with a great piece of cake in her hand says
she wishes Papa had it and tell Papa that she got the sweet kisses
he sent her and returnes them also to say she's a nice good girl.
Nessa by the doctor's thinking a change of air benifisoll I hope
that you are no worse than when I was out now I want you to let
me know when there is the least thing in the world the matter
with you. I gave Jack a prettie good April fool this morning he
has just come in and says that where you are is the best place for
you and you had better remain for the war as you are sure not to
be hurt if you want more vegitables you can or we will write to
that merchant and send him money to send you more. My page
has run out and I must stop all well and send there love to Nessa.
Good bye. Yours ever. Katie

Alex April 4th/64

Dearest Nessa

Your letter of the 28 acknowledging the receipt of mine of the
22nd has just been received, and Oh Nessa you cannot immagin

my feelings on reading it I feel as if I had commited a crime that I hardly dare ask forgiveness for but I know how good and kind you are Nessa and that you will forgive me and never think of it again.[27] Tomorrow, Tuesday is my regular day for writing to you but I feel so badly about that letter I cannot wait. Nessa you must not think anything more about it for I ment no harm. Oh that I had followed my own thoughts was after I had it sealed and tore it to pieces. I am so sad that I do not feel like writing about anything else. Dear Nessa we will send you a box soon. I have t[w]o calico shirts to make for you as soon as they are finished we will send it. Do you receive the paper from New York or not. I did not know that I was imposing a tax of two cents on you for every paper I send until this morning I must close Nessa now please don't write me another such mornful letter it were not for the kind affectionate manner in which you finished your letter I do not know what I would do. All well and send there love I delivered your kiss for Lillie. Oh that I could have one from you too. Good bye. Yours Ever Affectionately

    Kate

The archaeological evidence for clothing is abundant at Johnson's Island. Hundreds of buttons have been recovered from latrines and within the block areas. The most common button found is the prosser button. These ceramic buttons are typically plain white; however, a number with

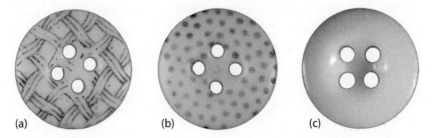

(a)   (b)   (c)

Fig. 10. Examples of prosser buttons recovered from Johnson's Island: (a) calico button (FS5334, dia. 10.5 mm); (b) calico button (FS1286, dia. 10.5 mm); (c) plain dish–type prosser button (FS0394, dia. 11 mm). (CHMA. Photographs by author.)

patterns, called calico prossers, have been found. The calico buttons were probably from shirts like the ones Kate indicated she was sending to Wesley.

Alex April 8th/64

Dear Nessa

I suppose you all are fasting to day as it is fast day in the South.[28] But we poor creatures have so little to eat from day to day that if we go without one day I don't know what would become of us the next.

Nessa why so long about writing. I have been getting your letters so regular lately that I have become spoilt and don't know hardly how to wait when they don't come regular. Will Fred and Purdy came down yesterday evening. All are well up home Purdy send his respects to you and says take care of yourself. Al had company the last time Purdy was down some of those what do you call them. Mosby Guerrilles stoped at the table, Al says he thought the horses were gone but they disturbed nothing but told him he was the doggedest fellow they ever saw.[29] That a body could not get anything out of him about ether side then turned round and said that was the best way. Lillie is standing by me but says she realy don't know what to say to Papa but sends you a kiss says wants to see you and that she is going to sent you her picture soon. All are well and send there love to you. please Nessa write soon will you. Good bye. Yours affectionately and Devotely.
      Katie

Alex April 9/64

Dear Nessa

I am most afraid that you wont like my writing to so often only three times this week that's not so very often, now if you promise that you wont scold me this time. Ill promise you that I will not write to you again before next Wednesday. I received your letter of the 2nd yesterday directly after I had sent mine to you. I hope the long walks you take prove beneficial to you. I would like very much to be there to walk with you provided we could walk where we pleased. Dear Nessa I cannot promise you all the letters I write but the greatest portion are for you they are very few that I write that are not sent to a certain Capt Makely at Fort Johnson. Tell Capt Ginevan I sent those rings by express to his sisters but have never heard weather they received them or not perhaps he has heard. Mrs. Jane Simson has just left. She asked me plese say to you give her love to her nephew Lieut Simson and say that his cousin Mr. L. S. has got about again and all are well escept his Uncle James.[30] But Nessa what I want to come at by writing this letter is do you know who James W. Parker. Co D 18th Confederate Cav is he is now a prisoner at Fort Delaware he wrote to Ma mentioned her christan name and stated he boarded with her a short time. no one ever boarded with Ma and we cannot inimegin [imagine] who it can be if you know write immediately and let us know. Look out for a box next week Lillie insists on sending her Papa some fish. All well and send there love to you Jack gone home this morning got letter from Doc yesterday talks about coming home. I send you 6 stamps write very soon and often.

Good bye Ever affectionately Kate

Johnsons Island April 16th/64

Dear Kate

I have received your letter of the 9th also the postage stamps you sent me. You wanted to know if I knew any one by the name of James W. Parker, Co. D. 18th Confederate Cav, but there is no one by that name in my Co., unless he has joined, since I was taken prisoner.[31] I am of the opinion that the gentleman is trying to pass himself on you under an assumed name. I suppose he is writing to you for something and, wants to try, and make you believe he is an old acquantance. I would not pay any attention to any such letters. I am very confident there is no such a regiment in the Confederate Servace. The 18th regt of Confederate Cav would mean, regular Confederate troops, belonging to the regular C.S.A. and not the provisional army of the C.S. Several of my boys were at Fort Delaware, but none by the name of Parker. Kate have you heard anything from my lady friend of Wheeling Va. She spoke of writing to you some time ago. Tell Jack I have received his letter and will write to him soon. Give my love to Father and Mother and with my best wishes for you all,

I am your affectionate

Wes

Toward the end of this letter Wesley talks about his lady friend in Wheeling. It was not uncommon for prisoners to correspond with many different individuals while in prison. This is the only time Wesley mentions his lady friend, and Kate does not seem to know anything about her. Many women were providing comfort by sending needed supplies to the prisoners. I have no information on how the prisoners at Johnson's Island came into initial contact with these benevolent women.

William Peel, a resident of Block 8 at Johnson's Island, wrote on April 26, 1864, about his interactions with several women in Baltimore with whom he had been corresponding.

I was favored, by the morning mail, with a package of late Baltimore papers, accompanied by a letter from Miss Dona. The letter informed me that I had fallen into another egregious blunder in my correspondence with her. It will be remembered that I recd., by express a few weeks since, a couple of anonymous—if the expression is admissible—boxes. I was somewhat perplexed to decide exactly from whom they had come, but being unable to settle it elsewhere than on Mrs. M + Miss Dona, + , as I had written but a day or two previous to the former lady, I at once determined to pour my store of gratitude at the feet of Miss Dona, content, for the time being, through her to express my thanks to Mrs. M.

My letter today leaves me almost as much in the back ground as ever, simply informing me that Miss Dona "was not the good angel who sent me the box of good things" but that "the credit—was entirely due a fair lady, with blue eyes + light hair." This is a partial picture of Miss Maggie, but to write to her would be another "leap in the dark." Shall I make it? (Wilds 2005:168–69)

Dear Kate

Your letter of the 9th has been received. I am not at all supprised at your thinking, strange of my not writing oftener. My
health has been very bad lately, and in fact there is so little to
write about heare, that I almost hate to write. A great many of
the prisoners heare think we will all soon be sent on exchange
and from what I have seen in the papers, I cant help but think,
that there may be something in it.[32] Though I am still afraid to
place much confidence in the reports we have heard. Tell Lill I
received her mesage, and will be very much obliged to her, for her
photograph. You may also tell Kate, hers would be very gladley
received, though I hope it will not be long before I may have the
plasure of seing you again. Give my love to all.

Your affectionate,

Wes

At this time, Union surgeons were selecting the sickest prisoners to
be exchanged. Wesley may have emphasized his illness to convince
the doctors to put him on the list. As for there being nothing to write
about—the prisoner minstrels who called themselves the Rebellonians
had performed for three hours just a few days earlier, new prisoners
had arrived from St. Louis, the weather was breaking, and the prisoners
were starting up their baseball games in the yard. Additionally, the beef
being given to the prisoners over the past week had been rotten (Wilds
2005:160–63; Stakes 1864:54–57).

Alex April 14th/64

Dear Nessa

It has been a long time since I wrote you last way last week,
although it has been some time you will have to excuse me from
writing much of a letter this time for I have a very sore finger
again it is very painful. I have the luck of having gathered fingers.
Jack's ice has arrived also my machiens. I had given it up for
lost thought those bad Rebs had got it but all arrived safely last
Tuesday evening. Nessa we send you a box by express started it

yesterday I hope it will reach you safely I will write a list of what was send on other side. I hope the gauntlets will suite Capt Fountain they are the best and smallest I could get I gave $2.50 for them I hope your things will suite you. I wrote a line under neath the list sent in box to the Major who superintends to the boxes and all such I do not know his name that he was to let all pass with out confistocating as Lillie says or he and I would have a qurrell. Lillie says she hopes Papa will enjoy the fish for she sends them says she knows you love fish because she does also sends you a kiss. Will F, and Purdy are down. I wrote to Mollie Monday sent a small bundle also stated that you had written to her if you

Fig. 11. Food storage jar, patent September 1860 (FS1050, height 18 cm). (CHMA. Photograph by author.)

want vegetables write to that Mr. Robinson and son in Sandusky. All well and send there love write soon. Good bye.

Ever affectionately Kate

2 shirts calico, 4 collars,
2 pairs yarn socks, 4 pair cotton also
1 pair gauntlets, 2 bundles for Lt's somebody
1 ham, 4 bolonies, 2 cans tomatoe,
1 can peaches, 1 jar pickled onions,
1 can blackberry wine, 1 bottle Hosteters bitters,
2 boxes sardines, 1 bottle horseraddish,
3 pies, some smoked herring, oranges,
lemons, sugar, nuts, 1 pound cake

The list of contents for the box Kate sent had the potential for leaving evidence in the archaeological record. Most discarded items would have been placed in the police cart (think of this as the garbage can for the block). Some broken items may have had pieces reach the soil, while others might be tossed directly into a latrine. With the number of items found over the years, it is apparent that many kinds of items were bought at the sutler's or sent to the prisoners.

Alex April 19th/64

Dear Nessa

I am so very sorry to hear that you have been sick again, then I am glad to hear that you have gotten better again, Nessa I am afraid that you do not take the proper care of yourself that you should you did not say what was the matter with you, I am glad to hear that you have a sutler out there now, I hope that you have received your box by this time.[33] Ma was afraid that you would be sent off before it arrived out there, but I told her not to be uneasy about the leaving part, I have just got back from market. I wish you had some of the nice fresh fish I got we get beautiful large shad at 50 and 60 cts a pair as nice as I ever saw, but they have been very high until now. Nessa I just feel like getting a letter from you this morning and would give ever so much for one just to know how you are, you I suppose have heard nothing of the exchange the report here was that all were to be exchanged after the 18th of this month but the papers say not a word about it. Lillie is asleep yet though it is after 9 oclock but I will send a kiss for her, all are well and send there love to you write soon and if ever such a thing should be that you are to leave out there let me know and I will be in Balt. Good bye. Ever affectionately yours Kate

Alex April 22nd/64

Dear Nessa

I have just received your letter of the 16th of course you had not had time to have received your box at that time, but hope by this you have it, you seem to think by your letter that Mr. Parker is a sort of imposter. I cannot but think there is something in it myself but how did he know Ma Christen name. There was quite an excitement in town yesterday about the provost marshalls on account of some Rebel prisoners brough[t] in they are rair things here now that is in town, but the soldiers say they within a mile or two of town every day nearly amoung those yesterday were Phil Roche cousin of L Green I did not get to see them, they belonged to different commands, Whites, Mosby's and were at a wedding of a certain Confederate Col's when caught, but the worse part was the Col had to make his escape without getting married that evening that was too bad now was it not, Nessa who in the world is this lady friend of yours I cannot immagin. Jack went up home yesterday and does not expect to be back for three or four days. I received a letter from Millie yesterday she and her child are well but did not say anything bout getting a letter from you, Doctor expects to be home by the 28th of this month. Lillie is in a kind of fret this morning and says she is going to write to Papa that Mama is a bad girl, but that I must tell you she is a good girl you know how much truth there is in all that Ma sends her love to you and says you must be a good boy and take care of yourself and keep up. Nessa you did not say one word about how you were and you know that is the most important part I want to

know about all well and send there love. Good bye Ever affectionately yours Kate

Johnsons Island May 2nd/64

Dear Kate

I have the pleasure of acknowledging the receipt of your letter
the 26th of April. I am glad to hear that John Smith has goten
home again. Mrs. Smith must have been very uneasy about him.
And poor Miss Mary, I don't expect she has got don talking about
it yet. I suppose everything begins to have the appearance of
Spring. About Alexandria, trees looking nice and green, and your
nice little flower gardens, are beginning to look very prety. I wish
I were there with you, instead of being heare on this oald island. I
don't think this war will last much longer, and I will try and content myself, and wait patiently for the happy time. It will come,
and I think very soon. Tell Mother I am in hopes I will soon have
the plasure of enjoying the nice treat she promised me when I get
home. Kate I am almost sorry I spoke of my health, as I heare you
have been very uneasy and imagined me much wors than I wer.
I am glad that I can releive you of any futher uneasyness about
that, as my health is tolerable good at presant. Kate do not allow
yourself to be troubled about anything. Look on the bright side
of everything. The time cannot be very far off when I will be with
you all again, and have the pleasure of enjoying many plesant
walks with you, such as we used to have. Oh! what enjoyment
in the indulgence of such thoughts. Think of them my dear Kate
and be happy. Give my love to Father, and Mother, and Lill a kiss
for me.

Yours affectionately,

Wes

His thoughts of spring were spurred on by the changing appearance
of the island. Prisoners talked about the advent of grass, leaves on the
trees, and birds coming back to the island, all of which set them pon-
dering about life back home. The prisoners planted gardens, especially
behind the even numbered blocks on the west side of the compound.

Wesley noted in his letter to Kate hearing from others of her concern for his health. As we have seen, there was certainly cause to worry, since many prisoners died of sickness in prisons. Wesley probably heard from his brother or other relatives concerning Kate's anxiety. This letter expressed a very positive tone. No doubt Wesley was trying to present a sense of control, giving hope to himself and to Kate.

Alex April 28th/64

Dear Nessa

Your letter of the 21st came to hand yesterday. I was extremely sorry to hear that your bitters was lost and that Capt Fountain did not get his gloves, they were certainly put in the box for I did it myself and they were certainly taken out there when the box was examined, did you inquire about them, they might you know have sliped behind something, if you do not get them let me know.[34] I have rendered Gen Terry a favor and I think that he will do me one. Yesterday was a wonderful day first I received your letter which was very agreeable indeed, next who do you think walked in, nobody but Dr. William Triplett of Mt. J himself which was not so agreeable 3rd in walked Doc just from Bloomfield he staid with us untill this morning when he went up home he is looking very well though he is not. And grows more and more like yourself if I had not of seen his face first I would of made sure that it was you. 4th and lastly I saw a yankee soldier that I knew before the war that is the first that I have seen that I ever knew before, Will T said that Mrs. Fountain was very anxious to come on but you know how much to believe of what he says, she wrote me that she was looking every day for Capt F return he said also not that he heard but that Capt F was very destitute, is it so, Nessa I send you the only sable hair brushes I can find in town I can get more but they are too large two of them are sable the other four are camel perhaps you can use them, if they do not suite let me know and I will try to get you more in Washington or Balt. Nessa I sent a list of the things I sent in the box written on the back of the letter I wrote you the day the box was sent, I have been wondering why some of you have not been painting each others faces, I shall be looking for yours before long now. I would like like [sic] to have all my and your friends faces. Write to me soon and always say how you are, all well and send there love to you. Good bye

Affectionately yours Kate.

Kate's letter of April 28, 1864, brings up a point worth commentary here. Although we are fortunate to have such a large collection of letters from their correspondence, there remains continual evidence that this assemblage of letters does not contain all that were written. Kate mentions his letter of April 28, which is missing. There are gaps in the historical record, for which detail sometimes can be inferred but at other times remains lost.

Kate notes sending sable and camel brushes for painting. Wesley never mentions his painting but does commission other prisoners to paint his portrait. Possibly he traded these brushes for their service. Archaeologically, there is no direct evidence of paintbrushes. It is possible they were made of wood and would have deteriorated if lost in the ground.

Nessa I send you 6 stamps[35]

Alex May 3rd/64

Dear Nessa

Your welcome letter of the 24th has been received and in it you spoke of Capt Ginevan's receiving a letter from his sister stating she had not received the rings I sent them by express to Cumberland directed to the care of a Mr. J Wickart at that place[36] I have been to the office several times about them and went again last Saturday when the clerk told me that they had been delivered to Mr. Wickart, I'll not rest until she gets them. Nessa have you received the letter containing the paint brushes I sent you yet and has Capt F received his gauntletts yet. I received a letter from Mollie a few days ago also heard yesterday by a lady friend just from there she and her child are well, her husband is a duty detective, realy Nessa I do not know what to write there is so little to write about. There is pleanty too but then you know is what do you call it contraband, there was 3 or 4 waggon loads of that article come in Saturday young and old the first negro troops that I have ever seen passed through here a few days ago then more on Sunday and more again yesterday. Realy I never was as scarce of something to write in my life before so I hope that you will excuse me for this uninteresting and short letter and I will write in a few days again and do better I have two more letters to write yet this morning one to Mrs. Ginevan one to Balt. For Pa the last I don't much mind writing for they are short. Take care of your self write soon all are well and send there love to you. Good bye, Ever affectionately yours

Kate

Johnsons Island May 8th 1864

Dear Kate

I have received your letter of the 3rd. Capt Ginevan has just got a letter from his Sister. She had received the rings you sent her. Kate I am going to write to Jack to morrow, to have ma[de] a pair of pants, and coat. I want a brown coat something like the one I used to ware, or my brown over coat. And I want you to get me some nice shell and if you can get some pearl. Perhaps you may find it in some of the Stores there it is sometimes kept in store. If there is none there, don't trouble yourself about it. If you can get any you can send it when Jack sends my coat and pants. I wanted to have some nice cuff butons made, but none of our jewelers had any nice shell, so I put it off untill they got in a new stock. We have had very nice wether for some time. The trees are beginning to put out, and the grass looks nice and green, and I imageon that all those that are at liberty must be enjoying themselves. I never wanted to get away from a place as bad in my life. We can only wait patiently, and hope for a beter time. Give my love to Father and Mother

Your affectionate,

Wes

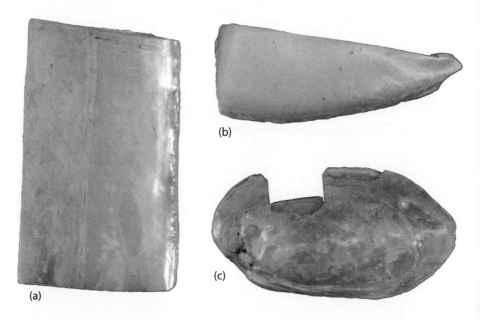

Fig. 12. Shells showing evidence of use in craft: (a) carved shell for possible set (FS0856, length 25.6 mm); (b) shell exhibiting use as source for shell set (FS1173, length 71.4 mm); (c) edge of shell exhibiting cut marks (FS0497, length 36.2 mm). (CHMA. Photographs by author.)

Hundreds of cut shell specimens have been recovered from the prison. Examples of both freshwater mollusk shell and marine shell have been uncovered at Johnson's Island. Some shell has a very high opalescence quality, sought by the prisoners making jewelry.

Alex May 7th/64

Dear Nessa

I received your letter day before yesterday threatening Lillie with no more messages until you received her photograph so I though[t] I had better hasteing up the matter. I would have written yesterday you know it was my regular day for writing but could not get the photograph until this morning they were taken by Elick R. I had them taken three different stiles. I do not know which is the best so I send you one of each one double and two single. Nessa if you have any sort of an artist out there do have yours painted and send it in. Well Nessa I believe the great fight has realy begun how it will go no one can tell, I am very sorry that you are in prison but realy Nessa I feel thankful that you cannot be in the fight for I can tell you that it is going to [be] an awfull one. I am so very sorry to hear that you are not so well again. Nessa I have had the last cross you sent me made into a pin and it is very beautiful. Mr. Frichell made a very nice and substantial job of it put a band of gold clear across the back well riveted and the pin on that he put your and my own initials on it I am very proud of it. Father has been quite sick since I wrote you last and is very poorly yet. The rest of us are all very well Purdy was down this week and all were well up home. Old Mrs. Entwisel is very sick poor old Lady I fear she will not live long Lill is very attentive to her Miss Mary is well. I have never received any letters from your friends yet all send there love to you take care of yourself and I hope this may find you better than you have been. Write and let me know if you get the photographs Good by. Ever affectionately yours. Kate

In this section the conversation shifts away from exchange. Both Wesley and Kate have resigned themselves to the fact that Wesley will be confined until the end of the war. Although this is not something Wesley would proclaim, Kate is undoubtedly thankful he is in prison and not with an active military unit. This was the time when Grant was attempting to defeat Lee's Army of Northern Virginia. The Battle of the Wilderness had just taken place, and further conflicts in Virginia were in the works. Casualties were high. No doubt Kate was nervous about the entire affair and glad Wesley was not in the fray. Kate's last few letters do mention some developing military actions, but she is careful not to say too much and have her letters considered contraband. Wesley's, on the other hand, are concerned only with his comfort and interest in the craft on the island. He appears either completely ignorant of the developing military campaigns (which is highly unlikely) or choosing not to mention these to his Kate.

Sending Images

(May 11–September 15, 1864)

If the women of a nation never lose courage, the men never can be conquered.

General Isaac Ridgeway Trimble, from Johnson's Island, February 8, 1864

Kate informing Wesley she was sending him photographs of their young daughter Lillie is more than understandable. Her request that Wesley try and get his portrait painted and sent to her, however, may seem an unusual request of a prisoner-of-war, but the desire for personal images to be sent home was quite common with these prisoners. How does this behavior become a widespread occurrence?

The prisoners at Johnson's Island reflected the best of the southern gentleman. These men were enculturated with a deep sense of entitlement. They valued their own education, their status in society, their military rank, family, and their religion. They were the protectors of their women and children. If nothing else, each wanted to make sure his family could count on him, even while in prison. The importance of letters in relaying this position in southern society is easily seen as Wesley briefly discusses family concerns. His need to find the perfect image of himself speaks to the overarching influence of his upbringing. No matter how the image was created, whether drawn, painted, or photographed, there was always the sense of stateliness. There was an assuredness about these portraits, letting family and friends know the men were doing well, even in the hands of the wretched enemy.

At various times both Wesley and Kate discussed sending or receiving images of the other. Wesley wrote about several artists among the prisoners but seemed dissatisfied with their abilities. Although many prisoners mentioned having their portraits drawn or painted, only one

Fig. 13. Pencil drawing of Colonel William E. DeMoss, 10th Tennessee Cavalry, by Major J. C. Smith, 12th Regiment Arkansas Volunteers (3 × 3.75 inches). (By permission of Rick Warwick.)

of these portraits has been located. The portrait is of Lieutenant Colonel William Eldridge DeMoss, 10th Tennessee Cavalry. He was captured in Tilton, Georgia, on May 13, 1864. DeMoss was at Johnson's Island from May 23, 1864, until May 21, 1865, when he took the Oath of Allegiance (NAGRP 1865). During his stay on Johnson's Island, he had his picture drawn by Major John C. Smith, of the 12th Arkansas Infantry. Major Smith was drawing portraits for a fee. Once drawings were finished, Wesley mentioned that he had them photographed in Sandusky to have multiple copies to send.

In a population of more than twenty-five hundred Confederate officers at Johnson's Island during the later stages of the war, it was not surprising to find men of varied and special talents. The letters made reference to their talents as artists, poets, musicians, and jewelers. Prestige was achieved in prison but for different accomplishments than on the outside. Officers who commanded a certain amount of respect due to their rank (and its ascribed status) found that in prison, rank was of secondary importance. Their military position was not easily recognized as they were forbidden to wear their uniforms. The only exception to this was the imprisoned generals, whose reputations did not require their uniform. The prison population knew who these men were and granted the generals their utmost regard. Other prisoners found that desired talents helped them achieve a higher status in prison, both in prestige and wealth. A good artist was sought out for his ability to provide a fine portrait to send home to the family.

Having your portrait painted or drawn was not the only means of having an image available to send to your loved ones. One prisoner brought photography to the island. Lieutenant Robert M. Smith of the 61st Tennessee Infantry was a prisoner at Johnson's Island from June 5, 1863, until February 24, 1865. He was captured at the Big Black River Bridge battle on May 17, 1863 (NAGRP 1865; Smith 1864). During his time at Johnson's Island, he created a photographic studio in the attic of Block 4 and covertly photographed prisoners for a fee (Smith 1863–65). No doubt he paid a complicit guard to furnish some needed supplies and ignore the operation. It is unclear how many photographs he provided, but many prisoners talk of his taking pictures during this period.

Colonel Virgil S. Murphy, 17th Alabama Infantry, wrote:

I visited an attic in the third story of a block, partitioned off from the main vacuum, by boards box tops and other rude material and forming a deguerreau room. An enterprising rebel, through some purchased tool has succeeded in running in plates chemicals and an instrument and has his studio here. Rebs in crowds visit him daily, to have (in consideration of paying one dollar) their traitorous countenances faithfully delineated upon canvass. Vain as the balance I sat for a picture and when it was developed and presented, I found to my astonishment that the plates were to[o] small to take all my beard which now reaches to my waist, I concluded to submit to this curtailing of my most cherished + manly feature and concluded to receive it anyhow. The picture otherwise is very good. (Virgil Murphy 1865, entry for February 2, 1865)

Robert Smith's camera held a plate two by two and a half inches in size. On these copper plates he used a wet plate process for creating portraits. His "studio" had light only from an eighteen-inch window in the gable of Block 4. Thus many of Smith's photographs were dark, probably from the lack of good lighting in the attic. Kate Makely notes in her letter to Wesley on January 30, 1865, that the picture she received was a good likeness but dark. This evidence suggests Wesley had his picture taken by Robert Smith.

Unfortunately, the photograph Wesley sent back to Kate is not part of the historical record. It would have shown Wesley much like Captain Francis Marion Jackson (figure 14), well groomed, well dressed, and

Fig. 14. Photograph taken by Lieutenant Robert Smith of Captain Francis Marion Jackson, 61st Tennessee Mounted Infantry (2.5 × 2 inches). (By permission of Nancy Feazell, granddaughter of Robert Smith, and Geoffrey Feazell, grandson of Nancy Feazell.)

projecting an air of confidence. Robert Smith even used a red dye for highlighting the cheeks of his subjects, a common practice of the time.

Wesley too set about acquiring a self-portrait. He was determined to attain an image he felt reflected his position in life. From the letters it appears that he had at least two portraits either drawn or painted (and then photographed to allow multiple copies) and had one photograph taken. It is unfortunate that these images have not surfaced with any of the descendants. Vanity was part of the dialogue between Wesley and Kate. Both were complimentary about each other's images and at the same time critical of their own. The demand for images to send to family was pervasive. Robert Smith had a thriving business, allowing him to send two hundred dollars back to his family (Smith 1864, entry for April 22, 1864). The demand also kept several other artisans quite busy. The assurance a well-composed image portrayed to the family was undoubtedly worth any expense in its production. These portraits were composed by the artist for no other purpose than to assure the eventual recipients of the image that their man was healthy and strong and would return. When posing for these portraits, the men were dressed in their finest. Smith may have lent appropriate attire to his clients for the photographs. Of the nine images attributable to Smith, the men were all wearing either uniforms or dress coats, some with vests.

Wesley's letters continue from May 11, 1864. Colonel Charles W. Hill was the commander at Johnson's Island, replacing General Terry on May 9, 1864 (Frohman 1965:12–13). Colonel Hill remained commander at the prison until after the war ended.

Johnson's Island May 11th 1864

Dear Kate

I had the pleasure of receiving your letter of the 7th to day. And am very much obliged to you for the photographs you sent me. I think they are very good pictures. Tell Lill she has fulfilled all her promisis, and will be glad to correspond with her again. I hardly know who I am indebted to for the other photographs, whether Lill or you. I rather expect I am indebted to you both, and to you particularly not only for the photographs, but for many other things you have so kindly sent me. Kate I would

Fig. 15. Photograph of Kate (Catherine) Makely with her first daughter Mary Louise (Lillie), ca. 1861. (By permission of The Library of Virginia, Makely Family Papers.)

gladly send you my picture if I could get one fit to send. There
are several very good painters heare but none that ever tried to
paint portraits. It is a very hard matter to paint a good picture,
especially for one that never don anything of the sort befor. I had
mine taken the other day, but it was not fit to send. I don't think
you would have known who it was taken for. I will have a pencil
sketch taken tomorrow or next day, and if it is anything like a
good one, I will send it to you the last of this weak or the first of
next, with some other things I have to send you.[1] Kate I supose
the City is all excitement and anxiety to know the result of the
big fight. You say you are sorry I am in prison, but am glad that
I will not be in the fight. Kate I know your kind and affectionate
feelings for me, and they can never be forgoton by me. You can
scarcely know how much I esteem them, and how much you de-
serve my kindest wishes. But Kate I would almost rather be any
ware els than in prison. If I could have my own wishes I would be
at home with you. Give my love to Father and Mother, also a kiss
to Lill for me.

Yours most affectionately,
Wes

                                        Johnsons Island May 16/64
Dear Kate
    I expect you have been looking for the so long promised pres-
ent for some time. And I fear it will not fill your expectations.
Could I get any thing nicer or better, I would take great pleasure
in sending it to you. The package contains a book, sett of chess
men, a ring, and the picture you wanted. The book contains
the names, and rank of all the officers in this prison. And some
poetry wri[t]ten by some of the prisoners here also a list of all
the generals in the Confederate army. And in the front you will
find a very good drawing of the prison. The ring is a very indifer-
ant one, and scarcely fit to send. I had a very pretty sett. I gave it
to the gentleman who made it, but he lost it and put this thing
in. I dont think the picture is a very good one, but it is a very
hard matter to get the expression of any one with a pencil. I had

one taken some time ago, and sent it over to Sandusky to get it photographed, and have not got them yet. I will send them to you as soon as I get them. I dont think it is as good as this. I wish you would have this photographed, and send me a coppy. I want to see how it looks after being photographed. I wish I had something nice to send to Lill, as I suppose she will expect something Kate if you have any nice setts for rings, breastpins earrings, or anything of that sort, that you want made up, mount kind of jewelry here, send them to me and let me know how you want them made.[2] Give my love to Father and Mother.

Any many thanks to Lill and C__ [Catherine] and I will also add a few kisses for them, for the nice pictures they sent me.

Yours most affectionately, Wes

On May 16, 1864, Wesley sent Kate a book with several mementos of the prison. Contained in the book, as he noted in his letter, were listings of all the Confederates being held at Johnson's Island and of all the Confederate generals. The book also included a list of the island's deceased and the autographs of many prisoners. The poetry in it was written mainly by George McKnight. Wesley probably purchased the book with the lists already written inside. The handwriting for the poetry and mortuary list is the same hand; but not Wesley's. Either the sutler or an enterprising prisoner sold the book to Wesley. Autograph books and books with listings of prisoners were popular, and a prisoner or guard, perhaps working with the sutler, created these books for prisoners-of-war to take or send home to recall all those imprisoned at Johnson's Island. Had Wesley been the one collecting all this data, it would have taken him weeks. He would certainly have mentioned the process to Kate, as he had done so often with the jewelry.

There was also a pencil drawing of the prison compound in the book. During Wesley's stay on Johnson's Island the prison was expanded and two large mess halls were added. This image was created prior to these changes. The map was probably an added attraction for the sale of the book, and once he had purchased the book and sent it South, Wesley had no real inclination to have another rendition of the prison complex drawn. He was focused on Kate's well-being and not on documentation of his experiences on Johnson's Island.

Alex May 11th/64

Dear Nessa

Jack brought me a double treat from you yesterday in the shape of two letters. Oh! Nessa if I could get one every day. They were dated the 2nd & 4th [both missing] you were glad to hear John Smith had gotten back. I was very glad on poor Mrs. S. account. I am sure that if Miss Mary could see eather of us she would not be done talking about it yet. Nessa everything realy does begin to look like spring here. I am afraid that we are going to have an intensely hot summer here for the weather is unusually warm now. I think I never spent so much warmer day in August than last Sunday was, Lillie is invited out to a partie this evening. It is her little friend Mollie Herriek's birthday. Poor little thing she is in fine spirits, oh if we all could be as free from care and trouble as she. I am glad you do not think the war will last long I hope your thoughts may prove true. Nessa you need not regret telling me know about your health for I always feel better satisfied when I know how you are I am releived to hear that you are better and that the thoughts of old times and those that are to come gives you pleasure Nessa I often think of them, and lighten, my heart. Nessa in your letter of the 4th you spoke of wanting to send me some thing. Dear Nessa nothing would give me more pleasure if I cannot see your own face than to receive the picture of it. I shall look ansxiously every day for it until I receive it I supose you have received Lillies and mine by this time, tell Capt. F. I am glad to hear that what Will T says is not so. He said, that he was coming to see me again before he left but he has not made his appearance, yet but I got that nobody was disapointed. I am sorry Capt F. has not gotten his gloves for I certainly put them in the box myself right on top. Jack has sent on for your paper again. I think Doc is the one to feel complimented you have always known my thoughts about yoursself.

All well except Pa. Lillie sends a kiss and her love to Papa all send there love to you. Good bye

From your affectionate Kate

Johnsons Island May 18th/64

Dear Kate

I have at last started the package I promised to send you some time ago, and hope it may reach you safely, as I know you will receive it gladly though it be worth but very little. One of the officers here has been kind enough to attend to it for me, and have it expressed.[3] The package containes a book with the names of all the officers in this prison, and a sett of chess men made by one of the prisoners here, a ring and the picture you wanted me to send you.[4] I don't think the picture is a good one, but you can judge about that yourself, as it has not been long since you wer[e] here, and saw me. You will see some change, as I have shaved off part of my beard since you saw me. It will look better after it is photographed. I wrote to Jack a few days ago to send some clothing

Fig. 16. Bone chess piece (top of knight, FS8349, height 24.3 mm). (CHMA. Photograph by author.)

to Lieut Pence and forgot to give his size.[5] He is about my size. I receive your letter of the 11th yesterday. I am sorry to heare that father is still sick. I hope he may be well by the time you write again. Give my love to him and Mother. I also send my love, and a few kisses to Lill and my other little pet.

Yours affectionately

Wes

As mentioned, inside the book Wesley sent Kate on May 11, 1864, was a drawing of the prison compound (figure 17). The drawing was not done by Wesley but by another prisoner at Johnson's Island. This bird's-eye view of the prison was typical of renderings of the complex in 1863 and early 1864. The artist was not well schooled in perspective, but the drawing has more three-dimensional aspects than do images of the prison completed by Captain Hogane and others in 1862. Captain James T. Hogane, topographical engineer, CSA, produced two-dimensional water color drawings of the prison compound for other prisoners in the summer of 1862. Drawings of the prison in later 1864 and 1865 exhibit a one-point perspective but vary according to the artist's skills. This drawing showed the thirteen blocks in which the prisoners were housed, the

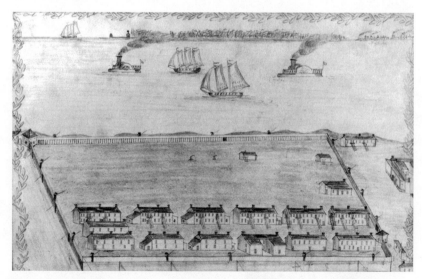

Fig. 17. Drawing of Johnson's Island inside an album Wesley sent to Kate. (By permission of The Library of Virginia, Makely Family Papers.)

sutler stand, condemned prisoner house, and water pumps. Shown on the outside were the stockade fence, guard, and a couple of buildings. In Sandusky Bay were depicted several boats, including the steamships that regularly serviced the island and a couple of sailboats, probably with sightseers. Wesley was housed in Block 1, the block farthest to the right on the bay side row of blocks. Block 6, the hospital block, is located in the middle of the opposite row with extensions running off the back toward the fence. One of these was the "dead house" and the other was the mess area for the hospital.

Alex May 14th/64

Dear Nessa

I have been looking so anxiously all the week for a letter from you. I don't know why, but I feel as if I must get a letter from you, perhaps it is the promise of that picture that makes me so impatient and then I kinder got the blues, there is nothing in the world to write about every thing is as still here as possible except it is the rattling of those mean carts and waggons. I wrote in one of my letters that Old Mrs. Entwisle was very sick poor old Lady is no better she has typhoid feavor, no one has been down from home for some time neather has Jack been up he is so busy he can not move. I believe he is about getting his brick machine in operation. Nessa I have just seen a sight that I hope I may never witness again I never before and hope I never shall again I am so nervous that I will have to stop writing for a little. Nessa have you received the photographs of Lillie and myself that I sent you yet. Poor little Lillie she talks a great deal about her precious Papa and wants to see him so badly. Oh Nessa we would all give any thing in the world to see you. There has been a great many wounded and sick soldiers brought up the river here the last two nights. I believe there is two or three confederate among them they are at the old lyceum hall I have not learned who they are. Nessa this has been truly a morning of arrests, Nessa I send you eight postage stamps are you getting your paper yet Jack wrote to have it go on. Do you want anything to wear or eat or money, if you do, write and let us know all well and send there love to you. Ma sends a message but I wont deliver it to day you know I have not the room to write Write soon, I remain affectionately yours

    Kate

Johnsons Island May 21st/64

Dear Kate

    Yours of the 14th was received yesterday. I am not in want of anything at presant. I wrote to Jack some time ago for some clothing, but have not heard from him yet. I am very much obliged to you, and you will pleas accept my kindest thanks for your kindness. It is very poor and inadequate reward, though what els can I give. Kate I heard from Dr. Triplett a few days ago, he was then in Philadelphia. I think he must be traveling for his health, for I expect it was geting rather unhealthy for him at home. Kate what in the world have you seen, or heard, or what misfortunes have you met with, to make you so unhappy. Oh! why will you embrace misery you aught not forfit your own happiness for any one. For heavens sake do not let any thing disturb your piece or happiness. Your enjoyment and happiness is very essential to your friends. Kate you say you have been looking for my picture for sometime. If you have not got it when this reaches you, I think if you go to the express office you will find it there. Give my love to Father and Mother.

    Yours affectionately.

    Wes

This letter is a good example of Wesley's concern for his family and attempts to provide the stability over which he has no control from prison. Kate's letter of May 14 does make one wonder what it was that she was observing; possibly something to do with the wounded soldiers. The conflict in Virginia was continuing at Spotsylvania. Wesley's mention of Dr. Triplett going to Philadelphia for his health may refer to the battles in Virginia.

Dear Nessa

Your dear letter came to hand yesterday it was a long time coming and I looked for it many a time before it did come it was dated the 11th that was a long time to come here, Jack also received your letter day before yesterday requesting a suit of clothes and stating that you had written to me to send you some shells for rings. Nessa I have never received the letter. I do not know why but I rather think there is a good many letters that are not delivered, Nessa the suit of clothes, Jack thought we could but [buy] ready made and cheaper, but I know your horror of Jew clothing so we went down to Mr. Murrey and selected the cloth and ordered them to be made it seems hard to get a nice adiena [?] color cloth every thing is eather dark or too light. Mr. Murrey says that he thinks that this is the most suiteable for and thinks it will suite you he knows it will wear well I though[t] it might be a little too heavy for pants but he says not, we did not order any vest as you did not send the measure though[t] you did not want it, Mr. M has your old measure yet, the coat and pants come very high but that is of no consequence if my Nessa wants anything he promised to let me have them this week. I am glad that you rec the photographs Lillie sends a kiss to papa and says that if I wrote to you that she is a bad girl she knows that you will write back that she is good. Al is staying down here now. All were well up home when he left except Doc from what Al say he must have erysipelas ask Capt Ginevan if he has heard wether his sister rec the rings I sent or not it makes me feel very badly about them. I saw the cleark at the express office he said that the letter had been delivered to Mr. Wickart in Cumberland in whose care it was directed. I wrote to them to that effectt and have never rec any answar. Nessa all prisioners sent to Point Lookout before the 30th day of Apl are declared eschange perk up your time will come next. All send there love to you and do write soon I am extremely sorry you could not get a picture to suite you that you could send me I am afraid that you want to be too good looking. Good bye.

Affectionately yours Kate

Johnsons Island May 24

Dear Kate

I received your letter of the 18th yesterday, and was there anything worth writing, I would have answered it at once. Everything is very quiet here. The weather is getting very warm, and I begin to feel a little lazy. You wanted to know if Capt Ginevan had heard w[h]ether his sister had received the rings you sent them or not. I thought I had writen to you some time ago that they had received them I am glad to see that you are in much better spirits than you wer when you wrote before. Give my love to all.

Yours affectionately. Wes

Many prisoner letters and diaries state at times that there was "nothing of importance to write." Some prisoners wrote pages about changes in the weather, different incidents related to the guard, or just about their accomplishments in the washing department. Having many examples of his letters to Kate, it seems probable Wesley's brief letter of May 24 covering only the bare necessities suggests he was not feeling well.

The USS *Michigan*, the only armed vessel in Lake Erie, was sitting in Sandusky Bay. She typically arrived at times when there were rumors of a mass escape attempt (Rodgers 1985:83–107). The *Michigan* stayed until May 25, steaming out that morning. During the last half of May 1864 the Union guard made their presence known to the prisoners by forcing their retirement into the barracks before sunset, by restricting access to certain newspapers, and by having them standing for hours during roll call. All this suggests that the Union was suspicious of potential escape.

Alex May 20th/64

Dear Nessa

I would like so much to write you a good long letter this morning but you can immagin how much I feel like writing having just waking it being most 10 o clock, but Nessa I did not lie down until ½ past 8 this morning I sat up with poor old Mrs. Entwisel last night poor old lady we did not expect her to live until this morning, Nessa I believe the fight has commenced again. I supose you saw by your paper that Imboden had, had, a brush with Siegel, Imboden, Echols, and Breakinridge were in the fight about New Market, poor Miss Mary I expect she shaked and quaked a little more. Nessa Mr. Murry promised your suite to be done this week so about Monday we will start the box. We have had a good deal of rain but the weather is warm and pleasant now and Nessa I heartily wish with you that you could be with me, Nessa I hope and cannot but think that, that, bright day is in store for us yet and not so terribly far distant though it may seem a very long time to us, I hope my poor boy is well and will continue so, this leaves us all well Pa has been very much complaining indeed you know he cannot stand the heat of summer well. Lillie send a kiss to Papa and word that she is a good girl all join me in love to you, write to me very soon and often Nessa. Good by.

Ever affectionately thine.

Kate

The battle of New Market, Virginia, started in earnest on May 15 and then, after a lull, resumed on June 1, 1864 (Boatner 1987:588–89). Major General Franz Sigel commanded the Union troops and General John C. Breckinridge the Confederates. Brigadier General John D. Imboden was also commanding troops for the Confederacy. His brother, Captain Francis Marion Imboden, 18th Virginia Cavalry, was captured in early June 1864 and sent to Johnson's Island (NAGRP 1865).

Alex May 23rd/64

Dear Nessa

I have just dispatched your box and hope it may reach you safely and prove satisfactory it is a nice box and I know you will say so, I hope the clothes will fit also the hat and shoes, we got everything of the best we could. Nessa I went all over town to day everywhere I though[t] I could possiblely get any shells but

Fig. 18. Hard rubber cross with indentation for metal set (FS5290, length 18.7 mm). (CHMA. Photograph by author.)

what I send you were all I could get. I hope you can use them, there is a small bundle in the box for Lt. T. B. Jackson.[6] Mrs. John Daingerfield sent it. Nessa the pruns I sent you must put them in a kettle and just cover them with water then boil them well put in some sugar and a little nutmeg they will be very good for you, and very nice if any of the men are sick, I would have sent you a ham but though[t] you could buy one out there there is so few things we can send now the weather is so warm that everything spoils so soon. I have received two letters from Lt. Pence in his first he wrote for a suite of clothing but a few days after he wrote again and stated we need not send the suite, but some other things he wrote for, so we shall send his box tomorrow if I can get the shirts made in time I will send him some shirts socks shoes and money what he wrote for and some eatables. Nessa a lady friend of mine wants you to get for her a cross like the last one you sent me you remember it don't you it was kind a round with a round pearl set in the centre you spoke of having some thing for me you can send the cross when you what you have for me send the price of the cross and how I must send the money so that you will be sure to get it also she wants to know what a set would cost earrings and pin of the gutta percha made round and set with pearls and gold[7] she could have the pin and the part that goes though the ear put to them here let me know about them as soon as you can Nessa poor old Mrs. Entwisel is gone she was buried yesterday, all well but Pa he hurt his leg yesterday and it is very painful All send there love to you. Lillie sends a kiss. I must bid you good bye now hoping this and your box may reach you in safety. Yours most affectionately Kate

turn over

1 coat. 1 pair pants. 2 pairs cotton socks. 1 hat. 4 neck ties. 50 paper collars, 1 pair shoes, 1 piece soap. Some shells. 1 bundle for Lt. T. B. Jackson. 1 fruite cake. 1 can blackberries. 1 can tomatoes. 4 lbs sugar, 1½ doz herrig. ½ doz orenges, 4 lbs dates. 4 lbs figs. 2 lbs pruens. 2 boxes of sardines ½ doz nutmegs. 5 bolonias, 2 lbs dried beef. 1½ doz lemons some small cakes, 3 lbs nuts, 1 piece jellie cake. K.

The archaeological investigations at Johnson's Island have produced hundreds of buttons. Buttons for fly or suspender attachment were normally of bone or iron. Although button failure due to breakage occurred, the large number of recovered whole buttons would suggest that failure of the thread holding buttons to clothing was more common. Most of the items supplied to Wesley in the box would not leave much of an archaeological record.

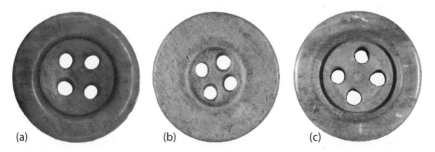

(a)   (b)   (c)

Fig. 19. Examples of bone buttons recovered from Johnson's Island: (a) FS0076, dia. 19 mm; (b) FS0058, dia. 16.5 mm; (c) FS0183, dia. 17.5 mm. (CHMA. Photographs by author.)

Dear Kate

I have the pleasure of acknowledging the receipt of the box you sent me. I am very much pleased with the clothing you sent me. They fit me very well, and are verry nice. I suppose I am indebted to Lill for the fish, as she sent me them before. They are verry nice, and so is everything els verry nice and good, and I scarcely know how I will ever be able to repay your kindness. Tell Miss Daingerfit I delivered the package as directed. I have also seen about the cross and earrings you spoke of. The pin and earrings will cost nine dollars. If she wants the earrings let me know. I am getting along here about as usual, though my health is better now than it has been since I have been a prisoner. I have almost given out all hopes of an exchange this summer, and proposed to my room mates to paper our room, and try and make every thing around us look as cheerful as possible.[8] I spend most of my time walking about and reading some oald books, though they interest me but very little, and occasionly I have the pleasure of receiving a letter from you, and I have had the pleasure of receiving three of those dear letters lately. Oh! Kate I must thank you for many happy minutes they have given me. The thoughts of a heart so fresh in the timeless purity of goodness is a luxury I could scarcely have expected. I daily find more to charm my interests and deepen my affection for you. Give my love to all, and with many thanks to you for kindness, and my best wishes for your happiness,

I am yours affectionately, Wes

The picture of Kate Makely in the collection at The Library of Virginia shows her wearing earrings and a brooch, both intentionally colorized in gold on the photograph despite their small size in the image. This touch and the nature of Kate's requests to Wesley indicate that she was associating with others of an affluent standing.

Fig. 20. This enlargement from the portrait of Kate Makely (fig. 15) shows her earrings and collar pin. These items were colorized in gold on the original photograph. (By permission of The Library of Virginia, Makely Family Papers.)

Johnsons Island

June 2nd 1864

Dear Kate

I am glad to hear that you have received the things I sent you, and to hear that you are pleased with them. I saw Mr Withers yesterday he is very well, and has not been sick that I know of. All the Alexandria boys are very well at present, and in fine spirits.

Kate I am much obliged to you all, for your flatering complements. Remember me to aunt Jane, tell her I have not forgotten her yet, and intend to send her something the next time I send anything and tell her, I want her to take good care of my two little pets. I will have the ring made you spoke of and send it with the other things. If you want the earrings you spoke of some time ago let me know at once, so that I may send them all at the same time. Give my love to father and mother.

Affectionately yours, Wes

Among the many styles of finger rings produced at Johnson's Island, one common ring style was made from hard rubber buttons with silver sets of a hand and heart. This style was probably one sent to loved ones. Figure 21 shows three rings with hearts as part of the overall design. Rings FS5387 and FS5531 appear to have been complete prior to being broken and lost. FS2164 may have broken before it was finished with insets. The differences among the three rings in quality of workmanship is quite apparent.

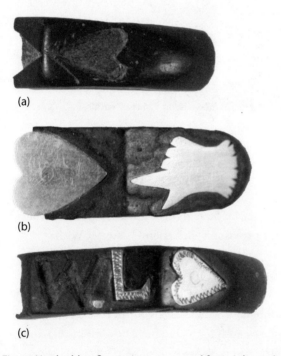

(a)

(b)

(c)

Fig. 21. Hard rubber finger rings recovered from Johnson's Island: (a) broken finger ring with heart and diamond shaped sets (FS2164, dia. 16 mm); (b) broken finger ring with pointing hand and heart silver sets (FS5387, width 5.2 mm); (c) broken finger ring with lettering and heart silver sets (FS5531, width 4.7 mm). (CHMA. Photographs by author.)

Dear Nessa

I have received the box of presents you sent me and am very much oblige to you they are all very nice indeed, there was one article I prize above all the rest I think it is an excellent likeness though Purdy wants to persuade me that it [is] to[o] good look-ing. Most every one recognizes it at once. Ma thinks you better looking than you use to be and says if you stay on Johnsons Is-land a little longer that you will be come very hansome, but I do not think there is any room for improvement. Aunt Jane knew it at once and says also that you are prettier and that you look like a man now. The chessman are very nice and I hope that we may live and soon meet and that we may play many a game together with them. Purdy was much pleased with and wanted to get them from me. Lillie loves the ring and says her Papa sent it to her she knows he did, she is not so well to day. Here she is just come from Miss Mary with a nice glass with handle that Miss M has given her to drink her milk out of. Nessa before I forget I want you to send me another ring like the one you sent in the box. I want it exactly like that one except the set make it for a set about the size of the one you sent. The set is to be put in here, a di[a]mond so the ring must be nice the one you sent just fits my third finger this one must about fit my first finger. In my last I ordered a cross for a friend also. I sup[p]ose you have received the letter it is to be sent by express you can send the ring with it and the pieces. Nessa why do you pay the express I do not think you have any more money than you want. Don't do it again. The book you sent I am much pleased with except one thing I did think to find a piece of your composition in it. Nessa I hope you have received your box by this time. Miss Withers was here inquiring after her brother who is a privet in Mosby Com. and but is held out there as a Captain John B Withers,[9] she heard two weeks ago or better that he was ill about that time she sent him a box and since she has written to him and others but can here nothing. I wish you would inquirer and find out about him and let me here as soon as possible his mother and sister are very much distressed about him I send you some scraps of gold there is four little pieces you can probably use it for some thing and when I write again I will send you more and better. Pa has a very sore leg he hurt it last Sunday and it has become very sore. I kissed L for you but that other pet of yours I could not get near enough to her but wont give it up. I will have those photographs as soon as I can get them All send there love to you hoping this may find you well. Yours affectionately,

    Kate

This letter, perhaps more than any other, illustrates how fortunate the Makelys were. Kate chastises Wesley for paying to have materials sent by express when he could easily have sent items COD (cash on delivery). She mentions the gold pieces she enclosed with the letter and requests a ring with a blank set to be used for the diamond she has. Although the war was continuing in northern Virginia, her letter all but ignores it. Kate finished the letter by stating she has had photographs made of his likeness. There is no indication in her writing that she had to cut back on her lifestyle due to Wesley being a prisoner-of-war or impacts of the war locally.

Johnsons Island

    June 4th 1864

    Dear Kate

    I have been looking for a letter from you for the last day or two, and for fear you might write more than we are allowed to receive. I thought I had better write to you at once and notify you of the regulations in regard to writing. There was a notice posted up inside of the prison a few days ago, saying that we would not be allowed to write or receive more than one page of comon letter paper. Everything is very quiet here at present, and there is very little said about the armies in Virginia, and even the exchange is spoken of very seldom. The weather is very plesant and cool. I offtimes think of you all and Oh! How much I wish I could only be with you all. What pride and pleasure I would take walking with you Lill. Don't forget about writing only one page of letter paper. Give my love to father and mother.

Yours affectionately

Wes

Posting the regulation restricting length of letters was a reminder to prisoners of who was in charge. It was a practical matter as well, since Union postal inspectors had to read through all their writings. On June 3, 1864, prison officials posted another notice restricting what the sutler could provide. This began a long series of retaliatory stances by the Union toward its Confederate captives. Wesley did not burden Kate with all the restrictions imposed on prisoners. Prisoners with enough credit at the sutler avoided these limitations by purchasing needed items or bribing the guard.

Alex June 1st/64

Dear Nessa

Your letters of the 21st and 24th have been received. I believe it is the first time that I have ever a second before answering the first it would not have occurred but that I waited for the photographs to send you I was to get them Monday evening but did not go for them until yesterday morning then I was to get them this morning when I went they were not done and would not be until day after tomorrow, but as soon as they are done I will send them I want to have a very large one taken, cause why you know its not every day that one comes across such a hansome picture that's my idea. Nessa I hope before this that you have received your box then that will be one subject for you to write upon. I send you in this letter some sets of different kinds you might worke them up into something. There is 18 or 20 wounded confed's here now, one of the young Carters belonging to Mosby's comand passed though here Monday wounded in the neck he was sorthy[?]. I tell you everything is very quiet here now and the weather very warm no troops passing here now except Negroes. I think if you were to rake the whole south over with a fine tooth comb you could not find any as black. Have you ever rec a letter of mine in which I spoke of a Capt J. B. Withers. His sister waited to here from him, I don't remember if I ever said anything about sending a box to Lieut Pence we sent him one the day after we started yours but have never heard from him since I sent him all he wrote for and some other thing also some eatables and fifteen dollars in money a pair of shoes no 8 like yours they costs $3.00. There are sixteen sets in all that I send hoping this may reach you safely and find you well and over your lazy fit I will close.[10] All are dragging about, Lillie is not well and is very fretful she sends her love and a kiss to Papa all send there love Good bye Yours forever Kate

write soon

Alex June 3rd/64

Dear Nessa

At last I have gotten your photographs and send you three of them I think them very good most every one does though the whiskers makes a difference since your old friends have seen you every one complimented you highly so highly that it does not make me resin[?] on the contrary it almost makes me begin to think that you are not realy as good looking as the picture. I wont tell you who all you are compared to for it migh[t] turn your head if it don't mine I don't forget that I am not so good looking my self. But don't think that I am getting any uglier because I am not going to do that for your sake, enough foolishness now. Have you received your box yet it is strange I do not hear from you concerning it or from Lieut. Pence about his it was started the day after yours and not half the distance to go I intend writing to him as soon as I get through with this. In my last two letters to you in them I sent you in one some pieces of gold in the last there was sixteen sets of different kinds[11] do you want anything I will have an opportunity of sending something in about a week or so if you do let me know when you get your photographs from Sandusky if they are different from these you must send me one, Nessa do you remember Frank Shurman that boy Pa raised at the commencement of the war he belonged to Pressman's artilery served his time out then joined some cav. Regt. Well he was brought in day before yesterday a prisoner looking very well fat as could be and well clothed.[12] I believe I have gotten to about the end of the race course and of course will have to stop but I just feel like I could rattle on all day. All send love. Lillie and somebody else a kiss Good by Ever affectionately yours Kate

Alex June 7th/64

Dear Nessa

Your letter of the 29th has been rec acknowledging the recept of your box also today I rec yours of the 8 the one you write the day before you wrote to Jack for the clothing just to think one month on the way Nessa I don't want you to thank me so much for what I do for you, is it anything more than my duty to do what I do. I wish I could do more I feel that I cannot do enough for my Nessa. Is the rumer that is afloat here now true that the prisoner are not going to be allowed to receive any more boxes or things until after the 1st of Oct. please find out the truth and let me know the last letter I wrote I sent you 16 sets of different kinds have you rec them yet. The set of jewelry I wrote to you about some time ago are for a lady friend of mine she wants a cross like the last you sent me then she wants a pair of earrings and pin she wants them made round with a cross of gold nicely carved in the centre of the pin and earrings please have them very nice for she is a nice lady.[13] Send the person's name who makes them as she wants to know and the price of all and I will send you the money. I rec a letter from Lieut Pence this morning he is well and has rec his box. Poor fellow he sent me his photograph and says that it is the only thing he has to send if I will accept it. Of course I shall not send it back it is an excellent likeness, I send you 6 stamps all well and send there love to you Lillie and K. a kiss I would send some sets in this but must hurry to get it in the mail for this evening I have some very pretty ones for you

Good bye affectionately your Kate

Dear Kate

I had the pleasure of receiving two letters from you this morning. One of the 3rd and the other of the 7th. And also the photographes. I have not been able to discover the beauty in them you speak of. They are nothing like as good looking as the ones you sent me some time ago. They are very pretty, but I cannot discover anything pretty about them. The setts you sent me some time ago came thru safely. They are verry pretty, and I am sorry I cannot get some slab gutapercha to make rings for them. The butons are to narrow for the setts, but perhaps they can be used for something els. I will attend to having the cross earrings and, pin made you spoke of. The gentleman who made the cross I sent you is not making any now, though I think I can have one made like it. I have not heard anything about not allowing us to receive

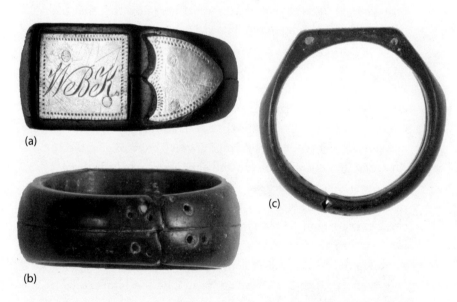

(a)

(b)

(c)

Fig. 22. Hard rubber finger ring with three silver sets: (a) top view showing decorative border on sets plus WBK inscription; (b) back view showing repair of broken ring plus both halves of the ring; (c) side view showing copper pins used to hold together two buttons used in making this ring (FS0034, dia. 17.6 mm, width 9.7 mm). (CHMA. Photographs by author.)

things from our friends. If I heare of any order of that kind I will let you know. My health has not been very good lately. I was taken sick the day after writing to you about being in such good health. I am much beter now and hope I will soon be well again. Give my love to all.

Yours affectionately, Wes

The prisoners were making many types of jewelry from hard rubber. The source of the hard rubber was through friends and the sutler. Wesley was probably talking about hard rubber chart rules, which were slightly thicker than hard rubber buttons. He may have been talking about a thicker hard rubber material. To achieve a thicker ring for larger sets, prisoners took two buttons and put them together with copper pins. Figure 22 shows a ring made in such a fashion. This style was popular at Johnson's Island for the prisoners to wear.

Alex June 10th/64

Dear Nessa

I have rec your letter of the 2nd also. The one written on the 6th of May only one month coming Nessa you are much oblige to us all for our flatterings your quite welcome for all the rest but you know that I am no flatterer, have you rec the letter I wrote you last Monday about that set of jewelry Nessa I could sell a great many things for the men if I had them so many want things made by the prisoners and I expect there is not a very ready sale out there for such things.[14] A lady friend of mine was here yester-day evening and requested me the next time I wrote to you to ask if that Capt or Col, I forget which it is and my book is not home to see however hes' a Mr Pipher she wishes to know if he was not formerly of Newbury S.C. I delivered your message to Aunt Jane she [said] she will do her best. Nessa you spoke of papering your room I supose it is to be with old letters,[15] I will sent you some more sets in this letter. The report is that the federal troops are in Stanton, do you still receive your paper from New York. There are a great many rumors afloat it is hard to beleave anything you hear there are quantities of wounded being brought up the river.

I supose you have heard of the death of Col Dulaneys son. We are all well at present. Your smallest pet is asleep yet so I send a kiss for her. Nessa I am going to Washington to day to see a friend I wish so much it was so that you could be here to go with me. I feel so little like going anywhere unless it is for charity.[16] All send there love to you write soon. Nessa several of us want to know who Asa Hartz, the author of 'will nobody send me a box' is, Nessa there are ten sets in all that I send 5 pearl. 4 white, 1 glass that will be very nice some of the men to put in a ring with hear [hair?] for some friend. Good bye. Yours affectionately Kate

Major George McKnight, also known as Asa Hartz, was one of the best-known prisoners at Johnson's Island. Along with the imprisoned generals, George McKnight was discussed in many autograph books, diaries, and letters. He was an assistant adjutant general on General Loring's staff. On June 19, 1863, he was captured at Hazlehurst, Mississippi. He arrived at Johnson's Island on August 10, 1863, remaining there until October 6, 1864, when he was transferred to Point Lookout. He was best known for the poetry he wrote, leaving examples of his work in many diaries and autograph books. The poem Kate mentioned can be found in various prisoner books (Frohman 1965:149–50). It was attributed to the Duce Klubs, who appears to be George McKnight. Given the similarity of the two versions that follow, it would be difficult to believe they were written by separate individuals. Kate referred to the second poem later in the letters as having been written by Asa Hartz.

Will no one send a box to me!
by Duce Klubs
Frank calls the list over every day.
The hungry crowd now melt away;
I linger still and wonder why,
No package come for me today.
Are all my aunts in Dixie dead!
Would all my cousins forgotten be!
What have I done—What have I said

That no one sends a box to me!
Tisn't Fair.
I watch the express most every day,
With hungry look for the list o'er run,
And damn him whose name is called
But love him, more who gets not one;
For I can sympathize with him,
And fell hoe keen his hunger must be,
Since I'm a prisoner on Johnson's Isle
And no one send a box to me
I'm in despair!
Away down in Alabama; sunny clime,
Where Musquitoes sing so sweetly;
There dwells a quiet happy cousin,
And many a box she used to send me freely
Now others from their dear cousins hear,
Beg goods and boxes, Expressed Free,
Yet here I've been almost a year,
And why not some one send a box to me!
O. My God!
Will no one just send one Box to me,
To prove that I'm remembered yet!
If you but know how much delight
I'd feel could I provisions get—
Could I but hear from some kind aunt,
Whose box I ne'er would forget,
Will some one now my hunger end;
If some one doesn't send me a box
I'll take the Oath!

And No One Writes to Me
by Asa Hartz
The list is called, and one by one
The anxious crowd now melts away,
I linger still and wonder why

No letter comes for me today.
Are all my friends in Dixie dead?
Or would they all forgotten be?
What have I done, what Have I said:
That no one writes to me?
Its mighty queer!
I watch the mails each weary day,
With anxious eyes the list o'errun;
And envy him whose name is called,
But love him more who gets not one.
For I can sympathize with him,
and feel how keen his grief must be
Since I am an exile from my home,
And no one writes to me.
I do declare!
Within a quiet-happy home,
Far, far in Dixie's sunny clime,
There dwells a quiet happy maid,
Who wrote to me in by gone time.
In tender letters, loving free
And why does she not write to me!
We're not estranged!
Will no one write me, just a line,
To say that I'm remembered yet!
You cannot guess how much delight,
I'd feel, could I a letter get.
Could I but hear from some kind friend,
Whose face I ne'er again may see,
Will some one now, my anguish end!
If some one doesn't write to me,
I'll get exchanged!
(Makely 1863–65)[17]

Nessa I send a piece of ring containing seven sets.

Alex June 14 [?]

Dear Nessa

I again seat myself to pen you a few lines it seems a long time since I wrote to you last though it was only last Friday. Though it seems so long I do think I never had less to write about. But one thing before I forget it. I want you to have made for Pa, a nice chain. I saw a beautiful one that was sent to Kate Smoot from Fort McHenry.[18] Pa will have it finished of with the gold himself. I have a large and very hansome shell for you and some very pretty sets also. I have been sending you sets in my last three or four letters have you received them. Nessa you are going to fin up so cheerful I wont go so far as comfortable, that I expect you wont want to leave Johnsons Isle soon. Can you not persuade your landlord up make room for the whole family or am I to remain at home this summer. You know I never spent the summer in town I believe the watering places in Va are not to be opened this summer and as there is one at Johnson's Isle that I prefer being nearer than any one else, and as you say that the weather is so warm that it makes you lazy it is quite different here it seems that old Alex is turned into a northern city is so cold that a fire is comfortable. I wrote in my last I think to knowing if Nessa wanted anything. I asked Col Hoffman in Washington Friday about what I had heard about the boxes he told me I could send when I wanted and as many I must not forget your caution about the one page, all well and send there love to you. Kate has so much to send that she will have to send a box by express. Good bye dearest. Ever affectionately your Kate

Some of the prisoners were skilled in making necklaces and watch chains. Figure 23 illustrates a portion of a chain made by Robert Smith, the same Robert Smith producing prisoner photographs. This particular chain was made by cutting a slit into every other link, and opening it up enough to allow the adjacent links to slip inside. The link was then closed to give the chain a continuous appearance. Archaeologically, a number of individual links have been discovered. Figure 23(b) shows

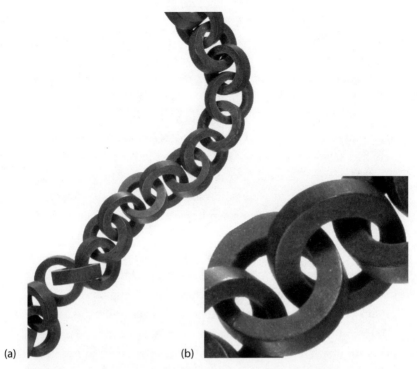

(a)   (b)

Fig. 23. Chain made from hard rubber tubes: (a) larger section of chain made by Robert Smith; (b) close-up of chain links showing every other link has a break, allowing them to be interlocked (diameter of link 6.5 mm). (By permission of Nancy Feazell, granddaughter of Robert Smith, and Geoffrey Feazell, grandson of Nancy Feazell.)

the cut link on the left side of the image and the uncut link on the right. Additional examples of hard rubber chains are illustrated in chapter 6.

Alex June 17th/64

Dear Nessa

I have just rec your letter of the 8th also one from Lieut Pence. He says that he wrote you and sent you his photograph but that he had not heard from you since. I will deliver Capt Winsor message the first time any of the family come in his Father sent him a box yesterday. Nessa I wish you could have been here this morning Purdy came down yesterday and has just gone I only wish you could have seen him. I wanted him to tell me where he gets his liqures from as it is a very difficult article to get here now I told him that perhaps we could get a little too. He says that when he comes down is the only time he gets any and as I told him this morning he makes pretty good use of the time. all were well up home but Doc. I am going to try to get up there next week if I can. Nessa have you rec any of the sets that I sent you, in the letters yet. I sent some in several letters, Jack wrote to you yesterday. Nessa have pity on me I know you will for I have got to have one of my double teeth extracted how I do dread it. The ladies of Alex are having a festerval for the benefit of the poor at the second door from us Lillie tormented me last night so I had to go with her. Nessa if you were only here to go about with me I could enjoy myself as it is I seldom go any where and when I do it is no pleasure. All are well except Jack he has your old complaint and is very much complaining all send there love to you. Mine you have Good bye Affectionately yours Kate

Johnsons Island June 22nd '64

Dear Kate

I have just received yours of the 17th, and as you expect to visit the country soon, I thought I had better write you one more letter before you started, as perhaps I, might not have an opportunity of writing to you again before you return, or at any rate I shall wait untile I hear from you again, and know ware to direct. I would have writen to mother some time ago if I had known her post office. Every thing has been changed so much since I were home that I do not know ware their post office is anymore. I received a letter from Jack this morning. He says he supposes I am getting quite tired of prison life, but thinks I am much better off here than I would be in the army. If that's the way he talks I don't think he knows much about it, or at any rate I would much rather be in the army, or almost any ware els than in prison. I am sick and tired of this kind of life, and would be very glad to make the change. The earrings and pin you spoke of will be finished in a few days, and I would send them to you as soon as they are finished if I knew what kind of a chain you wanted. When I send them I will write to Jack and ask him to attend to getting them, and leave them with your father for you. I hope you may enjoy yourself and have a pleasant time up country. Give my love to all. Affectionately yours, Wes

It seems Wesley was trying, in as nice a way as possible, to share the fact that being imprisoned, and losing one's ability to move about freely and be responsible for one's day-to-day actions, was worse than almost any other fate. John Taylor, 7th South Carolina Cavalry, shares the same sentiment in a letter he wrote to his brother on July 30, 1864: "If you wish my horse take him, or any thing else of mine you want. I believe we are in prison for the war, & altho' I had rather lose a limb & be free, I now see no alternative, nor have I for some time" (Meissner and Meissner 2005:39–40).

Wesley heard about Kate's social activities, and her and his brother's travels, and all he could do was offer affectionate words and serve as a conduit for jewelry. How surreal to be sharing the struggle of prison life at one moment and then immediately switch to the status of earrings.

The prisoners had been allowed to bathe in Lake Erie during the previous few days. Several blocks were allowed to proceed each day, with small groups spending up to twenty minutes in the lake. Many prisoners talked about how much they enjoyed this privilege. Bathing was curtailed on June 22 but resumed on June 24.

Alex June 21st/64

Dear Nessa

Your letter of the 15th was rec to day on my way to the dentist's I called at the office and was treated to a letter from you. I did not have my tooth extracted the other day Dr. Denelt though[t] he could kill the nerve and save the tooth for me I though[t] that would be much better for I knew that you would not want a toothless wife.[19] Nessa the sets I sent you I am glad you rec and there is more on the way for you Nessa I am going to send you a box soon and I will try to get some of the slab gutta percha for you I have a beautiful shell to send to you when I send the box. I could of send Nessa a handsomer boquet than I did

but the deffinition of what I sent suited me best. Nessa I made
a mistake in inquiring the name of the person I did. Kate Smoot
was here this morning directly after I rec your letter and I gave
her as I thought the desired information but it was the Duce
of clubs she wanted to know, she has my book and I have not
seen the other young lady since so I cannot tell you the rank or
anything else about the gentleman in this the young lady liked to
went into conniptions when she saw his name in the list, Nessa
well you know that I am not of a jelous disposition I knew that
you had rec the or rather it had been sent to you I say myself it is
hansome but I do not think so much so as the one I rec sometime
ago any ways the ladies are after me for the first but nobody asks
for the second[20] and Jack rec your letter requesting some money
and will attend to it all send there love and Lillie and myself
return the kiss but I do not know who you will get to give it you
I wish I could write a whole sheet. Good bye. Yours affectionately
Kate

Johnsons Island June 26th 1864

Dear Kate

Yours of the 21st was rec yesterday. I had not been expecting
to hear from you so soon, as you have been contemplating such
a plesant time in the country, though I hope you may realizing
your expectations; Every thing is about as usual hear. It is the
season for visitors to be coming in here, and they are arriving
constantly.[21] Some of my old acquaintances arrived hear a few
days ago. They were from the valley of Virginia. Among them
that arrived here was Capt Imboden brother of the generals, and
Lt Ream of my company.[22] He has but very little news. He says
Mr Hagsheads family are all well the last time he heard from
them, and he also informs me that some straggling soldiers have
stolen my horse. He says they tride very hard to find out what
had become of him and get him for me. But could not heare
anything of him. He says he was in good order, and was the finest
horse he ever saw. I am sorry to loos him for I don't believe I can
get another horse like him in the confederate.

Kate I went to se Rebellionans the other day, it was a grand affair. I will send you one of the bils.[23] Perhaps it is not as good as some you have in the city, but you must remember that this is only a place of resort for Southerners traiting the north, and of cours we cannot have everything as nice as you do in the citys.

You was speaking of sending me a box. I will mention something you may send me if you can get them conveniently. The Bible says give strong drink to those that are ready to perish, and wine to those that are of heavy heart you will find it in the last chapter of the proverbs, old testament, and I am both sick and of heavy heart and besides the doctor says I ought to have something of the sort. Instead of sending me nice fruitcakes you may send me some porter's blackberry wine or Hosteters biters if you can get it conveniently also send me some tea. Give my love to father and mother and Lil a kiss for me.

Affectionately yours, Wes

Alex June 24th/64

Dear Nessa

Your letter of the 18th came to hand this morning acknowedgeing the receipt of the sets. I have more for you but if you have more that you know what to do with I will not send them. Nessa I am so sorry that you are becoming so dissatisfided and that your health is so bad again it makes me sick myself when I think about your situation but Dearest Nessa do for my sake try to content yourself your health depends so much on your spirits you think a change would be benifitial to you Nessa we all know it would, but not a change to the old Capitol. You have no idea of the place I have spoken to several persons about a transfer and all think you are better off where you are the Capital they say is alive with the vermon.[24] Then you would be confined to a close room altogather That is if it were possible to get a transfer but I know we could not for there is no officers kept there now the privet and all are being sent away from there now to Fort Delaware none are to be kept here but guerillas and they in very close confinement. Ma Pa Jack and myself all think you had better content your self where you are as long as you have stood it this long try it a little longer. Nessa I think there is brighter times close at hand *one way or another*. When Nessa will be released and we can be together again and I truly hope never to be separate again. Nessa there is no slab gutta percha to be had in town. Ma is going to Baltimore next week and will try to get some there, for you then we will send you a box I am going to send you some medicine too that I think will cure you if you have the diorrah the chain I spoke of seeing was simply the plain round links, linked together she had it mounted here. Now Nessa remember your Kate and keep up those spirits I know you will say it is very easy for us to say so but Nessa we feel and deeply feel for you, all send there love to and Lillie a kiss. Good bye. Ever affectionately yours ever.

Kate

Johnsons Island July 10th/64

Dear Kate

I expect you have been looking for your things for some time, and if they had made them when they promised I would hav sent them some time ago. You will find a small box for Miss Stewart sent by Lt Knicely. I did not have the earrings and pin you wanted for your friend made exactly as you wanted them. I did not think they would be pretty the way you spoke of. If they do not please her keep them and I will get her another sett. The pin and and [sic] earrings cost eight dollars, and the cross two dollars and a half. They wer[e] made by Lt. W. H. Wasche.[25] There are two sets of earrings, and two pins, one set for you, and one for your friend. I also send you several other things, A sett of cuff buttons, a collar button, the ring you want to put a diamond set in. It will have to be dressed after the sett is put in, a chain with an a cross and a nice little fish to it. You will have to get some open rings to fasten them to your chain, a fan, it is all made of one piece of wood, and a nice cross, and had Kate and Wes engraved on it.[26] It was not engraved exactly as I wanted but it will do. I think it is very nice. The cross is emblematic of our saviors love, and the sett is an emblem of life, checkered. The other chain and cross is for Pa. I had a latten motto engraved on his, the translation is (By this sign we conquer).[27] The two rings and the pin with a redish collor is for Lill. The other two pins are for our mothers one for each. And the pin with the black cross in it is for aunt Jane. I don't know wether it will please her or not. If it dos not, tell her to let me know what she would like to have and I will get it for her. Kate I would like to send something nice to your mother. If you know of anything that she would like to have let me know so that I may get it for her. I sent her a plain pin because I thought it would suit her better than any other I could get.[28]

Give my love to all
Affectionately yours, Wes

Alex June 27th/64

Dear Nessa

Your letter of the 22nd as rec today and Oh Nessa how I want this answer to fly back to you. I have not left for the country yet nor do I know when I shall go. I did think that I would go up to see Ma this or next week. But your wife is of so much importance at home she cannot get off, and if I should go you need not stop

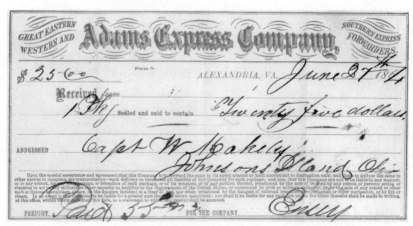

Fig. 24. Adams Express Company receipt for $25, dated June 27, 1864. (By permission of the Friends and Descendants of Johnson's Island Civil War Prison.)

writing for I would not be gone longer than 4 or 5 days. I would be afraid to stay 12 miles out in the country. Mosby might carry me to Richmond Al can not get off conveniently eather. Don't be alarmed about writing if I should go to stay any time your letter could be sent for some one is down every day or two. But I am very much afraid that I will have to spend the summer in town and a hot one it will be for the weather is almost intolerable here now though it is a little more pleasant this evening. Nessa Jack has just gone to the express office to send you some money. He sends 25 twenty five dollars. I gave him your letter to read and he says he think he does know something. Nessa do you rec your New York paper yet or not. I rec a letter from Lieut Pence this morning he wants more money. Has Capt Fountain heard from his family lately I wrote to Kate sometime ago and have not heard any thing from her since. we are all tolerable at present and I hope that by this time you are well again all send there love to you. Affectionately your Kate

Johnsons Island
July 11th/64

Dear Kate

I have at least got the jewelry I promised to send you sometime ago started. I sent it by express this morning. The package contains the pin earrings and cross you wanted for your friend. I also send a set of earrings and pin, a sett of cuff buttons, a collar button, a chain with an acorn and a fish to it, the ring you wanted me to get you to have a sett put in, a fan, and a cross with our names engraved on it for you. The two rings and the pin with a redish sett are for Lill. And the other two pins that look very much alike are for our mothers. The pin with a gutapercha cross in the sett is for aunt Jane, and a cross and chain for Pa. I hope these things may reach you Safely, and that I may hear from you again soon. I have not heard from you for some time. The last letter I got from you was the one you wrote to me on the 27th of June. Tell Jack I received the mony he sent me, and am very much obliged to him.

My health is somthing better than it was some time ago, and I
hope I may soon be well again

Give my love to all

Affectionately yours, W. Makely

Alex July 8th/64

Dear Nessa

Your letter of the 29th June was rec yesterday and by it I see
Dear Nessa that you are becoming more and more dissatisfied.
I spoke to a friend of ours yesterday who says that if you get a
certificate from the surgeon in charge out there to the effect that
your health is bad and he thinks a change would be benefitial
and send it to me that he will do all he can for you and Nessa if
any one can have anything done I think he can all shall be done
fore you that can be neither money nor pains shall be spared to
do what can be done for you. You may get worried sometimes
and think we don't want to do for you but Nessa there nothing
in this world that we would not do for your benefit that we could
do all we do and why we think is for your good. however, you get

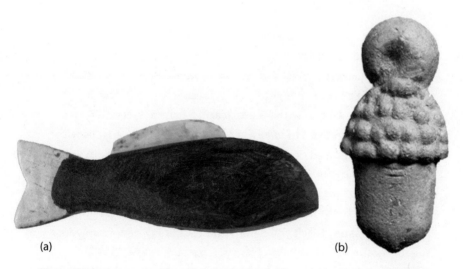

(a)   (b)

Fig. 25. Trinkets recovered from Johnson's Island: (a) carved hard rubber and shell
fish (FS1533, length 23.5 mm); (b) copper acorn (FS3610, length 21.4 mm). (CHMA.
Photographs by author.)

the certificate if you can and send it then we will see what can be done and if anything can be do will meet you in two or three weeks at the Old capital Nessa Old aunt Jane left us day before yesterday and I suppose the balance will go Saturday night after they get paid off. Purdy has not brought Lillie back yet so I cannot deliver the kiss. I wont send your box until I rec a letter in answer to this which I want to have very soon. Have you rec the money Jack sent you. Yes we are all well except Pa and he is so overcome with the heat that he can scarcely get along. All send there love and best wishes to you. Good bye

Yours affectionately,

Kate

The Library of Virginia does not have the June 29 letter to which Kate referred. It is possible she mistook for June 29 the June 26 letter, in which Wesley requested blackberry wine or Hostetter's bitters because he was "sick and of heavy heart." Her letter indicates that paid servants for the household were leaving. Aunt Jane had been referred to several times in previous letters, but no other servants were mentioned. This reference, plus her indication that "neither money nor pains shall be spared," suggest the Makelys were wealthy.

Johnsons Island

July 16th/64

Dear Kate

Yours of the 8th was received a day or two ago. It is the first letter I have received from you since the 27th of last month. I am sorry to hear fathers health is so bad, and feel for him as I know something about what it is to have bad health. I have been a prisoner upwards of 12 months, and have had very little good health during that time. Prison life is bad enough on a person in good health and is much wors[e] ware a persons health bad. I would like very much to se you but I don't think there is any prospects of seeing you soon as you could not leave home while your father is so unwell. Kate I will not trouble you with the certificate you spoke of, though I could get it very easily as the doctors say a change to some other prison would do me more good than any thing els I could do, and I know you would do anything in your power for me, but I do not want to be to troublesome to my friends.

Kate I sent the guttapercha jewelry I promised you on the 11th by the U.S. express. Let me know w[h]ether you have received it or not. Tell Jack I received the mony he sent me, and am very much obliged to him.

Give my love to father and mother

Affectionately your, W. Makely

Wesley continued to choose not to write about the many changes occurring at the prison. The Union surgeons suggesting Wesley would do better at some other prison were probably only trying to lighten their own load of sick prisoners. Major Eversman, the Union surgeon in charge of prisoner health, often cited how his work was eased when prisoners were transferred to other prisons (Eversman 1865).

On July 12, 1864, the prison yard was expanded about ninety-five feet to the west, behind the even numbered blocks (Wilds 2005:228). Prisoners took advantage of the added space to plant gardens (Wilds 2005:228–29). Wesley never mentioned the prison expansion. Possibly his living in Block 1, on the other side of the expansion, meant the increase in space had little significance to him.

On July 14, 1864, the USS *Michigan* again anchored off the shoreline of Johnson's Island (Stakes 1864:79–80; Wilds 2005:229). As noted, this typically happened at times when the Union suspected possible large-scale escapes. The guard was also firing into the yard for violations of the rules, which always made the prisoners nervous.

Johnsons Island
July 19th 1864

Dear Kate

I have been looking for a letter from you for some time. The mail has arrived again and still no letters for me. The last letter I got from you, you were still in the city, though I hope by this time your fathers health may better, and that you may yet have the pleasure of spending part of the summer in the country. Kate if you should go up country or have a good opportunity of sending, I wish you would take the hair out of Lills best pin and give to mother. Tell Lill I will send her some more as soon as my hair gets a little longer. All your your [sic] acquaintances here are well. There is a great many prisoners here complaining but not a great very sick. I suppose Lill has grown very much since I saw her last and perhaps is learning to read and write. Tell her I should look for a letter from her soon. Give my love to all.

Affectionately your, W. Makely

Providing a lock of hair was quite common. Archaeologically, one locket, with braided hair contained inside, was discovered at Johnson's Island. Hair is preserved in an archaeological context only in close proximity to copper. This brooch had a picture on one side (deteriorated) and the braided and coiled hair on the other.

Fig. 26. Locket with preserved coiled and braided hair, tied with ribbon (FS0187, dia. 42.8 mm). (CHMA. Photograph by author.)

Dear Nessa

At last we have started your box which I expect you have given out ever getting but Nessa you know by this time why it was not sent we had it and one for Lieut Pence packed a week ago to send but the railroad being torn up there was no express but I hope it may reach you safely now and that it may please you. I put a little tobacco in for Capts F and Imboden. Nessa the last letter I wrote you I noted that an influential friend of ours said that if you would get a certificate from the surgeon out there to the effect that your health was bad and he thought a change would benefit you and send it to me that he would do all he could for you. Nessa I do not know if you ment the scolding you gave in your last letter for Jack or myself anyway I don't take much of it to myself because you know I always let you have your own way now don't I. I want you to have it in this matter anyway if it can be had. Nessa I rec the box you sent today and we are all so much pleased and all send so many thanks I cant tell all. I cannot thank you enough for the beautiful cross and chain and set you sent me. I will send Ma's to her the first opportunity I have I don't know when that will be as orders are very strict here now and no one allowed a pass. Lillie is still up home, Miss May Rooch is very much pleased with her set and cross and send many thanks to you for them. I send you some money today for the things I do not know if it will pay for all but you will find inclosed twenty dollars, Nessa do write soon and let me know if you rec all safely. All send there love to you and Kate sends her's and remains ever affectionately yours,

Kate

Attached to July 18, 1864 letter

List of articles in box,

1 fruite cake	2 doz onions
1½ lbs coffee	1 can wine
1 round beef	1½ doz herring
½ lb tea	2 boxes sardines

1 can tomatoes	1 do black berries
1 shell	1 bundle for Adgt J B Jordan
½ doz lemons	crackers

1 lb smoking tobacco, 4 papers chewing do.

1 doz oranges, loaf sugar, fine do.

1 can peaches, figs, 1 small pond cake,

pears, candy, raisins, prunes,

dates, small cakes, 5 bottles + 1 box medicen

Nessa please take the medicine in the bottles by directions I feel confident it will help you

Fig. 27. Patent medicine bottle, Adams and Fay, New York (FS0273, height 13 cm). (CHMA. Photograph by author.)

6 stamps

Alex July 22/64

Dear Nessa

Your letter of the 16th came to hand to day I am astonished to to [*sic*] hear that you have not rec but one letter from me since the 27th of June for I seldom if ever miss my regular days for writing Tuesday's and Friday's and if I should I always write the next day but then when I think some of your letters are 2 weeks and even a month on the way it is not at all strange. Dear Nessa I am very sorry to see that you are a little mifted about your transfer business now don't say that you are not for Kate can tell. Nessa all that any of us said we thought was said for the best. Now if you think it will benefit you any I want you to come. Nessa if it would be of any thing could be done for your benefit and it was not done I should be miserable I could never forgive myself for ever writing anything to the contrary to you. You say that you do not expect to see me soon. No Nessa not unless you could get a transfer to some nearer point do I expect to see you soon unless there is a great change and it would be next to impossible for me to leave home now for such a long distance. I would like so much to see you but Nessa unless you get the certificate spoken of I fear that pleasure will not be soon granted. If you could get it I assure you it would give no one any trouble. Nessa I don't think that you ought to think hard of me or give yourself any trouble about what Jack says or does. I am glad you rec your money I will tell Jack. I hope before this you have rec your box and the letter I sent you containing twenty dollars. Lillie is still up the country. I rec the box you sent and all are much pleased with our presents. Pa is better one of those hot days last week he had a slite attack of sunstroke balance all well and send their best love to you now if you want to come and can get the certificate do so and send it to me and don't have any more to do about it. I am a little poorly myself but I believe I am more sick to see you than any-thing else. Good bye

Most affectionately yours Kate

Alex July 25th/64

Dear Nessa

Your letter of the 19th has been rec and in it you again complain of not receiving any letter from me for so long I do not know how it is Nessa, I assure you it is not my fault for I have always written as usual except the week that those terrible Rebels were in Maryland. I do not expect to go to the country this summer. I cannot well leave home. Pa's health I don't think any better though he may feel somewhat so for a few days but it altogether depends on the weather how he feels. he is very low spirited. You spoke of some hair being in Lillie's pin being taken out and sent to Ma. I did not see any hair among the things. I hope by this time that you have rec your box and that it will please you. I wrote you word that Col. Dulaney said that he would do all in his power for you if you would get that certificate and send it on. Lillie is still up at her grandmas Col D. promised me that he would bring her home today but he started last Sunday morning and hearing from the Reb's he thought it wise to turn back so now he says he will bring her home Thursday or Friday. I am so anxious to see her has been more that three weeks since she went away she has grown a great deal since you saw her and talks a great deal about her Papa that the Yankees have got. She can neither read nor write yet, some time ago she got a book and was very fond of it for a while but soon tired of it I do not trouble her much with learning yet I do not think it well to task children much with books while so young however, she shall write you a letter soon. All send there love, you write soon and take care of your self Good bye Yours Most affectionately

Kate

Kate mentioned Lillie's grandmother in this letter. She was probably referring to Wesley's mother, who was living in Fairfax County, Virginia. Both of Kate's parents were alive as well.

Lillie's exact birth date is unknown, but she appears from the family records to have been born in either 1860 or 1861. She was at least three years old and perhaps close to four.

Alex July 29th/64

Dear Nessa

There is nothing in the world to write about but then I must
let you know how we all are. Pa is better the rest of us all well
and I heartily hope that you are the same. Purdy came down last
Tuesday evening but did not bring Lillie with him he said that he
would be down again in a few days and bring her. I wrote him a
letter by Col Dulany to bring her to Anadale and the Col. would
bring her in town as it was so hard for persons to get passes to
go out but Purdy met the letter this side the court H. as he was
on his way down.[29] He said that from my letter he thought that I
was distressed to death and had a notion to go back for her. You
cannot imagine how much we miss her. Purdy says that he does
not believe if I were to go after her that I would get her to come
home she is so well satisfied. Doctor goes blackberrying with
her and the children. I don't know why she likes Dixie so much
or how she knows a difference for whenever she gets reproved
for anything she allways threatens me that she will go to Dixie
we still have no one with us since Aunt Jane left. The weather is
extremely hot here now and very dry, everything burnt up and
everything is so very high. I wrote a letter to McSmith the other
day and sent word for Caroline B. to come down if she could
Nessa I have been looking every day for a letter from you but
every day a disappointment now write soon and often will you.
All send there love to you and say take care of yourself

Goodbye Most affectionately yours

Kate

Johnsons Island

Aug 8th/64

Dear Kate

Your letter of the 29th of July has just been received, and
I take pleasure in answering it at once, as it is your request,
though as you say there is scarcely anything to write about.
Kate I am sorry you have been disappointed in hearing from
me, though I I [sic] assure you it is not my fault, for I have been

writing to you regularly. I hope you may be more successful hear-after and think you will as the mails are running regular again, though I sometimes think I will not write to you as often as I have been doing, and try and think less about home while I have to remain in prison. I have no doubt you will think it a strange notion in me to try and keep from thinking of home, and I al-most think so myself, or a useless one I don't know wich. I might keep from thinking or forget almost almost [sic] anything els, but cannot forget, nor keep from thinking of my ___ [here he drew a blank line]. Kate you must not think I do not want to write to you, nor that I am not as anxious to hear from you as ever: when I do not hear from you regular I am as uneasy as I can be and fear something is the matter with you, and am uneasy until I hear from you, and when I receive your letters I read them over and over, and think of you all and long to be at home. I would give al-most any thing if I could only see you sometimes, but I must not think about that. I must try and content myself with my home on Johnsons Island. Kate, I am glad to hear that fathers health is better and hope it may continue to improve. Give my love to all. Your affectionate Wes

Wesley's referral to Johnson's Island as "home" was telling. For their own survival, prisoners created a familiar space and tried to regain some sense of ownership. This may have been his way of coping with prison life and managing the loneliness encountered from missing loved ones.

Two fairly major events had taken place in the prison compound prior to Wesley writing to Kate on August 8. The Union constructed two large mess halls on the bay side of the prison compound to pull the messes out of the barracks and give more room for additional prisoners (Wilds 2005:259). This work started on August 4, 1864. The activity within the prison compound did not go unnoticed by the prisoners, and upwards of thirty took advantage of all the men passing in and out to gain access to the outside world. Their efforts were discovered by the Union on August 8 and skirmishers were dispatched to recapture the escapees.

The second event was closing down the sutler. Mr. Johnson was fi-nally removed as the sutler because of his price gouging. A new sutler

U.S. MILITARY PRISON JOHNSON'S ISLAND, LAKE ERIE, OHIO.

J. A. Bergin

Fig. 28. Bird's-eye view of the Johnson's Island Prison compound, 1865, from the autograph album of Captain James S. Moreland, 17th Alabama Infantry. (By permission of Manuscript and Special Collections Library, Duke University.)

was not available until August 13, when many new restrictions were in place. No eatables or clothing were sold to prisoners, and items that the prisoners wished to purchase had to be preapproved by the guard.

I send eight stamps

Alex Aug 2nd/64

Dear Nessa

Just think this is the 3rd or 4th letter I have written you since I rec one from you. Do you write or not. I eather go or send to the office every day expecting a letter and every day am doomed to disappointment.[30] I have never heard wether you ever rec your box or the letter I sent you containing twenty dollars or not. I heard from up home yesterday all are well I am looking for Lillie home tomorrow or next day and Doctor with her. I also wrote

Ma word that I had a nice present from you for her but that she would have to come after it. Nessa was the hair you spoke of fixed in the pin in any way I know Lillie will be so much pleased with her presents. I would so much rather that Lillie would stay up the country if I could get to see her sometime for it is so very unhealthy in town amoung the little folks a great many die, but Col Wells our Pro here says for my own safety and good he cannot give me a pass that there are too many guerilla's about.[31] Jack Barnes was sentenced to be hung then it was commuted to ten years imprisonment. Ann came down and went to Washington yesterday to see him. The wether here is almost intolerable. I do not think that I ever felt so warm weather before. You remember that breaking out I used to have on my throat. I have been taking medicine for it and it has sent it all over my body my arms are very sore but I believe that it will cure it intirely it is like the worst kind of heat and annoys me sometimes most to death. Have you any mosquitoes out with you. They are very plentiful here. Nessa you will have to write me 5 or 6 letters to make up for this space. All are well and send there love to you. Do you want for anything let me know write soon and often Goodbye

    Yours affectionately

    Kate

Johnsons Island

Sept 15th 1864

    Dear Kate

    I have been looking very anxiously for a letter from you for the last month, but have not received a single one since the 5th of last month. I am very uneasy and cannot help but think you are sick. I received a letter from Jack several days ago saying that you were at home, and well, and that you had written to me. I felt very much relieved for a time, and felt sure that I would have received a letter from you before this, but I have been disappointed, and am geting very uneasy again. I wish I could be with you, that I might know how you wer, and give you what little assistance I could, but as it is I can only hope that heaven will ever guard and protect you. I would have written to you sooner after received Jacks letter if the mail was leaving here every day as it has been doing heretofore. The mail only leaves here twice a week now, (Mondays and Thursdays), though we receive the mail every day. Tell jack I cannot answer his letter at present as we are not allowed to send more than one letter by each mail. He wanted to know if he could send me some mony. Tell him that we are still allowed to receive mony. Kate I am in hopes I will not be disappointed much longer by not receiving any letters from you. I want to heare from you, and heare that you are well. I don't see why they should not let me know if there was any thing the matter with you. It is true I could not do anything for you, but still they might let me know, and not keep me in fear, and uneasyness all the time. Give my love to father and mother, and with my best wishes for your Health and happiness,

I remain your affectionately
W. Makely

There is desperation in Wesley's letter of September 15, 1864. It had been almost six weeks since he had heard from Kate, to whom he wrote twice a week and whom he undoubtedly thought about daily. Kate expressed the same sentiments in her August 2 letter to Wesley. All the travel restrictions taking place in Virginia at this time must have affected the mail as well.

Union officials, in attempting to handle all the mail requiring inspection, restricted outgoing mail to two letters per week, one letter per prisoner on each day the mail left the island. Considering the mail had to be inspected, there was no guarantee letters would actually be sent on their way that day. Prisoners who wished to send more than one letter at a time could sign the second letter with the name of another prisoner.

Conditions at Johnson's Island grew worse as daily rations were cut and opportunities to purchase from the sutler were restricted. By this time Wesley had spent fourteen months at Johnson's Island. Hopes of exchange had vanished, and he had resigned himself to being captive at Johnson's Island. There was no clear expectation of exchange or release.

Kate tried to adapt to the newly imposed status for her husband. She freely shared her own discomforts with her situation, seemingly forgetting how much Wesley was suffering.

The month of September 1864 provided some interesting events and challenges for the prisoners. Wesley's focus turned, for the most part, away from exchange or transfer to a different prison. He realized exchange was not a viable option, and there was no prospect of acquiring better accommodations at another prison. The only advantage at a prison like Fort Delaware was being closer to Kate. Even if he were there, she would not have been able to visit him.

Wesley's attempts to provide an image of himself did meet with some success, and as we have seen, he wrote to Kate in May 1864 about papering his room, attempting to make it more cheerful. He was now resigned to surviving in this "home." Johnson's Island was no longer a temporary stop in his military journey. After almost a year, he took ownership of his living quarters.

The mail system was a constant source of frustration for both Wesley and Kate. He had no control over when her letters arrived. One way Wesley was able to connect with Kate on a daily basis was through fulfilling her jewelry requests. He did control the search for talented jewelry makers, which enabled him to provide Kate with fine examples for her, Lillie, Kate's mother and father, his mother, and friends. Hard rubber jewelry was central to both Kate's and Wesley's ability to endure the time apart. Wesley was able to provide for Kate, and Kate's sharing the prison jewelry created a network of people committed to Wesley's well-being.

Hard Rubber and Hard Times

(September 19, 1864–March 12, 1865)

The shell cross I want you or Lill to have, and the necklace I made myself expressly for Lill, and had a hart made for it, . . .

Wesley Makely to Kate, December 7, 1864

Wesley enhanced contact with his family by providing numerous examples of hard rubber jewelry. He was not a gifted jeweler but did have a discerning eye for purchasing fine examples for his Kate and Lillie. Hard rubber jewelry was about the only thing Wesley provided his family beyond the letters he wrote. He probably achieved some satisfaction of purpose in pursuit of the finest jewelry made at Johnson's Island.

Hard rubber jewelry was a constant topic in Kate's and Wesley's letters. Some prisoners mentioned hard rubber or gutta-percha jewelry in their diaries or letters, and others referred to presents sent to family members without the specifics noted by Wesley. Prisoners like Lieutenant Robert Smith and Captain William Peel discussed making jewelry, but these two were among those few prisoners paid to produce the finest quality items (Smith 1864; Wilds 2005). Wesley appeared to have become obsessed with finding Kate better and better examples of a variety of jewelry. The motivations behind his continued bestowment of jewelry on Kate can only be speculated upon. Perhaps it was a means of providing some enjoyment to Kate in the uncertain times. Possibly Wesley felt Kate wanted these items to share with her family and friends, reminding them of his own fate. It could be that Kate exhibited her status in society with these prisoner-carved pieces. Possibly Wesley gained status as a preferred customer of Lieutenant Waesche and others. Whatever the reasons, Wesley must have gained some pleasure through this activity.

His pursuit of the finest of jewelry items kept him constantly thinking about Kate's reaction to the next item sent.

Although Wesley and Kate talk of using gutta-percha in the making of jewelry, the material was actually hard rubber. Woshner explains the differences between these materials, noting that the majority of manufactured buttons, chart rules, and combs used during the Civil War were made of hard rubber (Woshner 1999:48–49). Patented in 1851 by Nelson Goodyear, hard rubber was molded into a variety of things useful to soldiers. The India Rubber Company, the Novelty Rubber Company, and the American Rubber Company were the main producers of hard rubber items (Woshner 1999:54). Prisoners used their carving skills to alter these hard rubber items into fashionable jewelry.

Archaeologically recovered from the Johnson's Island prison site are hundreds of examples of waste material from the jewelry industry. The most common items converted into jewelry were hard rubber buttons and chart rules, skillfully carved into finger rings, crosses, brooches, or other items desired by the prisoners and their families.

Fig. 29. Carved hard rubber "badge," broken and missing the inlays for three sets (FS4593, length 16.7 mm). (CHMA. Photograph by author.)

(a)

(c)

Fig. 30. Hard rubber chart rule pieces as raw material for jewelry: (a) example of complete hard rubber rule (by permission of Mike Woshner, length 30 cm); (b) edge fragment of hard rubber rule (FS0708, length 16.1 mm); (c) larger chart rule waste piece with melted edge (FS1605, length 36.4 mm). (CHMA. Photographs by author.)

(b)

Sets of gold, silver, gem stones, mother of pearl, copper, and iron were liberally used for decorating the jewelry made at Johnson's Island. The master jewelers carved the exquisite pieces sought after by many prisoners, and even some of the guard. The archaeological record provides some common symbols, including the cross, heart, hand with pointing finger, shield, acorn, fish, diamond, and various forms of scrolls. Many gold and silver sets also sported initials.

Every stage of the jewelry-making process has been discovered at Johnson's Island. Excavations at Block 4, a regular housing block, produced hundreds of pieces of hard rubber waste and abandoned pieces from this work. The prisoners' writings talk of hundreds trying their hand at jewelry making, and the evidence confirms both the numbers making hard rubber items and their varied artistic ability. "Some of the Prisoners, make rings, watch chains which are beautifully inlaid with shell and gold and realize large profits for their jewelry, the shell and guttaperche are sent to them by their friends" (Stakes 1864:25).

Figure 30(a) illustrates a complete chart rule (not from Johnson's Island) and (b) and (c) are two pieces of waste chart rule. The complete rule is an example of one of the source materials utilized by prisoners. Both long edges of the rule are sloped, facilitating drawing lines. The curved border was often removed.

Figure 30(b) is a waste fragment recovered from Johnson's Island illustrating the curved edge, and figure 30(c) shows etching for both a circular and an angular design (abandoned). This piece exhibits melting of the hard rubber on its far right surface, suspected of being used to cement shell and metal sets into finished jewelry.

The larger and thicker hard rubber buttons were the most sought after for use in making finger rings. The most common waste piece from creating rings was a sliver of hard rubber cut from the button's edge, producing a flat surface for a set. Often two additional slivers were cut

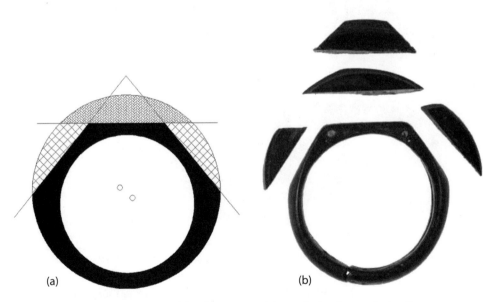

(a)   (b)

Fig. 31. Template for hard rubber finger rings: (a) ring design for producing finger ring with three facets; (b) finger ring plus examples of various waste pieces from carving a button. (Illustration and photograph by author.)

Fig. 32. Examples of hard rubber finger rings: (a) Silver center set from ring (FS0034); (b) similar finger ring design to FS0034, broken and with set missing (note silver rivet in top setting (FS3431, width 9.3 mm); (c) silver heart setting from FS5387; (d) interior view of FS7261 showing gold rivets; (e) hard rubber finger ring with three gold sets and initials (FS7261, dia. 15.9 mm). (CHMA. Photographs by author.)

from the main button to create two side-set surfaces. The result was a three-faceted ring allowing various types of sets. Many examples of button waste have been discovered. One telltale sign of a button fragment is a concave or sloped edge originally molded into the button face.

Figure 32 illustrates various set types found at Johnson's Island. The set with the initials WBK is silver, both cemented and riveted into the hard rubber ring. The two rivets are visible above the W and below the K. Figure 32(b) is of similar design with one of the silver rivets in the hard rubber base, but the set is missing. The heart-shaped set reveals the connecting rivet in the upper center of the heart. The interior view of a complete ring reveals the gold rivets holding three gold sets in place.

Placement of shell or stone sets into hard rubber jewelry did not include any form of rivet. These sets were attached to the rubber by heating a waste piece of hard rubber and using the heated substance as a form of glue. Close examination of sets reveals a small amount of slightly discolored hard rubber between the edge of the set and the edge of the jewelry item.

Johnsons Island

Sept 19th/64

Dear Kate

The envelope and stamps you sent me on the 18th inst came safely to hand, and I take great pleasure in acknowledging the receipt of them at the earliest opportunity. As for the letter I have not seen anything of it. Though I suppose there must have been one with it, as the envelope had written on it, "letter contraband in length," It is right hard after [2nd after crossed out] being disappointed several times, and waiting for upwards of a month for a letter from you to receive an empty envelope.[1] Though I can blame no one but myself, for I ought to have notified you of the regulations in regard to writing, and thought I had done so, but I am so absentminded that I scarcely know what I am doing, much less remembering what I have done. But as they say, there is no use grieving over spilt milk, so I will not say any thing more about it, and besides you can soon write me another, and in order that I may get your letters you must confine yourself to one page of letter paper. Tell Jack I have received his letter of the 9th, but cannot say when I can answer it, as we are only allowed to write two letters a week, and I am anxious to renew my old correspondence though he need not stop writing to me on that account. My health has been better for the last month or so than it has been for some time. Kate write soon and tell me if you have not been sick; I cannot help but think that something has been the matter with you, that I have not heard from you for so long.

Give my love to father and mother, and may God watch over my own precious treasure,

Ever yours affectionately,

W. Makely

September 19, 1864, was the day a major conspiracy to free the prisoners on Johnson's Island had been planned by the Confederacy. Captain John Yeats Beall was the Confederate in charge of a group from Canada that planned on seizing two boats and capturing the USS *Michigan*. The only armed vessel in Lake Erie, the USS *Michigan* was anchored off the shores of Johnson's Island. Captain Charles H. Cole of the Confederate Navy was positioned in Sandusky, Ohio, to board the USS *Michigan,* take hostage its captain (John C. Carter, Commander, U.S. Navy), and wait for those in Beall's command to arrive. The Union had learned of the plot and was waiting for Beall. Cole was captured in Sandusky before he boarded the USS *Michigan*, and on September 20 Beall and his men were pursued into Canada, leaving both boats they had commandeered (Frohman 1965:72–92). Almost all diaries from this time gave some account of the events surrounding this date.

Alex Sept 19th

Dear Nessa

It is very strange that I cannot hear from you. It will be three weeks tomorrow since I returned this is the fourth letter since and no answer. Jack has written 3 or 4 times since I came and said that I had come have I written to much or what. I never write more than one page and that seemed very little. I rec Frank Imboden's letter this morning you can tell him that his being taken a prisoner is the only thing that could restore so valuable a relation as I am, for I never intended to own him again but as long as he is a prisoner and in the land of strangers. in my last I do not know if you ever rec it or not I told you to say to him that I heard that cousin John had gone to Stanton with the chills say to him also that I will attend to getting the thing he wants with pleasure and immediately Have you heard of poor H Fosters death he died at Point Lookout about three weeks ago. Nessa could you get me two more sets of jewelry like or similar to the ones you sent if you can please send them it makes no difference about the price. All well and send there love to you, Lillie has gotten back and sends a kiss Goodbye

    Yours affectionately

    Kate

The previous letter Wesley had received from Kate had been written some six weeks before, on August 2, 1864. There was a long gap, and in that time Kate apparently took a trip to Stribling Springs. The letters she refers to did not arrive, for Wesley complained he had been waiting over a month and the one letter that came was considered contraband in length (see figure 33).

Fig. 33. Envelope from Kate to Wesley postmarked September 13, 1864. The postal inspector's note indicates the letter was contraband in length and was thus confiscated. (By permission of The Library of Virginia, Makely Family Papers.)

Kate's mention of Frank Imboden's letter was probably a request by him to have her pose as his cousin in order for him to be able to receive packages from her. At this time only close relatives were permitted to send packages to the prisoners.

Kate did not inquire about Wesley's health. She continued to request jewelry from him with no concern for cost. Apparently he had enough money to cover these costs or would be receiving more from Kate or Jack.

Johnsons Island

Sept 26th/64

Dear Kate

Your letter of the 19th has just been received, and I am glad to hear from you again. I began to fear you had almost forgotten me, or that you thought I had been exchanged and was in Dixie, as I believe you are one of the hopefull ones that always think we will be exchanged in a few weeks. I almost wish I could think as you do, for it certainly must be much pleasanter to think we will soon be exchanged than to think we will have to remain in prison perhaps for several years. Kate I am anxious to be with you all again, though I fear I will not have that pleasure soon, if I have to wait for an exchange,

Kate I see the papers say that Gen Imboden is dead, and a prisoner that was taken a short time ago says that he had heard before he was taken that he had died with fever at Staunton.

I will have the jewelry made you spoke of, and if there is anything els you want made let me know, so that I can send them all at one time. Tell Lill I am making her a nice present, and will send it with your things

Give my love to father and mother

Ever yours,

W. Makely

On the evening of September 23, 1864, a tornado hit the prison compound, tearing the roofs off several buildings and partially destroying

Block 6, the prison hospital (Eversman 1865; Wilds 2005:276–77). Although no prisoners were killed, several were injured. Many wrote of this incident but Wesley did not even allude to it.

Wesley vacillated on how he wanted Kate to respond to his imprisonment. At times he instructed her not to worry about anything. Here he seems to chastise her for being too optimistic. From how he phrased his comments, he wished Kate were more realistic about his fate.

Historical documents need to be read with the motives of the writer in mind. Due to the extensive historical accounts existing for Johnson's Island, we can see obvious gaps in the information Wesley chose to share with Kate. One set of letters cannot be seen as representing everything of importance that transpired; a multivocal approach is always more comprehensive. The following letter is included to illustrate how two letters from prisoners at Johnson's Island, written one day apart, offered distinctly different details. This letter was written by Lieutenant Alan Franklin Swadley, 31st Virginia Infantry, to his brother George, living in Denver City, Colorado Territory.

Block 11 Mess 2 Johnsons Island

Near Sandusky Ohio September 25, 1864

Dear Brother, I haven't received a letter from you since one dated August 5th containing five dollars, which I immediately answered returning my thanks for it. In that letter you said you had sent the same amt. to Cos. Geo[rge]. I heard from him the other day & he says it never came to hand. I expect I can do without, or with the little I have for sometime: but, if you send me any more send it by some man to the states & have him to express it to me.

We had a hurricane here night before last which unroofed three of the blocks or barracks. Although there are about 2600 men here & scantling planks etc. were flying thick, but 4 or 5 were hurt anything like serious.

I got a letter from home dated Aug. 26th All well at home Little John Bird has lost his arm in battle & is at home now. I will tell you what sister Annie says about you. She says we are real glad to hear from Bro. Geo. again & that he was enjoying good health. Do tell him that we all was so very glad to hear from him. Tell him we still live in hopes of seeing him again. She further says she thinks of writing to you soon. This is all she said about you. Cousin J. L. Shumate was well sometime since he sends his love to you. I wrote to you Aug. 28th in answer to yours of the 6th of that month. I ought to have written to you sooner, but still expected a letter from you before this time, but none came. A friend of mine request me to inquire if Judge H. P. A. Smith & Col Saml McLane Atty's at Law are still in Denver City. John Bird & Benj Hines Esqs were prisoners at Camp chase sometime ago. Let us know whether you are married or not for I have been asked this question several times. And could give no correct answer. I am well & the general health of the prison is good. I have never gotten you to consent to write to me once every two weeks. Hope you will. For I am always very anxious to hear from you.

Write as soon as you receive this & give me all the news you can. I remain Your Affectionate Brother

A. F. Swadley (address as Prison of War & as above). (Swadley 1864)

Adam Swadley's letter demonstrates how varied letters can be in their content. Had he been writing to his wife or mother, perhaps he would not have emphasized the severe nature of the storm. On the other hand, in the letter that the Union surgeon Major Eversman wrote to his fiancée the day after the storm, he emphasized the reactions of all surrounding him. "Last night we had one of the most terrific storms that I ever witnessed or ever care about going through again. You know my natural timidity when it blows but in spite of the terrible blowing—flying of timber—firing of guns, muskets and cannon and the screaming of woman and children, I had courage and even now words at myself how I passed through it" (Eversman 1865, letter of September 24, 1864).

Alex Sept 23rd/64

Dear Nessa

Your letter of the 15 was thankfully rec yesterday it is the first that I have rec from you since some time in July. I cannot tell you

how glad I was yesterday when Pa brought me your letter and
Ma seemed most as if as glad as I Nessa I am not sick you seem
to think that I must be neither have I been sick this is the 5th
letter I have written you since I have returned home. I tell you
in my last that while I was up I rode over to see your old friends
Mr and Mrs Fairal. They were all well Sallie is the same old Sallie
yet and sent her love to you all the naiboughers were well in that
nabourhood you knew Mr Wendel at the mill near Mr Fairar's he
lost a little boy very suddenly the day I was over, have you rec the
things you wrote for yet. We have rec a letter from the merchant
stating that he had sent all but the sweet potatoes and that they
were so very high he did not send any. Jack wrote immediately
to send some over I have just rec yours of the 19th acknowledging stamps. I am sorry you have been deprived of my letters after
waiting so long but we have to put up with a good many things
that's hard in this world all well and send there love
 Ever yours
 Kate

The manner in which topics were discussed is surprising in that Kate
mentioned the death of a small child, but her next statement switched
sharply to Wesley's request for a package. Many letters share reports of
someone's death, but the length restriction imposed on letters resulted
in little elaboration on any topic if the writer wished to relate information on multiple subjects.

Alex Sept 25th/64

 Dear Nessa
 I hope by this time that you have rec one of my letters, if no[t]
more if I must write such very short letters I will try instead of
two, to write three a week. I am so glad to hear that your health
is better and pray that it may continue to improve. Oh, I would
give world's this minute to see you, if it was only for a few minutes but, orders are so very strict that I can hardly hope for that
pleasure before you are released, Nessa you wrote me before I left
home that your horse had been stolen it was safe 4 or 5 weeks

ago. That, I am positive of. poor Al has gone home, left this morning he got a pass last Saturday to go. I never saw anyone so glad of anything in my life scarcely. I began to think that Caroline and Jack were thinking of making a match until Al was about leaving then I began to think differently Nessa if you can get four handsome sets of jewelry send them to me if you please no matter what they cost. Also ten or fifteen links like the one I send they must be ready linked and for which I send the pay two dollars. Miss Stuart wishes to know if Lieut Nicely rec $5.00 lately. Caroline sends her best respects to you All the family sent there love to you. Tell Cousin Frank I have just left the express officer and they will not rec any express for the prisoners with a special permit from the commanding officer then it must be directed to the Com Of. All send respects to Cousin Fr.

Affectionately Yours

Kate

Kate's statement regarding Wesley sending her sets "no matter what the cost" suggests they were affluent, as does the last letter noting that the merchant was to send sweet potatoes, again regardless of cost.

Kate had apparently adopted Frank Imboden into the family in order to send him some express packages. Her last statements indicate that the express office was unable to send anything to prisoners without a special permit.

Johnson Island Ohio
Oct 2nd/64

Dear Kate

I received your letter of the 25th of Sept yesterday. The two dollars you sent me has been received, though the link was lost in some way. I suppose it droped out some ware as it was loose in the letter. When you write again, send me another and sew it fast in the letter, though if it was like the links in the chain I sent you I think I can have them made without the link. I saw cousin Frank and told him what you said about sending the things. He wants the things sent to Col. E. A. Scovall, and mark them inside to him, though I suppose he will write to you, and send you the order.[2] Tell Miss Stewart Lt. Knicely says there has not been any money sent to him lately that he knows of that he has not received any notice of any having been sent lately. I have not received all the things I wrote for yet, and suppose I may give up all hopes of getting them.[3] Tell Jack to send me some money

Give my love to all

Yours affectionately,

W. Makely

Even though Wesley never indicated who his roommates were, Lieutenant Knicely was apparently one of them. Wesley had mentioned Knicely several times receiving money or goods but did not write about their sharing a room. Figure 34 is a letter Lieutenant Knicely wrote earlier in the year, in which he mentioned his block and room number. It is the same address as on Kate's letter to Wesley shown in figure 33.

No prisoner or guard account detailed how necklace and watch chains were made. Discoveries at Johnson's Island have provided the clues needed to reconstruct the process. Figure 35 consists of by-products from hard rubber chains. The two pointed hard rubber pieces are manufactured items (their original purpose or function is unclear) that prisoners cut into thin links. The two pictured links were made by two different processes. Figure 35(c) was made from a hard rubber tube. Figure 35(d) was carved from a solid piece of hard rubber. As noted earlier, every other link was cut and opened to allow the connecting links, which were not cut, to slip in. This process continued until the chain was completed.

Figure 36 illustrates a hard rubber chain with various diamond-shaped sets. This chain was fashioned by Robert Smith. The round links were made from black hard rubber and the diamond pieces were made with hard rubber, shell, and brass sets. The locket on the chain was carved from hard rubber with a shell inlay (Smith 1863–65).

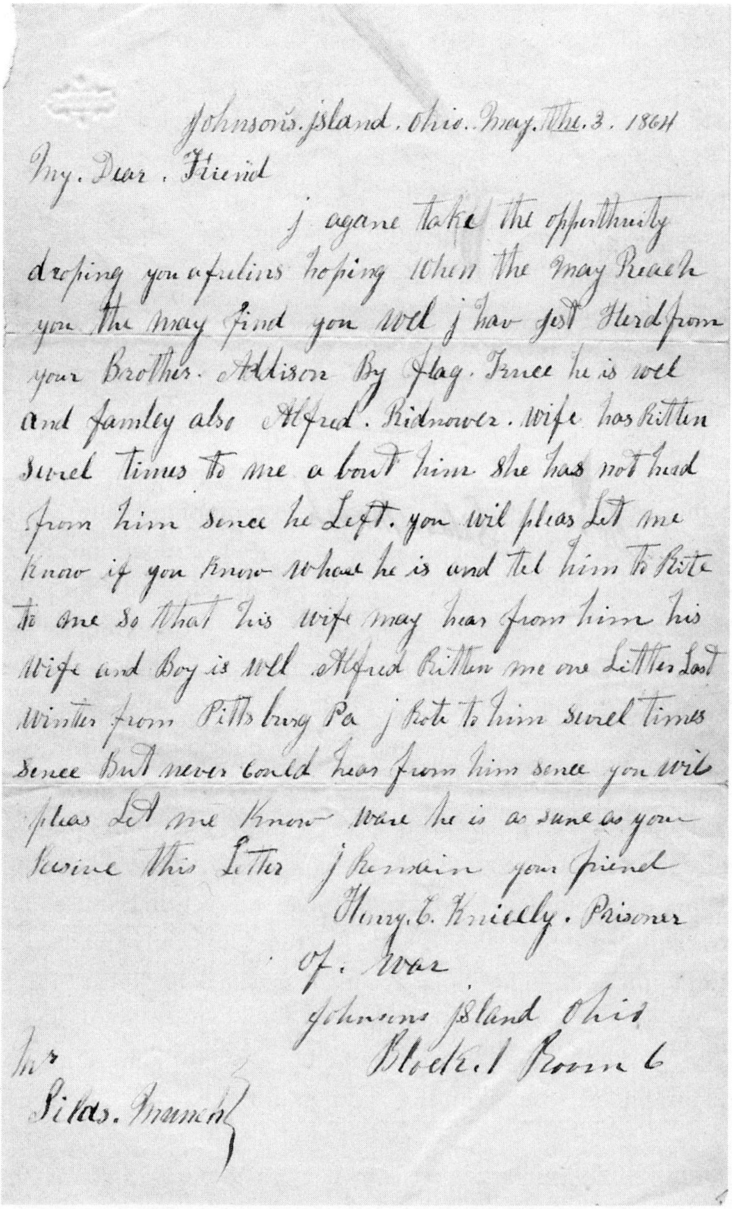

Johnson's. Island. Ohio. May. The. 3. 1864

My. Dear. Friend

j agane take the opperthunity droping you afulins hoping when the may Reach you the may find you well j hav jest Herd from your Brother. Addison By flag. Trnee he is well and famley also Alfred. Ridnower. Wife has Ritten surel times to me a bout him she has not herd from him sence he Left. you wil pleas Let me know if you know whare he is and tel him to Rite to one so that his wife may hear from him his wife and Boy is well Alfred Ritten me one Letter Last Winter from Pittsburg Pa j Rite to him surel times sence But never could hear from him sence you wil pleas Let me know whare he is as sune as you resive this Letter j Remain your friend

Henry. C. Knicely. Prisoner
of. war.
Johnsons Island Ohio
Block.1 Room 6

Mr
Silas. Branch

Fig. 34. Letter from Henry C. Knicely. Knicely is mentioned several times in Wesley's letters, and this letter shows he was a roommate of Wesley's, both residing in Block 1, Mess 6. (By permission of the Friends and Descendants of Johnson's Island Civil War Prison.)

(a)

(b)

(c)

Fig. 35. Various waste or lost materials from making hard rubber chain links: (a) probably the end piece to a hard rubber tube (FS3388, length 27 mm); (b) another end piece of hard rubber tube (FS3435, length 36 mm); (c) hard rubber link cut from tube (FS6187, dia. 9.4 mm); (d) hard rubber link carved from a solid piece of rubber (FS3990, dia. 11 mm). (CHMA. Photographs by author.)

(d)

Fig. 36. Hard rubber, shell, and copper necklace made by Robert Smith. The end hard rubber piece is a locket that opens. (By permission of Nancy Feazell, granddaughter of Robert Smith, and Geoffrey Feazell, grandson of Nancy Feazell.)

Dear Nessa

I have sent Cousin Frank's clothing and wrote to him yesterday the box was directed to Major Eversman M.D. as the express
agent would not take any express for prisoners unless directed to
Commdg Officer. I sent him two flannel shirts $5.25 1 net jacket
2.50. 1 pr shoes $3.50 1 hat 2.50, 2 prs yarn socks, let me know if
he receives them There is nothing going on to tell you so you will
find this a very dry letter Ma sent me 3 barrels of very nice apples
and Fred Tanner brought me a barrel of cider, and Caroline let
us have no peace until we had an apple butter boiling and it is so
nice. Do try to get permission to rec a small box. I want you to
have some of the butter so much. We are all very well at present
and hope you are the same Lillie sends Papa a kiss and has a long
letter for him. Good bye Dearest

Yours affectionately Kate

Major Henry Eversman took command of the medical responsibilities
for Johnson's Island in May 1864. As part of his duties, prisoners needed

Fig. 37. Major Henry Eversman,
surgeon, was responsible for the
prisoners' health at Johnson's Island
in 1864 and 1865. (By permission
of the Friends and Descendants of
Johnson's Island Civil War Prison.)

to get his permission to receive packages at this time. Major Eversman wrote to his fiancée:

> A prisoner in the yard has presented me with a beautiful watch-chain made of gutta-percha and shells it has several charms on it—one a small-fish another an acorn. It is very pretty—I will save it and bring it with me when I come home. I should have a watch now to use it.
>
> Since I had the only authority to approve their requisition for some delicacies, I received quite a number of small things—One prisoner has given me a whole package of the most elegant smoking tobacco—but all this petty kindness will not corrupt me and I shall only consider my duty. (Eversman 1865, letter of September 19, 1864)

Johnsons Island Ohio

Oct 6th/64

Dear Kate

I received your letter of the 28th of Sept yesterday, and as you say, there is scarcely anything to write about. I never was at a place in my life ware there was so little to write about, and hope I may not be here much longer, though I fear I will have to remain here a long time yet.

About fifty sick leave here to day, for Dixie, and I am sorry I am not one of the fortunate.[4] I know you will think very strange of my thinking them fortunate but we think any man lucky to get away from here alive. I have no doubt you all think it a small matter to be a prisoner, but you will not find anyone that has been in prison as long as I have that will think so.

Cousin Frank has received his things. Kate I am much obliged to you for your kind offer of sending me a box, and if I can get permission to receive something I will call on you, or Caroline for a box soon. I also want to get permission if I can to receive an overcoat from Jack. I have tried one winter here without one, and if I have to spend another here I would like to have one. Kate

I have been trying to get the jewelry made you want, but it seams to be difficult to get any one that can make nice work to doing anything, though I think I can manage to have yours made. Give my love to father and mother, and a kiss for my little pets.

Yours affectionately,

W. Makely

As noted earlier in this chapter, between the foiled Confederate escape attempt and the tornado striking Johnson's Island, it seemed Wesley should have had something to write about. He may have feared writing on the escape attempt would be considered contraband and would get his letter destroyed.

The "adoption" of prisoners was common, and many letters refer to cousins, one way to enable sending items to the prisoners. Wesley notes at the end of this letter the difficulty in getting jewelry made. As rations were cut and further restrictions on the sutler were enforced, the prison population must have slipped further into depression at the thought of never getting off the island. Some may have found jewelry making tedious. William Peel, a prisoner renowned for his jewelry making, switched to making fans because he became so tired of working with "gutta-percha" (Wilds 2005:226).

Alex Oct 3rd/64

Dear Nessa

Again I take my pen in hand to write you a letter but what will it be There is nothing in the world to write about except to let you know that all are well, that I supose is as much as you care about hearing. I have been quite sick for several days but am well again now or nearly it. at any rate I am going to carry this letter to the office and see if there is none for me. it has been some time since I rec one from you, the weather has been quite disagreeable for several days cold and rainy is it so with you Lillie send her love to you with a kiss says she loves papa best in the world and then Mama. sometimes I am almost tempted to jealousy but then it is you and I do not begrudge a bit of it. are you

well please let me know. all are well and send there love to you.
Good bye write soon Most affectionately yours

    Kate

Johnsons Island Ohio

Oct 9th/64

Dear Brother,

Your letter of the 28th of Sept. has been received. I have not heard anything of the money you sent me yet, though I suppose I will in a few days. I have only received part of the things I wrote for, there was a note in the box saying the rest would be sent in a few days, though he has not sent them yet. he must either have forgoten, or neglected to atend to it. I have not received the molasses, apples, nor potatoes, and wish you would attend to sending them to me. I have also goten permission to receive some clothing from you, and you might send them all together. Send me a big heavy gray coat. I don't care about its being fine, nor how it looks, so it will keep me warm. and two pr, socks, pr. of good heavy shoes that will keep my feet dry. this is the wettest, mudiest place I ever saw, and I find it almost impossible to keep my feet dry, and a nit jacket like the one Kate sent Frank. Tell Kate cousin F has received his things. Direct the things to Col. E. A. Scovall with a note inside stating who the things are for. If I can get permission to send for some eatables I will write to Miss Caroline or Kate for the box She has so kindly offered to send me.

    Give my love to all

    Yours &

    W. Makely

There is no explanation in the Makely Family Papers at The Library of Virginia as to why this was one of only two letters surviving between the two brothers during Wesley's imprisonment. This letter was a significant comment on Wesley's overall condition. As the weather grew colder, he was probably thinking about all those very cold winter days on Lake

Erie, when anything to keep one warm was welcomed. The Johnson's Island prison compound was a wet, muddy place. Water saturated the ground above the limestone bedrock and did not drain quickly. Earlier letters that contained requests for clothing were more concerned with style. All he cared about now was comfort and surviving another below zero winter. Maintaining the appearance of southern gentry was not as important as staying dry and warm.

Johnsons Island Ohio

Oct 12th/64

Dear Kate

I rec your letter of 5th today. I got permission to receive somthings, and wrote to Caroline several days ago, and hope I may soon receive the things you so kindly offered to send me. I was in hopes I would not have to trouble you much longer about sending me things but I fear I will have to spend another winter here. Kate, I wrote to you some time ago about a special exchange, and I fear the letter might not have reached you, I will mention it again. I want to be sent through to have an officer of like rank sent back for me. I will give bond to return myself in thirty days if I should fail. I think if you could get Col. Dulaney to attend to it, that arrangements might soon be made for my exchange. There has been several left here on special exchange lately, Two leave this evening. I am anxious to get exchanged, as my three years are nearly out, and I then intend to return home. Kate you remember you told me last spring when I saw you, that you thought you could have me released. I am anxious to get home, and if I cannot get exchanged I want you to try and have me released in some way. I wrote to Jack some time ago to see about it for me, but do not know what he has done as I have heard but very little from him about it. I now write to you, as I know you will attend to it for me at once. I often think of home, and how pleasantly, and agreeable I could pass away time, if I could only be there with you. Oh! Would it not be delitefull to have the pleasure of rambling about togeather as we used to.

How often has the flight of some bird passing by inspired me with the desire of being transported to you, that I might there enjoy the pleasures of life, if but for a moment. When I think of of [sic] all the pleasures; all that mortal could desire, and then think of this wretched life, it seams as a darkness was before me. It makes my eyes fill, and my heart sicken when I think of it. Kate you may say I ought not to let any thing trouble me, that I ought to take every thing easy, and make myself contented but you might as well say of some one who died, a fool he died, why did he not wait untill he recovered his strength, till his blood was calm, then all would have been well, and he might have been alive now. I know we are apt to complain that we have but few happy days. But human nature has certain limits, there is a degree of joy, grief, pains, which it is unable to endure.

May God bless you and make you happy.

ever yours,

W. Makely

Wesley had written to Kate on August 8, 1864, that he needed to avoid thinking about how much he missed home, that his home was now Johnson's Island. By October he had apparently failed at this approach. In this long letter Wesley shared his trepidations about being a prisoner. He revisited hopes of a special exchange, even though there was little chance of achieving success. What triggered him to raise his hopes of exchange yet again? Since their rations had been cut, many complained of being hungry, and overall, conditions had gotten worse. The famous "rat hunts" were now taking place, and many prisoners were for the first time eating rats as a means to supplement their diet.

Major Edward Thomas Stakes, 40th Virginia Infantry, wrote on September 12, 1864:

At 3 o'clock we dined which I can say with a clear conscience that I was as hungry when I left the Table, as I was when I went to my dinner. Towards sundown Lieut. Robuck fried two Rats, I ate the hind quarters of one which was as tender and good as a young Squirrel. I have concluded in my mind not to suffer again while I

am in this Prison for the want of something as long as I catch Rats.
(Stakes 1864:100)

Alex Oct 8th/64

Dear Nessa

Why is it you do not write you might try to make it so that I would rec one letter a week. Though I know how it is with myself nothing to write about and it must be worse with you then we are allowed to write so little you might if nothing else say how you are. I try to write three times a week which I believe I do. Caroline rec a letter from her home dated Sept 25 all were well Caroline sends her respects to you. We are all well at present and hope that you are enjoying the same blessings. Write soon. I have never heard weather cousin Frank Imboden ever rec the things I sent him or not. Lillie sends a kiss to Papa you are her sole talk, if your name is mention before her, she never lets it rest for an hour or two, all send there love to you

Most affectionately yours

Kate

Kate's writings suggest that she had no idea of the conditions Wesley was forced to endure. In October 1864 prisoners from Block 8 at Johnson's Island wrote to Colonel Hill, the commanding officer at the prison, complaining of inadequate rations and of additional hardship caused by Colonel Hoffman's orders curtailing delivery of express packages to the prisoners and restricting what the sutler could supply. The prisoners ended their letter to Colonel Hill with the following statement: "We will, in conclusion, respectfully urge you to increase our ration by an issue of anything eatable that you may see fit and which will make what is now given sufficient to satisfy our hunger" (ORA, ser. 2, 7:1021–22).

Alex Oct 11th/64

My dear Nessa

Your letters of Sept 29th and Oct 2 have been rec. I am sorry that you have not rec all the articles you wrote for they were all ordered and paid for perhaps you had better drop a line to Mr Robtson about them Jack will write to him in the morning The express Co would not rec money for you here so Jack went to Washington and sent you twenty dollars from there on the 30th Sept if you have not rec it by the time you get this let me know Nessa about an exchange or parole I do not know how it will be I have spoken to different persons myself but none seem to think that anything can be done for you. I assure you we will do anything that can be done for you. Nessa the link I spoke of was like mine. Tell cousin Frank I rec his letter and bill yesterday and that I will write him a letter too tonight. I have sent his things and thought he surely had them by this time they were directed to Major Eversman I hope he will get them Your Ma has been down staid [stayed] a few days. I was very sorry she had to return so soon and she so anxious to stay but the news Purd brought he thought she had better go. she is a good deal better and told me to send her love

We are all well and send love to you
Ever your,
Kate[5]

Johnsons Island Ohio
Oct 24th/64

Dear Kate

I have been looking for a letter from you for several days, but have not met with my usual luck lately. I had been receiving about two letters a weak for some time, and I fear it has almost spoilt me, as I don't feel satisfide when I don't receive them regularly. I am sorry to hear you complaining about time passing away so slowly. I can very redily see why a prisoner, or why a great many others, might complain but cannot see what should make you complain. I was in hopes time was passing away very agreeably and pleasantly, and that you were free of trouble. I must not forget to say something about my health, as you requested me to write often if only to let you know something about my health. My health has not been very good lately.

Give my love to all,

Yours affectionately,

W. Makely

Certainly from Wesley's perspective, Kate was living a life to be envied. Yet even if the countryside were not being torn up by war and travel restrictions were not in place, Kate was still feeling the effects of her husband being in prison. His comment about his health was so brief. Was he too sick to elaborate, was he depressed, or did he want Kate to be even more anxious?

This period was truly one of the low points for prisoners on Johnson's Island. James Wentworth, 5th Florida Infantry, wrote in his diary on October 21 how he was down to 128 pounds from a high of 174 pounds on April 20, 1864 (Wentworth 1990). Many wrote about the hunger they were experiencing. Edmond Patterson wrote during this time:

For several days some of the boys have been killing and eating rats, of which there are thousands in the prison. I have often been hungry all day long, indeed so hungry that I felt sick, and still I could not screw my courage up to the point of eating rats. But today after getting a few mouthfuls of beef and bread, and having been hard at work most of the day on kitchen detail I was constrained to try a mess of rats. My friend, Jones (not the renowned Bill Jones), had been very lucky and had captured a sufficient number of rats to make a big stew and invited me to try them, and it would have done a hungry man's soul good just to have seen me eat them. I cannot say that I am particularly fond of them, but rather than go hungry I will eat them when I can get them, though they have become the fashion to such an extent that from twenty five to a hundred are killed every night at each Block and they are already getting scarce. They taste very much like a young squirrel and would be good enough if called by any other name.

Explorations of the late 1864 latrines revealed a scarcity of materials and goods that had appeared earlier (Bush 2000:72–75). Even though there were more prisoners occupying the blocks, the amount of contraband items in the latrines was significantly less.

Alex Oct 14th/64

Dear Nessa

I rec your letter of the 6th yesterday. I wish very much that you could have been one of those who were sent on exchange, They certainly are fortunate to be exchanged but I think bad health is the greatest misfortune a person can have. I trust your time will come soon. It seems like ten years since we saw each other. You spoke in your letter of sending to Caroline or myself for a box if you could get permission send to Kate by all means anything in the world you are allowed to have you certainly shall have it sent. I am glad to hear that Cousin Frank has rec his clothes how does he like them I kissed one of your pets the other I could not.[6] Lillie is not very well I was afraid she was getting the mumps but I believe it nothing more than a cold. She sends you a kiss. All well and send there love to you. Jack is waiting for my letter so goodbye write soon

Most affectionately

Kate

Alex Oct 17th/64

Dear Nessa

I looked for a letter from you today. I do not know why but I felt as though I would get one. The town is all in a commotion to day on account of the arrests that have been made to day and yesterday. Doc has been down and left this morning on the train for home. He is coming down again in a week or ten days to spend some time with us. Nessa, Jack rec you letter Saturday requesting a coat and some other things must they be sent with out a bill or must we waite. Caroline rec a letter from Mr Jackson to day about a week old all the folk are well up there. I am going up to see Sec Stanton to see if I cannot get a pass to go to the valley if the Union troops remain up anytime The family are all well and send there love to you write soon Goodbye Affectionately yours

Kate

p.s. Lillie has gotten well and sends her love and a kiss to Papa

Kate's letter was quite short. She did not fill up the single page she was allowed. She may have had trouble finding subjects to write about or perhaps wanted to be sure her letters were never again considered "contraband in length." She was right to ask Wesley about whether he needed permission from the commanding officer at Johnson's Island to receive any packages of clothing.

Johnsons Island Ohio

Oct 26th/64

Dear Kate

I received your letter of the 21st to day. I am delighted to hear that there are some prospects of being with you again soon. I also received a letter from Jack dated the 22nd but as we can only send one letter by each mail, I cannot answer it at present. The mony he sent me has been received. He wanted me to let him know how I wanted to be released. You can tell him that, as I told you in the letter I wrote you some time ago. I received a letter from you a few days ago asking what to do about sending the clothing I wrote for, whether you should send them on or wait untill I send you permission to receive them. I got permission to send for them before I wrote, but it is not necessary to send it to you, as you would have to send it back to me before I could get the things, and besides it might get lost by sending backwards and forwards so much but if there is any prospects of getting released soon, you need not send them. Has Miss Caroline received the letter wrote her some time ago. I had expected I would have received the box you was speaking about sending me before this. I have not received the hair Lill sent me yet though I hope I may soon have the pleasure of being with you all again, and get a lock myself.

Give my love to father and mother

Yours affectionately,

W. Makely

Wesley's renewed hope of being exchanged or transferred was in part due to Generals Trimble, Frazier, and Beall being exchanged on October 19, 1864 (Wilds 2005:289). Prisoners continued to complain of feeling hungry and being deprived of some of the luxuries of life (tobacco, coffee). Rats were selling for one dollar apiece (Wentworth 1990, letter of October 22, 1864). Wesley's letters seemed to relay a bit of impatience.

Alex Oct 25th/64

Dear Nessa

I know you will think strange when I tell you that I have not been up to Washington yet. I got a pass on Friday to go up on Saturday also a letter Col D. sent me to the Sec. The Col was too sic to write himself so his daughter wrote for him but it was not what I wanted. Jack went to see Judge Underwood and he said that he could do nothing now but if you would waite until after the election he would certainly get you exchanged or released well to use his own words he told Jack he would do anything he wanted to do. I think Nessa that he is about the only person in town who can do anything. There is a lady friend in towne a relation of the Sec. who promised me to do all she could for you. I know you think strange of me and perhaps think Kate is like Jack, but Nessa you know how it was for a lady to go about before the war alone, it is more now though I know in most cases a lady can do more than a gentleman I wont quite yet awhile. We have the clothes you wanted ready to send but are waiting for the permit you said you sent to Caroline so all could go together if it does not come in a day or two we will sent the clothes anyhow. I ought to have written to you yesterday but I felt so badly because

I have done nothing for you that I could not write. All well and send there love to you write soon.

Very truly yours
Kate

When Wesley received this letter he probably felt exasperated with the delay in shipment of his clothes. He had just written Kate that he had not sent the permission note but was keeping it at the island for when his package arrived. Somehow, Kate was under the impression it had been sent to Caroline. No doubt this caused Wesley to feel his package would now be further delayed. Six inches of snow fell at Johnson's Island on October 22, 1864, a reminder of just how miserable winter could be on the island (Eversman 1865, letter of October 23, 1864).

Alex Nov 2nd/64

Dear Nessa

Pa has just brought me your letter of the 26th Oct. You say that you are delighted to think there is a prospect of being with me soon. Oh, Nessa that it could be so! Would I not give world's. But you will I suppose have to wait now untill after the election. Who do you think was to see us last night Robt. Beverly. He is one of the saftegards on the Manassas RR. The guard came up with him last night and allowed him to sit awhile he sends his kindest regards to you and says he often thinks and talks about you told me to say to you that all your friends up country were well and that you would be of good cheer he think that all will be well soon. I hope his words may prove true so far as that the war may end soon for I am heartily tired of it. Caroline has never rec your letter yet I think never will now, Nessa the clothes you wrote for were done up in a bundle and by express to you a week ago yesterday I hope you have rec them by this time. Jack goes up the R. Road tomorrow. I tell him he wont mind me untill the Reb's get him. It would be funny if he were taken to Castle Thunder and you were released and could go and find him there. he has permission from the government to do something up the

R.R. I must stop for fear my long letter will not be allowed to
pass so goodbye Dearest
    Affectionately yours
    Kate
    All well and send love

The Makely family must have been conflicted on their support of the
Union or the Confederacy. With Wesley as part of the Confederacy it
would seem Jack would not be subject to arrest, but all the circumstances are not known.

The election Kate refers to is the presidential election between Abraham Lincoln and George B. McClellan, which occurred on November 8,
1864.

Castle Thunder prison, located in Richmond, Virginia, was a group of
converted tobacco warehouses. This prison held many civilian prisoners
suspected of disloyalty, treason, or spying. Union prisoners-of-war were
also held at Castle Thunder. It had a reputation of being as bad as if not
worse than Libby prison (Casstevens 2005).

Johnson's Island, Ohio
Nov 9th/64

Dear Kate
Your letter the 2nd has been received. I am sorry to hear
that you have almost given out all hopes of getting my request
granted. You say there will not be any chance of having anything
don until after the election, though I think you had better said
after the war, as I would suppose that is what you ment, from
the way you write. In your letter of the 30th, you say that Jack
has been promised that my request Shall be granted if Lincoln
is reelected, but that I must not place any confidence in it, as
you do not believe they will do anything for me. I cannot see
what object they could have in promising anything they do not
intend doing, nor why you think they will do so. I cannot see why
you talk as you do. Kate you remember you talked in the same
way last winter. You told me then, that you had done all in your
power, but that they would not do anything for me, and to be in

good spirits, that we would all soon be exchanged, though when you came to see me in the spring, you told me that you could have my request granted. Now you say again that they will not do anything for me, but to be of good cheer, for this war will not last much longer. Kate I cannot see how you can know that the war will not last much longer, unless you had it in your power to stop it. I think you had better stuck to what you said first, that we will all be exchanged soon. Like the man who said, that if he had said the horse was fourteen feet high, he would still stick to it. Kate I know you are honest in every thing you say, or do, and that you would do anything in your power for me, but that you are led to believe all such nonsinse by other persons. Kate if you think you cannot, or do not want to undertake to do what I asked you, let me know, and if Jack does not succeed, I think perhaps I may find some one that can do something. Give my love to all. May God ever bless you, and that you may long be happy, are the wishes of Your affectionate,

W. Makely

Wesley seemed rather harsh toward Kate in this letter. Perhaps the cut in rations was affecting him. Rations at this time consisted of about ten ounces of spoiled beef or salt pork per day or possibly more of white-fish, a pound of bread per day, and a half pint of rice, hominy, or beans (Wilds 2005:289). The prisoners complained of shortages in beef and bread. Perhaps Wesley was concerned over the election, although prisoners were as yet unclear about who had won. The weather could certainly have affected his spirits. The past few days had been cold, windy, and rainy. Conditions at the prison were wretched from every vantage point.

Alex Nov 4th/64

Dear Nessa

Is it as cold out at Johnsons Island as it is here. If more so I do pity indeed you poor cretures for I am nearly frozen. Mosbey did not get Jack he returned home yesterday but is going up again today though I believe he is only going home this trip. All are well up home Al sends us a good many rabbits down. I wish you could enjoy some of them they are so nice. Mrs Browes and her two boys stayed with us night before last she has gone back to Philadelphia to join her husband. Nessa I want your advice about one thing and that is the cutting off of my hair would you if you were me it is becoming so thin it matters not how often I comb it I can get a bundle of hair bigger than my fist out you know you used to thin it out for me in the summers because it was so thick and I used some times to wish that I had not more than half as much as I had. I now wish I had it back. I am not going to wait any longer for to know what you will be allowed to rec but am going to send the box so you may look for your box next week, we are all well and all send there love to you. Write soon. Goodbye

Affectionately yours

Kate

The following letter is from Wesley's daughter Lillie to Wesley. It is the only one from her in the collection. Lillie was three or four when she "wrote" this letter. The handwriting is ragged in parts but at times is exactly like Kate's writing. The letter indicates Kate held Lillie's hand in writing the letter, and that would explain its rough appearance.

Alexandria Nov 6th/64

My Dear Darling Papa

I suspect you will fill your eyes when you rec my pencil sketch the next I will promise you a pen and ink one. Papa I want you to know that I write all this if Mama did hold my hand. I am a good girl and I am going to send to you in this letter one dollar out of my own purse. When your box is sent I am going to send you the nicest pone of cornbread you ever did see and some cake and candy.[7] Uncle Jack has got the yellow [word crossed out] jaundice. Papa Mama tells me that you have a present for me I am waiting patiently for it all are well and send there love to you. I send in this letter that long promised curl of my red hair and I want you to answer this letter soon. In this letter is a one dollar note a curle [of her hair] 1 stamp. Mama will write you a letter tomorrow I send you a kiss from myself and Mama and a hug of love from your dear little girl.

Lillie

PS Nessa are you allowed to receive boots now or not. Kate

It would seem that Kate wrote this letter with Lillie hanging onto her hand. Overall, the letter is very similar to Kate's others. The pencil sketch referred to was unfortunately not part of the surviving record. Toward the end of the letter, the lack of punctuation makes it difficult to separate out the different items included in the letter; one dollar, a curl of hair, and one stamp.

Alex Nov 9th/64

Dear Nessa

I have not rec my usual letter from you this week but perhaps it is owing to the election business report says that some of the rail road north was torn up I do not know how true it is. Yesterday was election day and a quieter one I never witnessed. Abraham is I expect reelected of course you all out there voted for him. There was a Lieut of the Federal Cav. here last night that had just come down on the train who told me all about the up country folks all about Piedmont, Rector T. Salem Plains & Woventon All were well he thought a good deal of the Fosters Shackletts and Payton's but thought that Mr Dr Payton a great talker and one that talked to the point to. Caroline rec a letter from Lieut Pence yesterday he is well but low spirited, he learned that Caroline was here by an officer who was lately captured he did not say who it was. Jack rec your letter yesterday and will answer it in a day or two he has been quite sick but is better now. You will rec a letter from Lillie I expect before you rec this as she wrote yesterday. All but Jack are well. All send there love to you. If I keep on I will fill out my long page then it will not be allowed to pass so Goodbye. Affectionately yours,

Kate

Kate mentioned several times the restrictions on the length of her letters. She seemed to do this to justify why her letters were not filling up the page. This is a reminder that institutionalization affects family and friends as well as those institutionalized. Although her letters could be twenty-eight lines long, hers typically were only twenty lines long.

Johnsons Island
Nov 16th/64

Dear Kate

Your letter of the 9th has been received, and I suppose I must answer it though I feel but very little like writing this morning. My health has been bad for sometime, and am very low spirited besides. I received a letter from Lill a few days ago. Tell her the money and lock of hair she sent me came safely. I am sorry to have kept her waiting so long for her things. I had expected to have sent them to her before this, but they are not ready yet, nor I cannot say when they will be, though I do not think it will be much longer. Kate you want to know if we were allowed to receive boots. We are not, nor I am not in want of them, I have a good pair of shoes which will do me very well here.

Give my love father and mother, Yours affectionately,
W. Makely

Wesley seemed curt in his letter. Kate's last letter had referred to a lieutenant in the Union Cavalry visiting her. Possibly Wesley disliked the idea of Union soldiers stopping by to call on his family. At the prison the Union guard was not allowing any privileges for the prisoners. For instance, prisoners were not even allowed to work with leather to make boots (ORA, ser. 2, 7:584). Wesley may have been harboring some resentment toward the Union military and did not wish to hear of his wife's interactions with Union soldiers.

Johnsons Island Nov 18th/64

Dear Kate

I had the pleasure of receiving your letter of the 4th yesterday. I am glad to hear that you are doing so well. You speak of all the good things that are sent you, and say you wish I could enjoy some of them. Do not let that trouble you. I will be satisfied for the present to get the necessaries of life, and leave all the luxuries, and delicacies, for others. The greatest enjoyment I could have would be in being released from prison, but that I suppose I need not hope for, for several years yet. I have spent upwards of sixteen months in prison, and have a good prospect of having to spend more than twice that many more, but I will not say any thing more about it, for it is enough to sicken any one to think of it. Kate you want my advice about cutting your hair. I would gladly give you my advice, or anything else in the world I could that I thought would be of any benefit to you, but I do not feel that I am capable of giving any advice, even about the most trifling thing, and therefore will beg to be excused. Give my love to all, That every happiness may attend you are the wishes of,

Your affectionate, W. Makely

This letter speaks to Wesley's frustration about no one being exchanged or released from Johnson's Island. He also alluded to the governmental policies of the day and the uncertainty that prevailed. Prisoners literally had no idea what would happen to them, even when the war ended. Their only hope, short of escape, was to take the Oath of Allegiance, and few seriously considered it an option.

Wesley may have been feeling too removed from his family to be of any assistance with Kate's dilemma concerning her hair. His institutionalization at Johnson's Island, and his effort to create more familiar surroundings at Block 1, created a separation he was not willing or able to transcend. He mentioned his wish to have the necessities of life, an indication of the overall suffering prevalent at Johnson's Island in late 1864.

Alex Nov 15th/64

Dear Nessa

By Saturday I supose I will hear your doom, if you are to be exchanged or not. I had expected to hear before this but one has to wait you military gentlemen's time when anything is wanting. I am afraid though that we will not be allowed to see each other before you leave if you should be so fortunate as to be sent off. But anything in the world to get you out of prison, Mrs Robedor from Turpen was here yesterday she is very anxious to go to see her son on the Island but believe she could not succeed in getting a pass[8] Doc is down but speaks of leaving again today Jack has gotten well again I believe Lillie wants every day to go to the office to get an answer to her letter from you. She is anxious to know if you have rec the letter yet and the curl also a one dollar bill. I also some days before enclosed a two dollars in a letter for you. Jack sent you $25 by express last Saturday[9] all well and send love to you

Ever affectionately yours
Kate

Johnsons Island, Nov 23/64

Dear Kate

I received your letter of the 11th some days ago. I expect you wonder why I am so long about answering it. I should have answered it sooner, but I thought I would write to Jack last mail day, and besides there is so little to write about here that I hate to write at all: Kate you speak of having some Federal Capts name who is prisoner at Danville, and is very anxious to get a special exchange, and say you are going to try and have me exchanged for him. Unless he has friends that have some influence at Washington, and will go and try to have it effected his name will not be of much service towards getting me exchanged. My health is very bad, and I am anxious to get home. I have almost given out all hopes of getting a Special exchange. Tell jack I have just received a receipt for twenty five dollars. I have not received any letter yet, though I suppose it must be from him. I will send the jewelry I am having made for you just as soon as it is finished. Give my love to father and mother. Yours affectionately,

W. Makely

Fig. 38. Hard rubber cuff button carved at Johnson's Island (FS2621, length 15.4 mm). (CHMA. Photograph by author.)

The main prisoner complaint at the Johnson's Island prison in November 1864 was the continued harsh treatment. Rations were short and little was allowed to reach the prisoners from the outside. With the demand on rats for food, by the end of 1864 even they were scarce.

Wesley, in spite of his health, managed to think about the jewelry he wanted to send home. He sent Kate several pairs of cuff buttons made from hard rubber. The carved hard rubber cuff button illustrated in figure 38 was recovered from the Block 2 area of the prison.

> Alex Nov 19th/64
>
> Dear Nessa
>
> I hope as you rec this that you will have rec your box which was sent off yesterday morning and I hope it will please you. I know you will think everything nice in it when you know that your Katie cooked everything in the box. Ma sends you the ham & turkey, Caroline the fruite cake, Lillie the pone of cornbread, apples, onions, and gumdrops. Pa sends the peaches the balance you may thank me for. I rec that scolding letter of yours yesterday but I forgive you for it because I scold sometimes myself. A friend went to see Stanton today for me and would have gone before but he has been quite ill. Doc is still with us. Lillie is looking with patients for an answer for her letter to you and talks forever about her present. All are well and send there love to you, write soon and often. Goodbye,
>
> Yours affectionately
>
> Kate

List of articles in box, 1 ham, 1 turkey, 1 jar pickles, 1 jar apple butter, 1 can peaches, 1 can pickle oysters, 1 lb ground coffee, 2 oz almonds, 2 oz pecan nuts, ½ gal chestnuts. 1 fruite cake, 1 ginger bread cake, 1 pone corn bread, 14 lemons, 4 oranges, 4 lbs loose sugar, ½ oz tea, [crossed out word], 64 bisquit, 25 puffs, 50 donuts, 5 mince pies, 3 lbs butter, 10 onions, 1 lb figs, 1 oz spice nuts, 6 apples, a few raisins, and gum drops.   K.

Figure 39 (FS0745) is known as a cathedral- or gothic-style pickle bottle (Lindsey 2010; Russell 1988:98–99). This design of pickle bottle was common in the 1860s and popular at the Johnson's Island prison site. It is possible the jar of pickles in Kate's list of the box contents was like the one in figure 39. This particular bottle was discovered from a late

Fig. 39. Cathedral-style pickle jar recovered from the 1864 latrine for Block 1 (FS0745, height 27.7 cm). (CHMA. Photograph by author.)

1864 latrine from Block 1. There are several slightly different types of gothic pickle bottles from Johnson's Island. Although this type of bottle is known as a pickle bottle, it was used for sauces and other contents as well.

Johnson's Island, Ohio

Nov 27th/64

Dear Kate

I am sorry to have to inform you that I have not recd. the box you sent me, It reached the Island on the 24th. I receipted for it, paid 70 cents charges on it from Sandusky here, but have not been allowed to receive one single thing it contained. I am sorry you sent it, though I suppose you know but little about prison regulations, and doubtless thought when I wrote to you that I was going to try and get permission to send for a box of eatibles, that I would have to keep the permission until the box arrived, in order that I might receive it when it arrived, as I wrote to you that I had to keep my permission to send for clothing until the clothing arrived, unless I could not get them when they came though a great many of the things you sent, we are not allowed to receive at all. You must have thought I was in need of dainties. I was some what surprised when I saw the list, as I had written to you several times last Summer about sending me fruit cakes, candies etc. Perhaps I might have been allowed to recd the box if there had not been so many dainties in it. It was a very nice box, and I would like very much to get it. Kate perhaps you might get permission from the Sec. of War, or the Commissioner of prisoners to send me eatibles occasionally, though I hope I may soon be out of prison and not have to trouble you so much. I have not recd the letter you Spoke of in the note you sent in the box. Give my love to all.

Yours affectionately, W. Makely

Thanksgiving Day was November 24, 1864. Wesley gave no indication that he or anyone in prison celebrated the day. Henry Eversman, surgeon for the Union, in writing to his fiancée, also did not mention any celebrations. Wesley continued his criticisms of Kate and even of the contents of the box. Certainly her goal was to provide good food, but Wesley never got to enjoy the contents. He had asked Kate in late June of 1864 to send to him some wine or Hostetter's bitters instead of fruitcakes.

> U.S. Military Prison,
> Johnsons Island,
> Nov 30th/64

Dear Kate

I received your letter of the 19th last Monday, and am Sorry the I cannot Say I have recd the box of provisions you sent me, and regret it still more since I have learned that every thing was cooked by you. I know the things wer[e] very nice, but there is no use grieving about it. I am sorry you sent the box, but I suppose you know but little about prison regulations. Although I was not allowed to receive the things, I am as much obliged to you as if though I had recd them all. Kate I am sorry to hear you spoke of my Scolding letter. I fear I said more than I aught to have done, as I know I Sometimes do, especially when I am not very well, but I assure you I did not mean anything of that sort and hope you do not think I would intentionally say or do anything that would wound your feelings in the least. Kate be assured that "I have not a hope that does not dream for thee; Nor joy that is not shared by thee; and have no fear that does not dread for thee."

Kate I Scarcely know what I did write, but I hope by this time you may have changed you mind about it. Tell Lill I am getting her things ready to send as fast as I can, and think I will get them started sometime next week. I have been waiting for some time to have a nice set made for you, but the gentleman who is to make them is waiting for some tools, he is expecting, and cannot make them until he gets them. If he does not get them in a few days I will send the other things on. Tell Dock I recd his letter this morning. Give my love to all.

Yours, affectionately, W Makely

Fig. 40. Carving tool set of Robert Smith. Additional attachments are in the wooden handle (handle length 12 cm). (By permission of Nancy Feazell, granddaughter of Robert Smith, and Geoffrey Feazell, grandson of Nancy Feazell.)

Historic and archaeological evidence has enabled the reconstruction of some of the tools prisoners used in making jewelry. There was evidence of a lathe, a table vice, various sizes of files, and a set of hand tools from a kit. Figure 40 is the tool kit Robert Smith used at Johnson's Island, probably purchased from the sutler.

Alex Nov 27th/64

Dear Nessa

I believe at last I have good news for you, the friend I told you that was interceding for you has Stantons promise that he will do all in his power for you. He sent your name also the names of too others who have lost there that is one leg a piece, who he also promised to have exchanged. The person who is to be exchanged for you is a Capt George L. Schelle Co I 88th Vols. captured at Gettysburg and is confined at the Danville Prison.[10] I hope now that it will not be maney days before you are released. Though we will still be deprived of each others company for some time, still you will not be in prison. Pa recd. a letter from Lieut Pence this morning, he is still in Deleware, and thinks that I have gone back south. Lillie is looking with patience for your promised answer to her letter think Papa is writing her a very long letter as it takes him so long to write it. Jack rec a letter from you yesterday and last night went to see judge U. I told him Jack what Stanton had promised to do for you. All the family are well and send there love to you. Have you rec your box yet. It was sent last Friday a week ago answer this as soon as possible when you start which I hope will be soon let me know, I will try to get to see you. Good bye. Ever Yours truly

Kate

Johnsons Island, Ohio
Dec 4th/64

Dear Kate,

I had the pleasure of receiving your letter of the 27th of Nov yesterday, and you can scarcely imagine how glad I was to hear that there is a very good prospect of getting a Special exchange, but I am not by any means as sanguine about it as you seem to be, although I think the prospects are very good. You Say my name has been Sent in, but do not Say ware to, or what for, though I hope it has been sent here, to have me sent through to effect my exchange for the officer you speak of, as I have no doubt but what I could Succeed in having the exchange made, but if they will not parole me to go through, and have sent my name to the Confederate Commissioner of exchange, offering to exchange me for the officer you speak of, and he Should refuse to make the exchange, I will write to Some of my friends in Richmond to See the proper authorities there, and try and have the exchange made at once. Write to me as soon as this reaches you, and let me know what has been don[e] and if it is necessary for me to write to Richmond I will do so at once. Tell Lill she must not look for a letter from me for some time, as I can only write two letters a week and it takes nearly all of them to keep up my correspondence with Kate. I will Send the things I am having made for you in a few days. Give my love to father, and mother.

Yours affectionately, W Makely

Wesley must have experienced a surge of hope every time discussion of a possible exchange arose, but as his December 4 letter also shows, he knew by now that his chances were slender. It is difficult to imagine Wesley's state of mind having to wait for the mail system to bring a response from his inquiries to Kate. Experience would suggest almost a month would pass by.

At the same time the conditions for the prisoners at Johnson's Island were at their lowest point. Many prisoners were complaining of poor and scant rations. The hunting of rats had made even that choice scarce. In contrast, an official report on the same day as Wesley's last letter gives insight into how the conditions at the prison were viewed from the Union perspective. It must be remembered rations were cut several times from April until November 1864 and the inspection report refers only to currently authorized provisions.

Inspection Report for Johnson's Island, December 4, 1864
by Lieut. Col. Edward A. Scovill
Conduct—good. Cleanliness—good. Clothing—comfortable. Bedding—about four-fifths of the prisoners not supplied with straw. State of quarters—clean, except one company in Block 10. State of mess-houses—fair. State of kitchen—fair. Food, quality of—poor fresh beef and some sour salt beef last week. Food, quantity of—prisoners' ration, except potatoes. Water—good. Sinks, fair condition. Police of grounds—good. Drainage—good. Police of hospital—very good. Attendance of sick—good, plenty of prisoner surgeons, nurses and cooks. Hospital diet—good and abundant. General health of prisoners—good. Whole number of prisoners, 2,755; no deaths since last report. Vigilance of guard—good. Remarks and suggestions.—The prisoners receive considerable clothing from relations, but many have no relations and are supplied by the quartermaster, as the following issue for November will show: Blankets, 598; shirts, 423; stockings, 748; greatcoats, 17; drawers, 465; bootees, 599. There has been beef returned to the commissary from the prison frequently, on account of its unfitness for issue. As the commissary has no authority to purchase potatoes I would recommend that the sutler be allowed to sell them to the prisoners. (ORA, ser. 2, 7:1186)

Dearest Nessa

I do not know why it is but it seems to me like a month since I heard from you though I rec a letter from you on Friday last which I answered immediately. I also wrote you one on Sunday last which I expect will please you more than any you have rec for a long time as it conveyed the information of Sec Stanton's promise for your release. Oh! I hope it will not be many days before it is fulfilled. Have you rec the box we sent you last Friday week ago, I [hope] it will please you if you are allowed to rec it. Nessa you remember I wanted you to have three setts of jewelry made if you think you cannot get them you had better send those that are finished as the parties are getting impatient and let the rest go. Do not forget the links of chain if you can get them about 10 links the size of mine, there is another set of jewelry wanted but of course it is no use ordering it. Doc is here and is going to start a school on Monday next. Mr W. Ford is also here the Rebs having run him off. We are all well except Pa he is complaining again. All send there love to you. Lillie sends Papa a kiss and says don't tell him that I am bad. Write soon. Good bye. Caroline sends her respects.

Yours most affectionately

Kate

Kate was under the impression Wesley would be either exchanged or at least transferred. The Official Records include no mention of Wesley Makely's name being sent anywhere. At this time several names were being discussed for exchange, and those individuals would eventually be granted transfers for exchange in January.

There was some urgency in her writing about jewelry. She had promised some jewelry to acquaintances of hers. Colonel Virgil Murphy, 17th Alabama Infantry, states well how this jewelry was viewed:

I wrote my wife and sent her a beautiful cross and mother a ring manufactured in prison. They will be objects of curiosity and precious relics some day in the distant future, when our sufferings are appreciated and our sacrifices acknowledged. It was all the token I had to send my loved ones, in value worthless but in sentiment and remembrance much. (Virgil Murphy 1865, entry for January 27, 1865)

This entry by Murphy provides great insight into the mind of the prisoner-of-war and the relationship with the jewelry. From Murphy's perspective, the sentimental and societal value associated with these items trumped their economic value, even those made with gold, silver, or diamond sets. The pleasure the prisoners gained through providing these "trinkets" was again something they could retake from the freedoms lost as a prisoner-of-war.

Johnsons Island Ohio

Dec 7th/64

Dear Kate

I have at last got your things ready to send to you and will start them in the morning. I will send you one shell cross, 1 guta percha cross, 6 breast pins, 5 rings, 3 watch chains, 1 chain with a hart to it for Lill a necklace, 2 sets of earrings, 1 set of cuff buttons, 1 heart, 1 fish and 1 acorn, I put some of the things in a Small box and directed it to you. I had intended them for Lill and you, though I leave it to you to select such things out of the box as you may want, and the rest you may dispose of among your friends. The shell cross I want you or Lill to have, and the necklace I made myself expressly for Lill, and had a hart made for it, but it did not please me so I had another made, though that has not got any place to fastin to the chain. I had intended having a clasp made for it, that She might either ware the other hart, or a cross to it as she might choose, but I thought best not to wait any longer, and send the things on as you seem, to be anxious to get them. The ring with M on it is for Lill, the one with K on it I had intended for you, but the man who made it, made a complete failure, it is not fit to ware, though I will send it along as I have no use for it here.[11] I hope the other two rings in your box may please you, I think them very pretty. Nearly all the things were made of the shell you sent me. The pin with the large white oval set in it, I had made expressly for the lady friend you speak of. The pin I don't think a very nice job, And perhaps you had better have another put to it before you give it to her. The chains I made myself, and the one with a hook to it I had intended for myself, also the fish and acorn, though you may do as you please with the things, and if you want any more like any of the things I send you let me now, and I will have them made for you. Give my love to all.

Yours affectionately, W. Makely

Breast pins were popular with the prisoners for sending to loved ones. The two breast pins pictured in figure 41 were made at Johnson's Island. Figure 41(a) was made by Robert M. Smith in 1864 and taken home with him. He wrote of it: "I made a beautiful breast pin [of] verigated shell with scoliped gurta-percha border" (Smith 1864, entry for April 30, 1864). The other breast pin was discovered in a latrine associated with Block 6, the prison hospital. It has the name Ella carved in the shell along with a leaf or vine border. Both have copper pins attached to the back.

The cuff buttons in figure 41(c) were also made by Robert M. Smith. He wrote in his diary, "I was working on buttons for General Trimble" (Smith 1864, entry for June 13, 1864). From the number of hard rubber items he mentions making from February through June, 1864, Smith must have been supplying many prisoners with mementos to send or take home.

The cuff button FS2994 in figure 41(d) was discovered in the soil underneath Block 4, apparently discarded or lost during the manufacturing process. The maker of this item had used a hard rubber chart rule that bore a portion of the maker's mark on it, from the American Rubber Company. Just below the word "American" was a portion of the Goodyear patent information. Nelson Goodyear patented hard rubber in 1851. Thus we know that some of the chart rule pieces found at Johnson's Island came from the American Rubber Company, a company operating out of New York (Woshner 1999:46).

Fig. 41. Hard rubber jewelry from Johnson's Island: (a) breast pin of shell and hard rubber (Smith collection, length 32.8mm); (b) breast pin discovered in an 1864 Block 6 latrine (FS0399, length 32.8 mm); (c) cuff buttons of hard rubber, shell, and brass (Smith collection, length 32.8 mm); (d) unfinished cuff button of hard rubber from Block 4 (FS2994, length 12 mm). (Items (a) and (c) by permission of Nancy Feazell, granddaughter of Robert Smith, and Geoffrey Feazell, grandson of Nancy Feazell. Items (b) and (d) CHMA. Photographs by author.)

Alex Dec 2nd/64

Dear Nessa

Your letter of the 23rd was rec yesterday and I tell you I welcome for it seemed a very long time since I rec one from you. but Nessa there is so little to write about at home I know how it must be with you. William Butler was brought in yesterday he has been a prisoner for 18 months and was released about 10 or 12 days ago. Came right round home. was home about four hours when he was again captured. I think if he gets out again he will be a little more careful about coming home. You stated that you had rec twenty five dollars. It was from Jack I did not know that he had not written but he said he was in a great hurry. he is the greatest business man you ever saw in your life building houses. I am very sorry indeed to hear that your health is bad again hope it will not be long before you are released then you will get better. All well except Lillie she has a cold and Jim is getting a very severe boil on the back of his neck. You remember the one that Kate nursed for you once. Well just such a one he is getting. All send their love to you. Write soon.

Affectionately yours Katie

Kate was talking about William B. Butler, a private in the 5th Virginia Cavalry and later of the 11th Virginia Cavalry. He was captured on May 24, 1861, at Alexandria, Virginia, and exchanged on August 21, 1861. On July 18, 1863, he was captured at Centreville, Virginia, and spent some time in prison at Point Lookout. He was exchanged on November 1, 1864, joined the 43rd Virginia Cavalry on November 15, and was recaptured, again at Centreville, on November 29, 1864, just a few days before Kate's letter. He spent the rest of the war at the Old Capitol Prison and Fort Warren, where he took the Oath of Allegiance and was released on June 13, 1865.

Johnsons Island Ohio

Dec 11th/64

Dear Kate

I expect you have been disappointed about getting your

things, and have been disappointed myself about sending them. I had expected to have sent them some time ago, but the weather has been so bad that we have had no express here for several days until yesterday, and I hope I may get them started in the morning. You will find a small box for Miss A. Stewart with two rings and a pin in it, sent by Lt Knicely, and another small box, sent by E. M. Stone for Mrs M. E. French there are two crosses and a ring in it.[12] The other two large boxes are yours. The box with your name on it has the things in it I intended for Lill and you. I send you two rings a piece, though one of yours was spoiled, and a cross for each of you. I had the pin with the acorns on it fixed so that you might use it to fasten your watch chain to. The other pin, cuff buttons, and ear bols[?] are for you also, though if you want any of the things in the box for your friends you may let them have them, and if you want any more made like any of the things I send you, let me know and I will have them made for you. I had the pin with the large white oval set in it made for your lady friend you speak of. If you think it will suit her have another pin put to it and give it to her. Kate you still seam to be very confident about my getting a Special exchange. I hope you may not be disappointed, though I am very fearful you will be. If I could have been sent through to make the exchange, I have no doubt but what I could have suc-ceeded, but have very little confidence in what I think has been done. Give my love to all.

Yours affectionately, W. Makely

The acorn was one of the images the prisoners favored in the hard rubber jewelry. Lieutenant Robert Smith, one of the recognized jewelers, carved a ring he brought home exhibiting an acorn on the side sets. The top of the acorn was made of gold, and the bottom, the nut section, was made from shell. The center was gold with his initials inscribed on it. He wrote in his diary, "I have made three finger rings today which I intend carrying to Dixie (set with gold)" (Smith 1864, entry for May 6, 1864).

Johnsons Island Dec 13th/64

Dear Kate

I expect you are becoming very inpatient about your things, as I have been talking about sending them for so long. I have had them ready to send you for sometime, but the bay is frozen entirely over, and there has not been any express from here for several days. I will send them through as soon as I possibly can. Kate I have been looking for a letter from you for several days. I have not received any since the 4th. I am very anxious to hear something more about my Special exchange though I have but very little hopes of getting a Special. Tell Jack I received his letter of the 27th of Nov several days ago, and will answer it soon. I am sorry to learn that father is in bad health again, and hope he may be well before now. Tell Lill I will try and answer her letter before long. Give my love to all. Yours most affectionately,

W Makely

Transportation to and from the island was difficult when the ice was not thick enough to support sleds. Ice had to be thick enough to transport over or thin enough for boats to plow through. There were times when two or more weeks passed without any reliable transportation to Sandusky. At these times, supplies were depleted and no mail was delivered.

Wesley does not mention it to Kate, but on December 11, 1864, a notice was posted on the prison bulletin board stating that prisoners were now allowed to write three letters per week. No rationale was given for this change in policy, but many prisoners were glad to write more to family and friends.

Johnsons Island Dec 15th/64

Dear Kate

I had the pleasure of receiving your letter of the 24th this morning, and was very glad to get it, as I had not heard from you for some time. Tell Lill I had intended the things I had made for her as a present, and not as a Christmas gift as She says, but everything is frozen up and there has not been any express from here for some time. I fear if I do not get them started soon they will not reach her in time for a Christmas gift. Tell her she must not be so impatient about not getting a letter from me. She must remember she was talking about writing to me a long time before she done so, though I must write to her soon as she will not write to me again until I answer her letter. I received a letter from Jack this morning, he speaks of receiving a letter from Lt Samuels about some money. I wrote to Jack some time ago asking him to send some money to Lt S- but I suppose he did not get the letter. Tell him to send it. Give my love to father and mother. I will also send a kiss to my two little pets. Yours affectionately,

    W. Makely

In the early morning of December 13, 1864, close to thirty prisoners attempted to escape. While trying to climb over the fence, Lieutenant John Bowles, 2nd Kentucky Cavalry, was shot and killed by the guard. Several men made the climb but were chased down by the guard and captured. Four made it to the mainland, but because of the severe cold and a well-armed farmer they surrendered and were returned to the island (Frohman 1965:52; Wilds 2005:305–7).

Alex Dec 3rd/64

    To Col. C. W. Hill,[13]

    Dear Sir,

    On the 18th of last month I sent my husband Capt. Wesley Makely a box of provision by express, which of course I understood him to have a permit to rec. he also wrote for some clothing which were sent before the box of provision, and which he received. To day I received a letter from him stating that he had rec a receipt to sign for the delivery of the box and had also to pay 75 cts. for the fraight from Sandusky. but was not allowed to see a single article it contained. the box was directed to Col. E. A. Scovall. I wish you would be kind enough to inquire about the the [sic] matter, and if Mr. Makely cannot be allowed to rec the box, have it returned to me at once. I went to see Gen. Wessel to day about it he gave me your adress and said the box would be returned if Mr. Makely was not allowed to rec it. and said that you would attend to it. The box cost rather more than I care about loosing and then the great disappointment to Mr. M. so I beg of you to please allow my husband to rec it, if not return it to me. by so doing you will confer a favor that will not soon be forgotten.

Respectfully,
Mrs. Wesley Makely

I give you a list of contents, 1 ham, 1 turkey, 1 jar pickles, 1 jar apple butter, 1 can peaches, 1 can oysters, 1 lb. coffee, 2 lbs almonds, 2 lbs pecan nuts, ½ gal chestnuts, 1 fruite cake, 1 ginger do. 1 lofe cornbread, 14 lemons, 4 oranges, 4 lbs lofe sugar, ½ lb tea, 64 biscuits, 25 puffs, 50 doughnuts, 5 pies, 2 lbs. butter, Onions, figs, and a few other little notions. a good many of the things sent by my little daughter to her Papa.

On the reverse side of Kate's letter about the missing box is the following note from the Express Officer:

Hd. Qu. U.S. Forces
    Johnsons Island
    Dec. 9, 64
    Respectfully referred to Capt. S. W. Bailey Inspect. Ex. Packages for information This package to be returned by Command of Col. Hill
    Express Officer
    Johnsons Island O.
    Dec. 9th, 64
    Respectfully returned with statement that I do not remember anything about the within mentioned box. But upon inquiry of the Hospital Steward find that the Box was sent to the Hospital at the time by direction of Dr. Eversman on account of the prisoner having no permission to receive it.[14]
    S. W. Bailey, Capt. 128th OVI, Inspect Ex. Prison of War

Dear Nessa

Your letter of the 30th Nov came to hand to day and with
this we will let the scolding letter drop. some day I will show it
to you with the rest some of these days. I have though[t] nothing
more of it since I answered it. though at the time it made
me feel quite badly for awhile but don't think or say anything
more about it and I won't either. I cannot help but feel badly
about you not being allowed to have your box. I have written
to Col Hill and if you are not allowed to have it I hope it will be
returned which I am quite sure any gentleman would do. Nessa
do not trouble yourself about having anything made for me.
Spend your money on yourself and be as comfortable as possible.
I have had the set of jewelry you sent me sometime ago mounted
and they are very beautiful. Lillie is waiting for her promised
present and wants to know if it is to be a present or a Christmas
gift. she has taken a notion that a present and a gift cannot be
one.[15] and poor little thing last night when I went up to bed
she wakened up and said Mama aint Papa a long time answering my letter. I would write him another and tell him what you
bought me from Balt but he would not answer it. So Nessa do
write her a little letter. Ma and I went to Balt yesterday morn and
came back last night. Nessa I would like to send you a Christmas
present but I know you would not be allowed to have it. write
soon all send their love to you. Goodbye Ever Affectionately
Yours Kate

Alex Dec 13th/64

Dear Nessa

Your letter of the 4th was rec yesterday. I would have answered it immediately but waited to see a friend of mine who
went to see Stanton about the exchange. I do not think it necessary for you to write to Richmond just yet at anyrate for Stanton
has promised your exchange. You say that I said in my letter that
your name had been sent on. but that I did not say where to or
for what why, fore exchange of course. but I do not know where

it was sent to. I do know that he promised to exchange you and sent your name out while the person whas there who went to see him about the matter. you seem to think that Capt. Shell would have to have some influential friend to effect the exchange. You must not forget that Yankee Officers have sweethearts who can have a little favor granted them by the higher dignitaries as well as you Southern Rebels. Capt. Shell's sweetheart wants Capt. Makely returned for her lover. So I think it will not be long before you are sent off you know there has been no flag of truce boat gone down lately. Nessa I wrote to Col. Hill about that box of yours and have pah[?] time to rec answer but none comes. I wish you would address him a note asking him if he rec mine and if he intends having the box returned. All send there love to you. Ma is quite sick with a cold. Lillie has a very bad one to. Rest all well. Good bye Affectionately Yours

    Kate

                                       Alex Dec 16th/64

    Dear Nessa

    I rec your letter of the 7th stating that you had the jewelry finished and would start them the next morning which would be 9 days ago. they have not arrived yet but they might not have been started just when you wanted them to be, but I hope they will get here yet. Our friend Mrs. H was here last night and sit with us until bed time. I told her that I was expecting a box from you and that there was a present sent for her. She said that Stanton had declared all those that he had sent the names of out exchanged and of course as your name was among them you will be among the number all that they wait for is arrangements for sending the prisoners off. they are to be sent down to Charleston for exchange. I believe I told you in my last that Ma was sick but she is up again today. the rest all well. Uncle John B. is dead. Died on Election day last. William Ford has been staying with us for 4 or 5 weeks but left this morning for Phila. Brower and family are living there. All send there love to you, Good bye.

    Affectionately Yours

    Kate

Johnsons Island Ohio
Dec 21st/64

Dear Kate

I have just received your letter of the 18th. I wrote to Jack on
the 19th and enclosed a letter to Judge Underwood asking them
to try and get me paroled to come home. I have heard of several
that have been paroled lately. Some I believe for the war, others
until exchanged. If Jack has received my letter he can tell you
what I wrote to him and to the Judge. If he has not received it
tell him to let me know at once. Kate it has been a month or upwards since Secty Stanton promised to do all he could to have me
exchanged for Capt Shell, and I can but think that he knows by
this time w[h]ether or not the Confederate authorities are willing
or not to make the exchange; at any rate I hope you will know by
the time this reaches you. I don't think the Confederate government will be willing to make the exchange, I have seen several
persons who have been trying to get Special exchange, and they
tell me that the Confederate government will not make any
more Special exchanges, and they will very likely think that the
Federal government has some special reason for wanting to get
Capt Shell exchanged. If I could have been paroled to go through
I think I could get them to make the exchange. For my part if I
could get a parole I would not trouble them about exchange, but
as the lady you speak of has been kind enough to do so much
for me, I must try and do every thing in my power to secure the
exchange of her friend. If Secty Stanton does not succeed in
effecting the exchange, and there is any thing I can do for her
friend, tell her, to let me know. I will be glad to do anything in
my power for him. Kate by the time this reaches you I think you
will know what has been don about my exchange, and as you had
influence enough to have my name sent through for exchange I
think you can very easily have me paroled, and hope you will lose
no time in attending to it. Col Hill received the letter you wrote
to him about the box you sent me. At the time the box came Col
Hill was away, and not in command. When he recd your letter he
looked after the box at once and found it had been turned over

to the hospital, otherwise, it would have been returned to you at once.

Yours most affectionately, W. Makely

This letter and the December 9, 1864, letter from Captain Bailey, Inspector of Express Packages, 128th OVI, provide information on the disposition of unauthorized packages. The illegal boxes were turned over to the hospital and Union doctors for use in the care of sick prisoners. This created a collection of goods not expected to appear at a prison hospital. Stemmed crystal glass, porcelain plates, fine tableware, smoking pipes, and a variety of liquor bottles have been recovered within the context of the prison hospital. For example, figure 42 illustrates an 1851 gravy

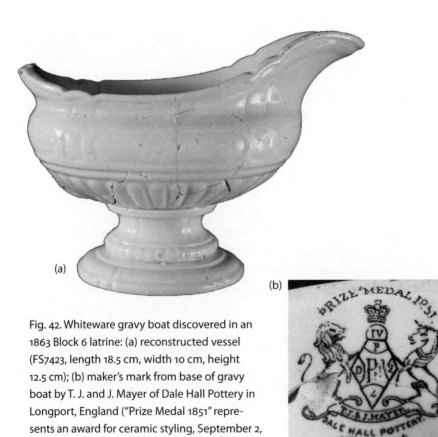

(a)

(b)

Fig. 42. Whiteware gravy boat discovered in an 1863 Block 6 latrine: (a) reconstructed vessel (FS7423, length 18.5 cm, width 10 cm, height 12.5 cm); (b) maker's mark from base of gravy boat by T. J. and J. Mayer of Dale Hall Pottery in Longport, England ("Prize Medal 1851" represents an award for ceramic styling, September 2, 1851—P = 1851, D = September, 2 = day). (CHMA. Photographs by author.)

boat recovered from an 1863 latrine behind Block 6. The maker's mark indicates manufacture by T. J. and J. Mayer, Longport, England (Kovel and Kovel 1986).

Alex Dec 19th/64

Dear Nessa

Yours of the 13th was rec yesterday you seem to think I am uneasy about the things you were to send me. I did begin to feel so before I rec your letter stating the bay was frozen over. Oh Nessa how much it grieves me to think that we cannot send you a box for Christmas and that you will have to eat the worse prison fare for your Christmas dinner. but Nessa I hope it will not be very long before you are released now and that will be better then all. I sent Lieut Pence $5.00 the other day also a box to Elmira and one to the Old Capital all without permits and all were rec. I cannot see why you were not allowed to rec yours. I have a list of articles taken from a northern paper stating what they were allowed to send to there friends in the South and it was nearly the same I sent you. I think they might do any how as they would like to be done by. Lillie says Mama cannot send Papa a box she must send him a Christmas gift and she don't know what so she sends a two dollar note which please find enclosed. All well and send there love to you, write soon. Good bye

Affectionately

Kate

One of the interesting points institutional research discovered was the inconsistency of governmental policy implementation at different prisons (Bush 2009:162–63). The commander of each prison facility had some latitude in interpreting the regulations sent by Colonel Hoffman.

Unfortunately for Wesley, his box was refused. William Peel, a prisoner in Block 8, was more fortunate. His roommate, Lieutenant Robert McDowell, 11th Mississippi Infantry (they had served together and were captured together) received a box on December 25, 1864, prompting Peel to write, "McDowell and I had, however, a very tolerable dinner. A piece of baked beef & baker's-bread (about two days ration of the former)

& thanks to Miss Dora—an apple pie & cornmeal pudding" (Wilds 2005:311).

The appropriate greeting for December 25th was "Christmas Best." Peel noted that the greeting was hardly used at Johnson's Island.

> U.S. Military Prison
> Johnsons Island, O
> Dec 27th/64

Dear Lill,

I expect you think I am very slow answering your letter and still slower about sending the present I promised you so long ago. I have had the thing ready to send you for some time, but there has not been any express from here lately until to day, and I am glad to day that I have at last got them started, and hope they may reach you safely by New Year. I expect that you have had so many pretty Christmas presents that my gutta-percha jewelry will scarcely be that enticing. I will look for a letter from you very soon telling me all about the pretty things you got, and how you spent your Christmas. I have had a very dull one so far, I spent part of my time reading and part walking about the prison, and oftentimes think how much I would enjoy being with your mother and you. It has been nearly two years since I have seen you, and I suppose you have changed considerable since then. time makes a great many changes, and I hope it may not be long before I will be with you again. Give my love to your mother.

Your affectionate father, W. Makely

This was the only letter Wesley wrote to his daughter while in prison. He tried to make everything appear as normal as possible for his little girl. There was no information available from the descendants of Wesley, Kate, and Lillie as to the specific jewelry sent at Christmas. From all Wesley said about obtaining fine jewelry items, he probably provided a finger ring similar to the one pictured in figure 43. This delicate ring, FS8035, consists of two side shell sets and an onyx center set. It is size 6, probably for a child or woman. The ring is only 2.1 mm at its thickest point by the sets.

Fig. 43. Hard rubber ring with sets of shell and onyx (FS8035, dia. 15.9 mm). (CHMA. Photograph by author.)

Johnsons Island, Ohio

Dec 29th/64

Dear Kate

I have just recd your letter of the 19th. I am surprised to hear you talk about being grieved so much because you could not send me a box for Christmas, and that I would have nothing but prison rations for my Christmas dinner. I thought from the way you wrote to me that you expected I would be in Dixie before Christmas, and was foolish enough to think so myself sometimes, but I have been badly disappointed, Christmas is nearly gone and I am here still, and for all I know may have to remain some time yet, not with-standing you wrote to me on the 16th that Secty Stanton had said I had been exchanged and that I would be sent South as soon as they made arrangements to send off some prisoners or, there has been some sent though on Special exchange since then, but I hear nothing about mine except what you write me. I hope though that I may soon be released in some way. I wrote to Jack some time ago to try and get me a parole and hope he may meet with more Success than you have with the Special. I am very tired of prison life and hope I may soon be released. Tell Lill I received the two dollars she sent me for a Christmas present, and am very much obliged to her for it. I wrote to her five days ago and have sent her the present I had promised her so long ago. I hope they may reach her by New Years, as she has been looking for them for so long. I suppose you and her have had a pleasant Christmas. Tell Lill she must write to me and let me know how she is pleased with the things I send her. Remember me to Miss Caroline. Tell her Lt Rosenberger talks a great deal about her.[16] He also sends his regards to her. Give my love to father and mother

Yours most affectionately W Makely

The following excerpt, from a letter written by Lieutenant Colonel Ezekiel F. Clay, 1st Mounted Kentucky Rifles, mirrors the impatience with prison life. He wrote to a woman friend of his and shared sentiments similar to Wesley's.

Don't know how in the world Kit ever got it into his head that I was to be exchanged. You will see from previous letters, that I have no hope of a general exchange, & but little of a special exchange. If I should be so fortunate I promise with all my heart to write- you very often and to think of you all the time. I had a good laugh at Miss D's question. Can't comply as much as I am opposed to being shot. She does not know the odium attendant on that office especially where one quits the line. I am very glad you denied the charge. Oh Mary why did you think it necessary to offer sort of apology for yr's of the 19th, am glad it was mailed before you gave it a second consideration. If it was not for y'r dear letters, I would say this is a most Dreary Christmas. Am so much obliged for the box as if I had rced. it handly either for something of this kind would be most acceptable Am sorry we are not permitted to receive. If my letters prove uninteresting attribute it to my illness for more I am suffering with much pains I can hardly write. As I have not the gift of closing my letter with those sweet words that are so dear to me in y'rs you must put up with mostly the best love of E.F Clay (Clay 1864, letter of December 27, 1864)

Alex Dec 23rd/64

Dear Nessa

Your letter of the 16th was rec yesterday. you say you were a long time receiving mine of the 9th you will be longer receiving this I am sorry to say. I have always thought that I would not neglect writing to you 3 times every week. I have kept up to it pretty well but rea[l]ly I have been so busy this week that I had to allow one of my regular days to slip around without writing even now it is after ten Oclock. Doc went to Balt. this evening to see Christmas. Al sent us a splendid wild turkey to day for our Christmas dinner. Oh! Nessa how I wish you were here to enjoy it with us. for myself I cannot enjoy much good things to eat or wear while my poor loved Nessa is lying where he is. Lillie talks so much about her Papa and says she does wish you would come home. Al sent her a tree this evening and she is going to have a Christmas tree and a very nice one it will be. her Uncle Jack has been preparing for a month a fence for it. Jack sent Lieut Samuels twenty dollars. I also sent Lieut Pence five today Jack has never rec your letter directing him to send to Lt S. I delivered your message and kiss to Lill. All well and send there love to you.

Ever Affectionately Yours Kate

Johnsons Island, O
Jany 8th/65

Dear Kate

It has been nearly two weeks since I received a letter from you, but I ought not to say any thing about not receiving letters from you, as it has been upwards of a week since I wrote to you, but I have been very unwell for some time, and am not much better yet, and feel but very little like writing, or I would have written sooner. Kate have you recd the guta percha jewelry I sent you, I sent it by express about the 27th of last month. I hope Lill and you have had a pleasant Christmas. I wish I could have the pleasure of being with you again, but it seems as if it is almost useless to think of anything of the sort. Give my love to father and mother.

Yours most affectionately,
W Makely

In contrast, the following was written by Major Henry Eversman to his fiancée Carrie on New Year's Day. As already noted, Major Eversman was the surgeon with the Ohio Volunteers in charge of the prisoners' health.

I have been homesick to day and have thought continually—what I was doing and where I was to day a week ago. I have felt sad all day and have frequently resorted to your picture to cheer me up. I hope you have had a very pleasant New Years—my best wishes and greetings to you all at home. We islanders spent it very quietly—a few fancy dinners were given among others—Mrs. Woodbridge treated us to a splendid goose and lots of other fine things.

Col. Hill, Col. Wisewell and Major Lee and their wives dined with us, we had a pleasant time and only took one hour and a half to eat our dinner; what a ruinous fashion you will say—but such is the fact. I took my time at carving—especially it being goose—a new thing to me—I thought I would be in no hurry. We got through at half past three I consequently eat very little supper. (Eversman, 1865, letter of January 1, 1865)

> Johnsons Island, Ohio
> Jany 10th/65

Dear Kate

I recd your letter of the 3rd this morning. I am glad to hear that your things reached you safely. Kate I am sorry you have given yourself so much trouble about getting me a Special exchange. I recd a letter from you a day or two ago in which you said that you had seen Judge Underwood, and that he had told you on what conditions he could have me released, but they do not seem to meet with your approval. I am perfectly satisfied with them and you may tell Jack that I want to see him and get him to attend to it for me at once. If you cannot attend to it for me let me know, and I will write to the judge myself. Give my love to father and mother, Yours most affectionately,

W. Makely

In the letters that mentioned Judge Underwood, the only one mentioning conditions for release was Kate's letter of January 2, 1864, instructing Wesley that Judge Underwood would intercede on his behalf only if he took the Oath of Allegiance. Apparently this was now agreeable to

Wesley. Wesley could have applied from Johnson's Island to take the oath, but he almost certainly did not want to face the ridicule and bodily harm from fellow prisoners. He hoped to get paroled from Johnson's Island and take the Oath of Allegiance at some other facility.

Alex Jan 17th/65

Dear Nessa

Your letter of the 8th was rec yesterday. I was glad to hear from you for I did not know what had become of you if you had been sent off or what. it seemed like a month since I rec a letter from you last. you complain of not receiving letters from me for so long a time I do not know how it is I think I have written to you as usual until last week. I did not know but what you had been ordered away as I know that your name has been sent through to Richmond for exchange and I heard that 150 prisoners had been sent from the Island. I have written to you two or three times since that was done Jack also wrote a week ago. I wrote that we had rec the jewelry and were greatly pleased with it. Jack sent the 50 dollars to the person you named also the money to G. Samuels. Uncle Davids wife died yesterday morning and is to be buried today. Geo Brighthapt is dead he was wounded before Petersburg and died of his wounds poor fellow he was a good soldier. Nessa I am so very sorry to hear that you are unwell. I hope by this time you are well. I would give anything if I could come see you but I hope the day is not far distant when we will not require a pass to see our dear friends. all the family are well. I have a bad cold but that is nothing strange for me. Several of my fingers are very sore. all send there love to you. May God bless and protect you. Good bye. Ever Yours Kate

Johnsons Island, Ohio
Jany 17th/65

Dear Kate

I had the pleasure of receiving your letter of the 9th yesterday. I am glad to hear that my name has been sent to Richmond for exchange, and am very anxious to know the result, which I suppose I will know in a few days, as I see the flag of truce boat came down on the 16th. Kate you say you would like to see me when I go, I would be very glad to see you, and think you could very easily get permission to see me at Baltimore on some point on the road. Capt Archer left here a few days ago on exchange, and had permission to stop in Baltimore a few days with his family, and I cannot help but think that you can get permission to meet me some ware on the road should I be sent from here for exchange, at any rate should I be sent I will try and telegraph so that you may have an opportunity of trying to get to see me. Kate I do not think you can think me so ungrateful as to be out of patience with you after your doing so much for me. Kate I hope I may never have such a feeling towards you, nor do not think I ever will, I have been troubling you so much, and you have been doing so much for me lately that I could not help but think it would be wrong in me to ask you to do anything more. Kate you seem to never tire and take pleasure in doing all you can for me. I hope to soon have the pleasure of seeing you. If the Confederate authorities do not agree to the exchange I want Judge Underwood to have me released at once.

Give my love to all. Yours most affectionately
W Makely

Captain Robert Harris Archer, brother and on the staff of General James J. Archer, was captured July 5, 1863, and transferred for exchange on January 11, 1865 (NAGRP 1865). Major Eversman mentions in a letter to his fiancée the transfer of 167 prisoners at this time. He told her they had only three thousand more to go.

Johnsons Island, O
Jany 26th/65

Dear Kate

I have just received your letter of the 21st and hoped I would hear something definite about my exchange, though I have very little hope of getting it, although there are some leaving here every five days on exchange. Kate I will do as you say. I will try and wait patiently until my time comes, which I do not think will be very soon. You have only to ask and I will obey. You ask me to try and wait patiently. I will do so, I will wait with all the patience I possibly can for my exchange, not for the Special you speak of, but until there is a general exchange of all prisoners, as I have no hopes of being exchanged soon. A great many have gotten Special exchanges, and very likely a great many more will get them, but I do not expect to get one. Kate I sent you my picture a few days ago I don't expect you scarcely knew who it was though they all here say it looks exactly like me, and I think myself considering the way they have to take them it is a very good one. Tell Jack his Cousin Andy from Payne says if he has received the permit he sent him for some provisions to send them as soon as he can, he has been quite sick and needs them very much. Give my love to father and mother, Yours most affectionately,

    W. Makely

The topic of exchange had crept back into Wesley's thoughts. A special exchange occurred on January 20, 1865, when a number of prisoners were transferred to Fortress Monroe. This special exchange had been in the works since July 1864 and included sixteen prisoners being requested for transfer to other prisons to oversee the distribution of clothing and supplies (ORA, ser. 2, 7:1227).

Wesley had his picture "taken" to send to Kate. Based on Wesley's stating "the way they have to take them," and Kate's response in a subsequent letter, the picture was probably taken by Robert Smith. It is unfortunate this picture has not survived. Wesley alluded to the process of how they were taken. It is fortunate that Smith left some information on how he managed to take photographs of prisoners. Here is Smith's own account, which he had placed in a small display of several of his pictures after the war:

THESE PICTURES Were taken by R. M. Smith Lieutenant Company E, 61st Tennessee Volunteer Infantry, while a prisoners of war on Johnson's Island, Ohio in 1864, the only light being from an opening about eighteen inches square in the gable of the garret of Block 4. This work was done without permission and contrary to the orders of the authorities. The camera box was made upon the style of what is known as a slide box; and was whittled out with a pocket knife from a piece of white pine plank taken from a dry goods box. The lens was composed of the front lens of two, small spyglasses about the size of a 25-cent piece of silver, placed in a small oyster can. The object glass, by which the camera was put in focus, was made by smearing soap over a glass. The chemicals used were brought into the hospital as medicines (Smith 1863–65).

Included with the description were photographs of four officers from the 61st Tennessee Infantry imprisoned at Johnson's Island. The photographs of Colonel James G. Rose and Lieutenant Lewis F. Rader are shown in figure 44. Lieutenant Rader's photograph is particularly dark, a common complaint associated with Robert Smith's work.

Fig. 44. Prisoner photographs taken by Robert Smith in the garret of Block 4: (a) Lieutenant Colonel James G. Rose, 61st Tennessee Infantry; (b) 1st Lieutenant Lewis F. Rader, Company C, 61st Tennessee Infantry (both 2.5 × 2 inches). (By permission of Nancy Feazell, granddaughter of Robert Smith, and Geoffrey Feazell, grandson of Nancy Feazell.)

Alex Jan 30th/65

Dear Nessa

Your letter of the 22nd containing your picture has been rec. I was much pleased with my present and think it a very good likeness though it is rather dark. Nessa Jack went to Washington Saturday to hear what had been done about you. Gen Hitchcock told him that Col Old [Colonel Ould] had been away and that so many papers had accumulated of his hands that he must have overlooked it. But that he Gen H. felt pretty certain that you would be exchanged. I declare Nessa it is provoking but when you rec this you will know what has been said and done and you can do as you please. I almost hate to write to you Nessa I have been promising and telling you so long and often what would and had been done that I almost imagine that you think I am made up of stories but Nessa I have done everything I could and would write you whatever these head Officers would tell and promise me until I have lost confidence in all of them. Ma is quite sick though she is a little better this morning and will I hope soon be about again as the Doc left no medicine for her today. Doc came from up home yesterday all were well. The rest of family well and send love to you. Lillie sends a kiss and Love to Papa. Good bye. Ever Affectionately Yours Katie

Johnsons Island, O
Feby 7th/65

Dear Kate

Your letter of the 3rd has just been received. I am sorry to hear that you are feeling so badly, and hope you have got[t]en entirely over it before now. Kate you say my name has certainly been sent to Richmond. I suppose you want to cheer me and make me think that I will soon be exchanged. If that is your object, I think you had better study up something else, for I ssure you that I have no more hopes of getting a Special exchange by having my name sent to Richmond, than I have of taking wings and flying away from Johnsons Island. It makes very little difference to me ware they send my name. As for my returning to Alex, I think very likely I will, but not very shortly. I sometimes think that if I was at liberty, and the war ended that I would never make it my home.[17] Tell Jack, Lt Washe has received the money he sent him.[18] You want to know why I don't get permission and send it to you for a box of eatibles. The only reason I do not do so is, they will not give me the permission. Kiss Lill for me, and tell her that I say she must kiss my other little pet for me. Give my love to all.

Yours affectionately, W. Makely

Johnsons Island, Ohio
Feby 9th/65

Dear Kate

I have been spending all the morning reading and was in hopes I would get a letter from you, so that I might spend part of the evening in answering it. My health has not been very good for some time, and the weather has been so bad lately that I scarcely get out of my room at all, and I am very much put too, to pass of the time. I sent out an application to send to you for some clothing, which I suppose will be approved and sent to me in a few days. As soon as I get it I will send it to you, and I want you to get me some books and send with them. We are allowed to receive prety nearly all kinds of books and magazines. I wish you would get me the Life of Mahomet and his followers by Washington Ervin [Irving], the Astoria, by Washington Ervin, Charles O'Malley Admiral Crichton by Hanison Ainsworth [*Admirable Crichton* by William Harrison Ainsworth], the Spy by [James Fenimore] Cooper, and Horse Shoe Robinson [by John Pendleton Kennedy]. Kate if there are any of them that you have not read you can keep them until you read them, and if you should get the permission and get the things ready before you get through reading them you can send them to me by mail. The life of Mahomet is said to be a very interesting book, and I think you would be pleased with it, and in fact they are all spoken of very highly. I would take pleasure in reading any book or magazine selected by you. Kate I will tell you how much you may write in order that your letters will come safely. You can write 28 lines of letter paper like this, or 42 lines of commercial note paper. Give my love to father and mother. Yours affectionately,

W. Makely

On February 5, 1865, the weather turned very cold on Johnson's Island. It remained below freezing and snowed off and on until the 13th, when the temperature dropped to 8 degrees below zero. Given the cold and wind, it was no wonder Wesley spent most of his time in his block. The temperature statistics for Kelly's Island presented in table 6.1 are comparable to what occupants of Johnson's Island experienced (ORA, ser. 2, 8:330–31).

The orders to restrict the number of lines per letter were posted on February 8, 1865 (Crow 1977:124). With the prisoners allowed to write three letters per week, restricting the number of lines was a way to keep down the work of the postal inspectors.

This was the first time Wesley mentioned reading books and his first request for books. In late November 1864 the prison officials requested Colonel Hoffman's permission to allow prisoners' families to send them books. Wesley may have heard this had been approved and decided to request some books.

Captain Edward Augustus Small, Company F, 11th North Carolina Infantry, was captured at Gettysburg on July 3, 1863, and arrived at

Table 1. Temperature statistics for Kelly's Island (degrees Fahrenheit)

Month	1860	1861	1862	1863	1864	Mean
January	28.6	27.22	27.22	26.48	32.36	28.08
February	29.17	32.42	26.73	29.00	30.02	29.47
March	39.96	34.73	32.93	32.00	33.98	34.72
April	45.25	46.82	44.70	43.03	45.02	44.96
May	61.44	53.28	56.83	59.92	59.95	58.28
June	68.38	68.43	64.80	66.51	69.71	67.56
July	70.69	70.69	73.14	71.42	76.17	72.42
August	70.72	79.82	73.39	72.16	75.00	72.62
September	61.26	65.28	62.46	62.46	64.41	64.10
October	53.40	55.42	54.37	50.14	51.23	52.91
November	40.07	41.04	40.40	43.07	41.00	41.11
December	26.95	35.8	34.39	34.37	28.67	32.04
Annual mean	49.66	50.24	49.65	49.70	50.03	32.04

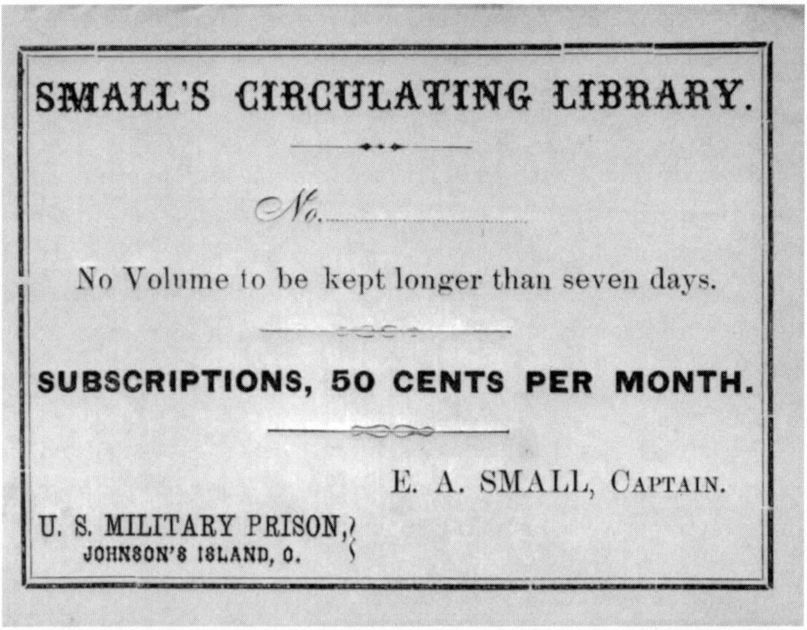
SMALL'S CIRCULATING LIBRARY.

No.

No Volume to be kept longer than seven days.

SUBSCRIPTIONS, 50 CENTS PER MONTH.

E. A. SMALL, CAPTAIN.

U. S. MILITARY PRISON,
JOHNSON'S ISLAND, O.

Fig. 45. Example of an enterprising prisoner providing books to fellow prisoners for a monthly fee. (By permission of the Friends and Descendants of Johnson's Island Civil War Prison.)

Johnson's Island on July 20, 1863. His stay was similar to Wesley's, ending by being transferred from Johnson's Island in March 1865 (NAGRP 1865). Captain Small recaptured some of his lost freedoms by creating a lending library for use by other prisoners. Prisoners brought various talents to Johnson's Island, and opportunities afforded to prisoners were partly dependent upon this diversity. Captain Small achieved a higher status by operating his library, and the prisoners, like Wesley, benefited.

There is at present no information on the extent of this library. Having access to reading materials was important to many prisoners. Some complained of not having much to read. Not only were there books in the possession of many prisoners, but various newspapers were delivered to the prison when allowed. There were reports of the prisoners creating "schools" in prison, with instruction in several foreign languages as well as law and medicine (Meissner and Meissner 2005:18).

Dear Kate

I have been looking for a letter from you for some time, and when the mail arrives, and I find there is no letter for me, I console myself thinking that tomorrow will certainly bring me a letter from you, but when the morrow comes I find myself disappointed again. I have been disappointed so often lately, and almost fear you are offended about something, and do not care about continuing our correspondence any longer, but as my sending you another little letter can, therefore, give you no other trouble than the trouble of reading it, which I hope you may find leisure time enough for some day, at any rate I will devote a few minutes in writing you another letter, this is the fourth I have written you since I have received any from you Kate we are all in very good spirits now, as there seems to be a prospect of getting exchanged soon. I think there will be a good many exchanged shortly, but when or how many I cannot say. One hundred will start this evening besides some who leave on special exchange, there have been a great many leaving here on special exchange lately, some who were not even expecting a special exchange. Kate I hope I may soon get out of prison and be with you again. I think it would be the happiest day of my life. Give my love to all.

Yours ever truly, and affectionately,

W. Makely

Wesley spent half of this letter telling Kate he had not heard from her. His ill health created the sense of despair apparent in this letter. The weather was also depressing. Following the low of 8 below zero on January 13 came a huge snow storm on January 15, after which conditions warmed enough to melt the snow and make everything muddy.

Major Henry Eversman noted on February 16 that 103 Rebels were sent on exchange, most because of illness. Eversman was besieged with requests by prisoners to be considered sick enough to be exchanged. Possibly Wesley was trying to convince himself he was sick enough to be sent with the next group.

Johnsons Island, O
Feby 16th/65

Dear Kate

Yours of the 11th has been received, the bay is open now and they have commenced sending prisoners off again. Three hundred were sent away a few days ago. I suppose another lot will be sent off about the first of next week, and I expect to be one of the number. Cous. Frank is still here. I don't think he will be sent off very soon as he is one of the late captures. Kate I have the jewelry I spoke of some time ago ready to send you, there are three rings, once bracelet, and one bust pin, One ring is for Lill. The other two rings and bracelet are for you, the pins Lill and you must disperse of as you please. I wanted to get a nicer one for you but could not. I think you will have to have hinges made to the bracelet before you even use it, they will not show much underneath about an inch from the end, though perhaps it will ad to the appearance of the bracelet to have them put on the top near the set. Tell Jack I have not rec^d the money he sent me yet, give my love to Lill. Yours affectionately, W. Makely

The importance of jewelry seemed to outplay the impending prospect of being exchanged off the island. Wesley was driven to see that the jewelry items were sent to Kate and Lill before he left. Figure 46 illustrates some of the variety of styles and forms for hard rubber jewelry. Some of the jewelry was exquisitely carved with designs and contained no sets. Other pieces were plain except for the fine gold or silver inlays. Those designs that are repeated may be the product of the same prisoner recreating a popular design.

Johnsons Island, O
Feby 19th/65

Dear Kate

I had the pleasure of receiving your letter of the 9th yesterday. I was very glad to hear from you, as it had been a long time since I received a letter from you, and I was beginning to feel very uneasy I received the letter Jack wrote me on the 8th Saturday

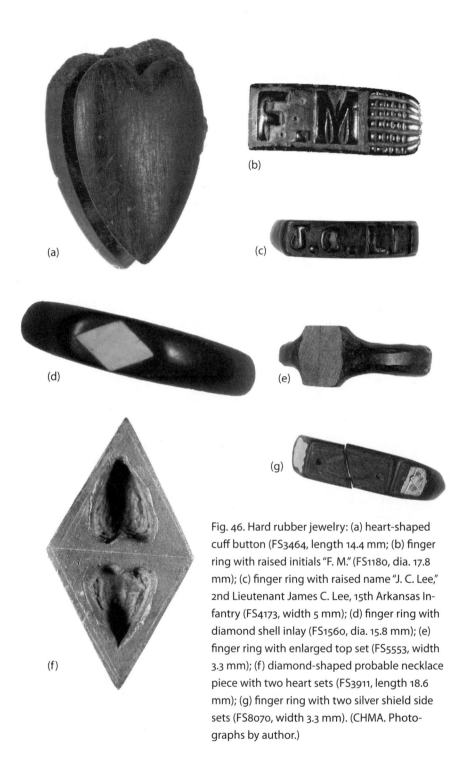

Fig. 46. Hard rubber jewelry: (a) heart-shaped cuff button (FS3464, length 14.4 mm; (b) finger ring with raised initials "F. M." (FS1180, dia. 17.8 mm); (c) finger ring with raised name "J. C. Lee," 2nd Lieutenant James C. Lee, 15th Arkansas Infantry (FS4173, width 5 mm); (d) finger ring with diamond shell inlay (FS1560, dia. 15.8 mm); (e) finger ring with enlarged top set (FS5553, width 3.3 mm); (f) diamond-shaped probable necklace piece with two heart sets (FS3911, length 18.6 mm); (g) finger ring with two silver shield side sets (FS8070, width 3.3 mm). (CHMA. Photographs by author.)

also, it was a long time on the road, though if it had reached me sooner it would have given me very little satisfaction, and I was very anxious to hear from you, and he did not even mention your name. I am always glad to hear from any of my friends, but I appreciate anything coming from you more than from any one else. Kate I hope you do not think I was offended. To the contrary I feel very thankfull, and am under many obligations to you for what you have done for me. Kate we are all in very fine spirits, and think we will soon be exchanged. You know I have been very slow in believing there would be a general exchange, but I cannot help but think that we will soon be exchanged now. A hundred left a few days ago, and a hundred more leave tomorrow. It cannot continue much longer without taken me. I would like very much to see you before I start, but I suppose it is useless to think of any thing of the sort. Give my love to all, and kiss Lill for me, and tell her that I will intrust her to kiss my other pressious little pet for me. Good bless you, dear Kate. Yours ever truly, and affectionately, W. Makely

Johnsons Island Feby 26/65

Dear Kate

I expect you have been looking for the permission I spoke of sending you some time ago for some clothing. The application has not been approved and returned yet, though I would not have sent it if it had, as I am in hopes I will be sent off on exchange before you could send me any. Kate I would like very much to see you before I go, but I hear there is very little hopes of my doing so, I will write to you and let you know whenever I am called to leave. I have been expecting to hear from you for several days but have not rec^d a letter from you since I rec^d yours of the 10th. I believe you only write one a week. Give my love to all. Yours ever truly, and affectionately, W. Makely

Given all the prisoners had experienced, the importance of receiving news from home always weighed on their minds. Wesley knew the mail system was unreliable; yet he still could not help feeling abandoned by his Kate. Regardless of the content, letters themselves provided comfort to both Wesley and Kate. Knowing someone cared enough to write gave assurance of a potential for life after prison. Many, like Wesley, uttered their disappointment at having no letters when the "express" was delivered. Kate also shared her disappointment with Wesley when his letters did not arrive. Almost every correspondence had a comparison of how many letters had been written by the author and how long it had been since the last letter from the other had been received. Even with the arrival of letters, there would still be accusations of indifference. Often Wesley and Kate were guilty of succumbing to their feelings of loneliness, clouding the reality of why letters were so erratic. Letters represented the most personal contact with the outside world to the prisoner-of-war. Their presence was a key aspect of how the prisoners managed to sustain themselves.

Alex Feb 15th/65

Dear Nessa

Your letter of the 6th has been rec and I would have answered it before, but Jack wrote day before yesterday and I thought that I would wait another day. yesterday I was very buisy so I neglected it then, I will write anyway to day, we are quite buisy now and I seldom ever go out unless it is on business, Caroline and I went with Doc to the theater the other night. The play was very good it was called the red knome. I would like to go often if Nessa were here to go with me. Nessa I believe I said in my last that I would not mention the exchange again but Jack was in Washington yesterday and went to see Gen Hitchcock who told him that there were several names sent on before yours that were not heard from yet, but there had certainly been an agreement made to exchange all prisoners every man of them. And that they would be sent off at the rate of 3000 per week and that the exchange had already commenced and there was nothing to stop every man from being exchanged now. Nessa that little book you mentioned Luciel I have never read it but will get and read it. Lillie is learning her lesson with uncle Doc. she sends her love and a heap of it to Papa. Caroline sends her respect to you and Lt R. she rec a letter from him one day this week. Nessa have you heard of M Pressman's death he was killed on the railroad near Danville. the family here are very much distressed. Purd was down this week all are well up home some Whites had him arrested last week for awhile. All well and send there love to you. Good bye Yours Affectionately

Kate

Johnsons Island, O
Feby 28rd/65

Dear Kate

Yours of the 10th has just been recd. I was very glad to hear from you, as I have not been getting many letters from you lately. I recd Jacks letter off the 14th today also. Kate I think that if Secty Stanton was asked, he would have me sent with the first lot of prisoners from here, as he has promised to do all in his power to have me exchanged. There are a great many getting special exchanges every day or so. I cannot see why they don't heare from mine. It is true the exchange is going on now and if they continue exchanging it will not be very long before it takes me, but I am very fearful something that something [sic] will happen to stop it. Kate you say Miss Caroline and you were with Dock at the theater the other evening, and that you would like to go often if I were there to go with you. I care but very little about theaters, but I would take great pleasure in accompanying you to the theater, or any ware els you might wish to go. I did hope some time ago that I would soon have that pleasure, but I have abandoned all hopes of anything of the sort very shortly. Kate I have two very pretty rings one for Lill and one for you. I want to get you some other things made before I send them. Give my love to all.

Yours ever truly and affectionately, W Makely

Wesley continued to provide various forms of jewelry to Kate and Lillie through the final days of his incarceration at Johnson's Island.

Dear Kate

I have just had the pleasure of receiving your letter of the
21st of Feby. I am in fine spirits and hope to soon be exchanged,
though I fear we may be delayed here some time yet on account
of the ice. There is to much ice for the boat to run, and it is not
strong enough for us to cross on, and has been so for some time.

We are all very anxious to have a big freeze or thaw. Kate I
have not got the things made yet that I spoke of sending you
some time ago. There is a great demand here for gutapercha jewelry, as most every body is trying to get some to carry south with
them. I have two very pretty rings for my two little pets, and am
having a bracelet made for you also.

Give my love to father and mother. Yours affectionately,
W. Makely

This letter was Wesley's only reference noting the "great demand" for
the hard rubber jewelry. There was indeed a high demand for jewelry
being made by prisoners-of-war. No matter when someone was imprisoned at Johnson's Island, hard rubber jewelry was being made. Finger
rings were the most common item prisoners mentioned sending South.

Alex Feb 28th/65

Dear Nessa

Your letter of the 19th was rec yesterday. I was glad to get it to
for we did not know if you had been sent off or not for it seemed
so long since I got a letter from you. This may never reach you
but if it should I want you to telegraph to me when you start.
Doc Windsor did to his friend and his brother Dave went on to
Baltimore to meet him. I have not heard if he saw him or not.
Caroline is anxious to know if Lt. R has been sent off or not. I
told Jack what you said about him in your letter, his reply was
that he did not think it worth while as I had written the day
before and that I was all the time writing to you. I delivered your
kiss to Lillie and told her that you wanted her to kiss your other

pet and asked her if she knew who it was, why says she, mama its you, certainly its you. I suppose you come on of course to the inauguration the 4th. I hear that Lincoln is going to let all the prisoners in the old Capital come out to see him take his seat. They having applied for the privilege. Ma & Pa health is quite poor now and has been for some time. Please if you can let me know when you start. All send there love to you. Now Nessa should you get back to Dixie do try and take good care of yourself. Give my love to all the folks down there. Now do take care of yourself and may God watch over and protect you.

Ever Affectionately Yours Kate

                                    Johnsons Island March 7th/65

Dear Kate

Yours of the 28th was received yesterday, and perhaps will be the last one I will receive from you while I am at Johnsons Island, for I hope it will not be many days before I am sent off on exchange. I was paroled several days ago and am ready to go at any time.[19] I am very anxious to get out of prison again, and hope will not be many days before I will be sent off. There are some five hundred who were paroled before me that have not been sent off yet. The bay has been in such condition for some time that none could be sent off, but it is beginning to open now and I hope we will all be sent off very shortly. Whenever I start I will be sure to try and let you know. Kate your braclet is finished, and I will send it to you as soon as I can. I fear though you will have some trouble putting it on and getting it off. If I had any gold I could have nice hinges put to it so that you would have no trouble getting it on and off, though if you find you will have to much trouble with it you can have it fixed. You will have to warm it a little before you try and put it on, and I don't know that it will open enough then, Tell Miss C that Lt R is not gone yet.[20] Kate I hope I may see you as I go through though I fear you cannot get permission to do so. Give my love to father and mother and kiss Lill for me.

Yours ever truly and affectionately,

W Makely

The archaeological record does not have any examples of complete bracelets. From the description Wesley provided, the bracelet sounds like a large solid hard rubber ring. Robert Smith wrote of making bracelets, but there was nothing in his collection resembling what Wesley described.

Alex March 3rd/65

Dear Nessa

You complain of not getting many letters from me lately. I do not know how it is I write as usual except last week I did not write but one letter. you say that you have written four letters without receiving one from me I cannot tell how it is for it is mostly the case that I write two for one of yours. though indeed this week has afforded me much pleasure for it has brought me three letters from you and this is only Friday morning. I wish it could always be so while we are parted. the one I rec on Monday I answered then Wednesday and Thursday I rec others which I answer today. I would have gone to Washington this morning but it is just pouring down and has been for two or three days so of course nothing can be done now before Monday. I intend going up to see the Secty. and also try to get permission to see you in Baltimore if I can find out when you are coming. Oh I do hope that he will grant me that one small privilege. Poor little Lillie, she does want to see you so badly you are her all. everything she wants part of saved for her dear papa. Nessa you say that you have a ring for L and me, as you have them send them but don't have any thing more made for we have most everything that can be made and I would rather you would keep your money for something else for yourself. All send there love to you. Jack sent the money you wrote for by Express yesterday. Ever Affectionately Yours

Kate

Over the years, all the hard rubber items associated with Wesley and Kate Makely have vanished. From the many letters that speak of jewelry, it is surprising no examples survived. After one or two generations passed, possibly the significance of the association with Wesley's imprisonment also vanished.

Alex March 6th/65

Dear Nessa

Your letter of the 26th of Feb was rec yesterday the 5th. I did look for sometime for the permit you spoke of some time ago and as it did not come I suppose of course that you could not get it approved. You say that you would like to see me before you go through. I know you would but dear Nessa not more than I would like to see you. I am going up tomorrow to Washington to see if I cannot get permission to see you. I do not know how it will be. I am rather afraid myself but however you must let me know when you are about leaving. Doc Windsor telegraphed home when he started which is a better way than writing as the letter might not come through in time. Nessa I do not know how it is you complain so much lately about not receiving letters from me regularly. I write as I have been in the habit of doing except week before last. I wrote only one. All are quite well at home now except Ma she the worse cough I have ever know any one to have. Some times she coughs of a night for two hours on a stretch. All send there love to you. Lillie and somebody else a kiss. Lillie says she is going to Dixie to see her Papa. That she is, be sure to write and let us know when you are to be sent. Good bye. Yours Affectionately

Kate

Johnsons Island, O

March 12th/65

Dear Kate

I have just received three letters from you, one yesterday and two to day. Kate I am sorry you could not get permission to see me when I am sent through, though I hope the friend you speak of may succeed yet in getting you permission to see me. At any rate I will telegraph to you when they start me from here, so that you may know when to start to meet me if you should succeed in getting permission to do so. Kate I expected to be on my way to Richmond before now, but the weather is so changeable here, freezing one day and thawing the next that it seems as if it will be summer before they will be able to get us across the bay. I hope though that you may hear from me on my way to Richmond in a few days. Kate I have the prettiest ring for you that has been made in this prison. I thought you would succeed in getting permission to see me I would keep it until then and give it to you instead of sending it by express. Tell Jack I have not recd the money he sent me yet, though I think I will in a few days. Give my love to all Yours affectionately

    W. Makely

The most elegant finger ring recovered from Johnson's Island was discovered underneath the floor of the prison hospital. Known as FS7261 (see figure 32e), the ring has three inlays of gold, riveted in, with the initials W, GS, and B. The ring is size 5, probably made for someone's wife. One of the challenges faced with this particular item is how to interpret the initials on the ring. Are the central initials the prisoner's or his wife's? Are the side initials his children's?

This is one of the finest examples of hard rubber jewelry discovered. Wesley claiming he has "the prettiest ring" for Kate, especially at a time when there was such a high demand for hard rubber jewelry, is a testament to his obsession with these materials and providing for his family.

Wesley's letter of March 12 was the last one until March 21, 1865, the day he left the island. Over the past six months, one major theme had been providing hard rubber jewelry. He mentioned all types of jewelry being sent. From January 6, 1864, through the end of February 1865 Wesley sent Kate at least 17 finger rings, 12 breast pins, 4 crosses, 4 sets of earrings, 3 watch chains, 2 sets of cuff buttons, 1 set of collar buttons, 2 chains with a fish and acorn attached to them, 2 bracelets, 1 necklace with a heart, a chess set, and loose trinkets (heart, acorn, fish). As is partially described in his letters, they were made from hard rubber or shell, with sets of gold, silver, shell, and probably other materials. The more than fifty pieces of jewelry speak to his having access to money, allowing him to purchase fine examples from Lieutenant Waesche and others. Wesley even talked of making some himself, which he notes to his family, presuming an added level of significance to those items.

Accurate estimates of how much hard rubber jewelry was actually made at Johnson's Island would be difficult to achieve. No doubt thousands of pieces of jewelry were made and sent or carried off the island. Diary entries suggest that most prisoners tried their hand at making jewelry. Excavations at Block 4 resulted in hundreds of waste fragments of hard rubber being recovered.

The level of involvement of both Kate and Wesley in the procurement of hard rubber jewelry helped them to weather his time in prison. She could share with her family and friends his "success" in obtaining beautiful pieces of jewelry, and he benefited by the knowledge of making Kate happy.

The significance Kate and Wesley assigned the jewelry was probably not the same for all prisoners at Johnson's Island. Wesley's letters seemed almost exclusively directed to his family, with little interjection of prison life or even mention of his roommates. He had to interact on a daily basis with many men, but those interactions were not shared with Kate. From the letters, at times Wesley seemed secluded and completely alone in surviving imprisonment. The jewelry he acquired was one of the few activities in which Wesley indicated interacting with other prisoners. The audience for his letters consisted of Kate and Lillie (and of course the censor), and thus it is necessary to consider whether Wesley was selective about the information he sent.

Investigations of the prison compound have provided data critical for understanding the craft activity. Recovery of hundreds of hard rubber waste pieces, discarded failures, and broken or complete jewelry items has allowed a greater appreciation for this prisoner art. The abilities some prisoners exhibited in the finished pieces were astonishing. Hard rubber jewelry was highly sought after by the prisoners as a means of sharing their imprisonment with loved ones. No doubt those wearing these distinctive items shared their sorrows of separation with anyone asking.

Going Home

(March 21–April 29, 1865)

In a short time I will be on my way from this hated Island. I will not at-
tempt to describe my feelings, although I feel as if I was relieved of
a great burden . . .

Wesley Makely to Kate, March 21, 1865

Wesley Makely spent one day over a year and seven months at Johnson's Island. The end to his loss of liberty seemed close at hand. Wesley had gone through the transition from captain of Company D, 18th
Virginia Cavalry, to just one of thousands of prisoners-of-war. In this
transition his loss of freedom meant significant changes in his relation
to power, property, prestige, and pleasure (Van der Elst 1999:138–39).
The choice of escaping was an option, but it was a dangerous one he was
unwilling to undertake. He could have assimilated by taking the Oath
of Allegiance, but that meant sure disgrace among his fellow Virginians
incarcerated at Johnson's Island. His long status as a prisoner-of-war
forced him to create ways to regain some of this loss as the only strategy
he had for surviving imprisonment.

In this final chapter of letters, Wesley faced even greater challenges.
He had developed means of coping while at Johnson's Island. Wesley
had altered his room, developed networks for acquiring hard rubber
jewelry, maintained a strong image to his family both in portraits sent
and information provided in letters, and weathered several illnesses. On
his journey to Fort McHenry, Point Lookout, and finally to Fort Delaware, he once again became the "fresh fish." He had to learn the nuances
of survival at these institutions. He was placed with new prisoners, in a
new setting, with different regulations.

Wesley had to cope with the defeat of the Confederacy and the assassination of President Lincoln. Wesley was ready to be home, but what would be the cost? How would his life be changed?

Alex March 8th/65[1]

Dear Nessa

I went the rounds in Washington yesterday trying to get permission to see you, but to no purpose as poor little Lillie says they are too mean to let her see her Papa. I shall try again though through a friend in Baltimore. I do not see why they are so strich with the confederates for some of there prisoners are paroled and at large in Richmond awaiting there exchange. Poor Lillie was so disappointed in not seeing you yesterday she knew that I went up to get permission and poor dear child she fully expected to see you yesterday. She says Mama I never want to go to Washington again unless I can see my Papa. There is nothing new in town to tell you. I never go out but what every one I meet and know has Mr Makely been exchanged yet. Oh Nessa I wish I could tell them yes. I have not heard from up home lately but all were well when I last heard from up there. I have been looking for Ma to come down for some time. Mother is still no better rest all very well and send there love to you. A kiss from Lillie and self. Good bye. Ever Truly Yours Katie

Alex March 11th/65

Dear Nessa

I received your letter of the 2nd this morning. I had begun to think that you had been sent off as the letter was so late in the week a coming. You spoiled me a little last week. Yesterday I was much disappointed that I did not get a letter from you. Last week by Friday I had received four letters and that you know is calculated to spoil most anyone. Nessa surely the bay must be frozen over now for it is very cold here. Yesterday was a bitter day. Nessa I see by one of the papers that Gen Imboden with his command has charge of the prisoners in Ala, NC. and Mississippi. I heard sometime ago that the Gen was dead. I think you wrote

me word perhaps the Col has been promoted. Has cousin Frank
I. been sent of[f] yet.[2] I think that Lieut Pense has been sent off
we never hear from him now. I heard from up home last night
all were well. Al sent us a very nice wild turkey. Ma cold is still
no better. Rest all well and send there love to you. Please excuse
me from filling the page as I want my letter to go in the 3 o'clock
mail. Hoping to hear from you soon again. I close and Remain
most affectionately Yours,

    Kate

Johnsons Island, Ohio
March 21st/65

    My dear dear Kate

    In a short time I will be on my way from this hated Island. I
will not attempt to describe my feelings, although I feel as if I
was relieved of a great burden, but I cannot be truly happy while
I am separated from those that are dearer to me than all els in
the world. I have tried in vain to forget those days spent with
you, the very memory of which sends an inexpressible thrill
of mingled pain and pleasure through my heart. Happiness I
have found to be out of the question while I am separated from
you. I have always looked to you as to a good angel, and all my
dreams of bitirn [?] and happiness are centered in you, and I
know you love me with an emotion pure and generous as such a
heart as yours alone is capable of feeling, and I well know what a
priceless treasure the love of such a heart is. I have spent many
unsettled nights and weary days since we have been separated.
I hope though it may not be long any more before I may be with
you again, Kate I think I would be the happiest man in the world
if I were with you again. Please excuse my writing to you with
a pencil. I would like to write you a long letter, but I have but
a short time to get ready and will have to close. I will have this
mailed at Sandusky, or some ware on the road. I will also try and
telegraph to you from Sandusky. Tell jack I recd the money he
sent me. I will also have your jewelry expressed to you. One ring
is for Lill, the rest for you. Kate many changes have passed over

me since I saw you, though I know of nothing concerning myself that would interest you much. I hope it may not be long before I may see you. Fair well my dear, dear Kate. May God watch over you and make you happy. My hand trembles as I write Fair well, but I hope it will not be long before you may hear from me again. Kate warever I may go or whatever may happen, you will live in my heart until it ceases to beat. Yours forever

Nessa

No doubt Wesley experienced many changes. Prisoners felt their time in prison was the most difficult period of their life. Perhaps he realized an adjustment would be required for his return to his family.

This is the only letter that Wesley signed Nessa. His last few sentences seemed to indicate his apprehension at leaving Johnson's Island. He definitely wanted to be off the island, but he did not know where he was heading or what additional hardships he would face.

Fort Mc Henry

March 26th/65

Dear Kate

I arrived here this morning after along and tiresome trip from Johnsons Island. I left there on the evening of the 21st. I telegraphed to you shortly after leaving Sandusky and hoped you could get permission to see me in Baltimore. Your rings and bracelet I sent to you by express and hope they will reach you safely. In the morning I suppose we will leave here for Dixie and hope to arrive Safely at Richmond Tuesday or Wednesday.

I will try and write to you again from Akins landing. Give my love to all. Yours ever truly and affectionately

W. Makely

The first stop on Wesley's return home was Fort McHenry in Baltimore, Maryland. Named Fort Whetstone during the Revolutionary War, the fort had been enhanced at the end of the eighteenth century and re-named Fort McHenry (Lessem and Mackenzie 1954). It was instrumental

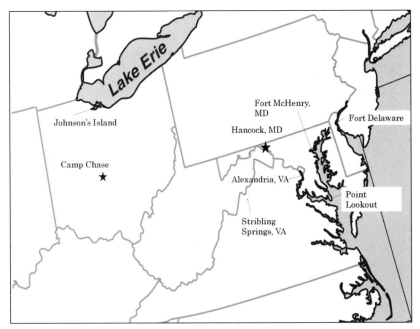

Map 1. Fort McHenry, Baltimore, Maryland.

in keeping Baltimore safe during the War of 1812. During the Civil War Fort McHenry was used for the transfer of prisoners-of-war as well as some long-term confinement (Casstevens 2005:83–96).

Major Henry Eversman wrote to his fiancée on March 22, 1865, that three hundred prisoners had been sent off the island the day before (Eversman 1865). One of the prisoners accompanying Wesley was Lieutenant James Wentworth, 5th Florida Infantry (NAGRP 1865). Wentworth described the journey in his diary. He noted that the prisoners took the steamer *Reynolds* to Sandusky, Ohio, where they boarded a train to Mansfield, Ohio. They traveled to Newark, spent the night, and continued the next day to Zanesville and Cambridge, crossed the Ohio River at Belle Aire, and changed cars. Taking the Baltimore and Ohio Railroad, they arrived in Baltimore on March 25 and marched to Fort McHenry on the 26th. They left Fort McHenry on March 29, boarding on the steamer *Star*, then transferring to the steamer *New York*, and passed through heavy storms for two days to reach Point Lookout, where they were put ashore on April 1, 1865 (Wentworth 1990).

Pt Lookout
April 1st/65

Dear Kate

I arrived here this morning and have had a long and tiresome trip from the Island. When we will leave here is uncertain,
though I do not think we will have to stay long. I had the rings
and bracelet I promised you expressed on the road, and hope
they have reached you safely. I will enclose the receipt to you.
Give my love to all Yours affectionately
    W Makely

Point Lookout is located in southern Maryland, protruding into Chesapeake Bay. Originally the site was used for a large hospital complex,
but in 1863 an additional forty acres were added as a prison. Officially
known as Camp Hoffman, the prison was always referred to as Point
Lookout and became known as one of the worst prison facilities in the
Union system. Tents were used to house the prisoners on the flat tracts
of sand (Casstevens 2005:162–67).

This letter only has four sentences. Two of the four are dedicated
to the jewelry sent to Kate. It suggests that jewelry continued to be of
great significance to Wesley, serving as the constant thread back to his
Kate.

Pt Lookout Md.
April 3rd/65

Dear Kate

We are making a much longer stay here than I had expected
when we arrived here last Saturday. I have not been able to learn
anything about how long we will have to remain, though I hope it
will not be long, for I am getting very tired of being in suspense.
We are quartered in the hospital buildings and am very comfortable. I am getting very anxious to hear from you, and as it is
uncertain how much longer we may have to remain I want you to
write to me here. Tell Jack to write to me also. I will try and write
to you whenever we leave here. Direct to Capt W M, Prisoner of
war, Hammond General Hospital, Ward IV, Point Lookout, Md.

I hope though before any letter may have time to reach here from you I will be in Richmond, but we may have to stay much longer than we expect. Give my love to all

Yours affectionately

W Makely

Wesley was fortunate to be housed in the hospital complex and not the general prison compound. The hospital complex was a series of fifteen buildings arranged in circular form and afforded much better living conditions than the tent camp. Hammond General Hospital was constructed for use by the Union troops injured in battle. In early 1865 it was used to house Confederate officers in the Union's prison system. Point Lookout's reputation for cruelty and inhumane treatment stemmed from the prison compound, composed of a fenced twenty-three-acre area where the best accommodations for prisoners were tents. With a capacity of ten thousand, it was beyond overcrowded when numbers within the compound reached twenty-two thousand (Casstevens 2005:162).

Pt Lookout Md
April 5th/65

Dear Kate

I am making very slow headway getting through to Dixie, it is upwards of two weeks since we left Johnsons Island and have only gotten this far yet, and I fear it will be some time yet, before we will get any fa[r]ther. We have very good quarters and a nice place to walk about, but still I am a little low spirited and have blues the worst sort. I spend most of my time walking about and watching the boats passing up and down the river. I would give almost anything if I could go on one of them to Alexandria to see you. I am very anxious to see you, but I fear I will not have that pleasure very shortly, for I expect it would be almost as difficult for you to get permission to come to see me as it would be for me to get permission to go to see you. I have no doubt but what you would have plenty of time to come to see me before we are sent away if you could get permission to do so, for I suppose they will have to agree on some other point to deliver prisoners as

Richmond is now in the Federal hands. I hope though that they will not be very long about deciding on some point for I am very tired of being kept in suspense and uneasiness. I want you to write to me, Tell Jack to send me fifty dollars. Tell him to direct, Prisoner of war, Ward IV, Hammond General hospital, Point Lookout, Md, care of Maj. Brady Prov Marshall, and write a note to the Maj asking him to return it if I should be sent on exchange before it reaches him.

Give my love to all Yours affectionately
W Makely

This was the most money Wesley requested in his entire time in prison. He may have been concerned about having money to purchase his transportation home once he was released. Many prisoners, suspecting they were about to be released or exchanged, borrowed money from other prisoners to enable them to travel home by boat or train.

Wesley continued to make no references to his fellow prisoners. There was no indication of the specific living conditions he faced while at Point Lookout.

Major Allen G. Brady was provost marshal at Point Lookout in April 1865. He had been major of the 7th Connecticut Infantry until wounded at Gettysburg. He joined the 20th Veterans Reserve Corps in November 1863 and was assigned to Point Lookout in May 1864.

Pt Lookout Md
April 8th/65

Dear Kate

I have been waiting all the morning for the mail, hoping I might get a letter from you, the mail has arrived at last but no letter for me though I could scarcely expect a letter from you as it has only been some five or six days since I wrote to you and it is rather soon for an answer yet though to me it seems as if I might have received an answer from London before now. I have been here but one week today and it seems as if though it had been a year. Time passes off very slowly and each day seems to be at least a month long I hope though we may not be kept here

Fig. 47. Photograph of Major Allen G. Brady, provost marshall, Point Lookout Prison. (By permission of Dale E. Call.)

in suspense much longer. Write soon direct your letters Prisoner of war, Ward IV, W. S. Gen Hospital, Point Lookout, Md. I gave you the direction some time ago but as the letter might not have reached you I will give it again, there is nothing here at all to write about. Give my love to all.

Yours affectionately

W. Makely

His proximity to Alexandria, Virginia, must have made it seem letters to Kate should have reached her within a day or two. His anticipation of exchange or release must have made it difficult to sit idle at this new location.

In Kate's letter of April 4 she did not ask any questions about his surroundings in prison. Wesley did not share information about Point Lookout, and Kate did not inquire. Wesley seemed careful not to talk at all about his living conditions, which from all historical accounts were more severe than at Johnson's Island.

Alex Apl 4/65

Dear Nessa

How glad I was to rec your letter of the 3rd this morning. it was not more than five minutes before I had said to Caroline that I wondered where poor Nessa was at, we were all sure that you had been sent through, when Pa called to me that he had a letter Pa Lillie and I went to Baltimore last Monday to see you but you had gone.[3] Oh! how I would like to see you. Ma is very anxious for you to come home. I would love to have you with me above all things in the world if you think you would come you say you hope to be in Richmond before an answer to your letter can reach you. I hardly think from that that you know that R[ichmond] has been evacuated and now in possession of federal troops. Where will you be sent to. I feel so uneasy about you. Nessa I hardly know how to or what to write. I am half sick I have another very sore finger. Last night I could not sleep for it and it is quite painful today so you must excuse this writing it is on my right hand. Nessa whatever you do or wherever you go do try to take care of yourself and may God help and protect you. All well and send there love to you. I rec the jewelry you sent me it was realy beautiful and I am so much ablige to you. Good bye Ever affectionately yours,

Kate

Wesley may not have been aware of the plight of Richmond. On April 2 the Union troops defeated the Confederates at Petersburg. This allowed the Union to take Richmond on April 3, 1865.

Kate's illness may, in part, have been due to her overwhelming concern for Wesley. There was growing uncertainty about the fate of those captured by the Union in the ever increasing optimism of the war's end. Almost as an afterthought, Kate still manages to thank Wesley for the exquisite jewelry he sent.

Fig. 48. Hard rubber finger ring, two views (FS1843, dia. 15.5 mm). (CHMA. Photographs by author.)

April 9th/65

Dear Kate

I had the pleasure of receiving yours of the 6th this morning.
It seemed as if it had been almost a year since I heard from you.
I am very sorry you did not get to Baltimore before we left. I am
very anxious to see you, and hope you may get permission to
come here to see me. You say you are very anxious for me to be
with you. I assure you, you do not wish it more than I do. Nothing in the world could give me as much pleasure, and could I have
had my wishes i would have been with you long ago. You spoke
about wanting to know ware we would be sent now since Richmond is in possession of the Federals. I have no more idea ware,
or when we will be sent than than [sic] you. I am very anxious
about when we will be sent and uneasy for fear we may not be
sent very shortly. I wrote to you five days ago and asked you to
tell Jack to send me some money. If you have not received it tell
him and to send it in care of Maj Brady, Prov Marshals. Give my
love to all. Yours affectionately

W Makely

Wesley once again mentions to Kate his need for money. He does not relay the amount requested earlier but asks Kate to have his brother send
it. Wesley does not indicate if it is for transportation after he is released
or to purchase needed supplies while at Point Lookout.

Pt Lookout Md

April 18th

Dear Kate

Yours of the 13th has been received. I would have answered it
sooner, but I supposed there would not be any mail for several
days, I am sorry that president Lincoln was killed, it is a great
loss to the country. I think he would have been very mild with
the south. I hope though that President Johnson will be equally
as good. Kate you say you are very anxious for me to come home.
I assure you, you cannot be more anxious than I am, and I wish

you would ask Jack to attend to it for me as soon as he can. I do not see any use of staying in prison any longer.

Give my love to all,

Yours affectionately

W. Makely

Two major events transpired between Wesley's letter of April 9 and that of April 18. General Robert E. Lee surrendered the Army of Northern Virginia to Lieutenant General Ulysses S. Grant at Appomattox on April 9, effectively ending the war. The second event Wesley mentioned was the assassination of President Lincoln on April 14. This was one of the few times Wesley mentioned any event outside his circle of friends and family.

His comment about not seeing "any use of staying in prison" must have referred to the downfall of the Confederacy. There still needed to be some accounting for all those who were prisoners-of-war. On Johnson's Island, the prisoners were struggling with the realization that the only way to be released was by taking the "Amnesty Oath." Captain John Reece, 1st C.S.A. Georgia Infantry, noted in his diary that many were "conferring with their friends as to what is best under the circumstances" (Reece 1865, entry for April 25, 1865). It was not until late May that most prisoners at Johnson's Island finally decided to take the oath and prepare for release.

Alex Apl 21st/65

Dear Nessa

I see by your letter of the 15th that you have rec the ten dollars I sent you. I am very glad for I had thought that you would never get it. You say you would like to be at home with us. Oh! Nessa what is it I would not give to have you so. I feel so badly to see my friends husband's coming in and you cannot. Tom Perry was to see us yesterday he is looking very well. they all ask after you and want to see you. Oh how I wish you were here. I saw Jack again this morning and told him to go again and see what he could do but I expect I will have to start out again myself. Capt Sam Johnston and a good many other Alexandrians came in yesterday. I do not know how it is they are paroled men yet they are kept imprisoned.[4] We are all quite well at present except Ma her cough seems worse these few days. I must stop for Lillie bothers my life out to let her write a little to you, all send there love to you. Affectionately Yours

Kate

My very Dear Papa

We all well and I am a tolerable good girl. I want you to come home. I want to see you very much. Papa I sent you 2 dollars some time ago and you never wrote that you got it so now Grandma and I send you two more. Good bye Your most affectionate little daughter Lillie

Pt Lookout, Md
April 25th/65

Dear Kate

I have just recd yours of the 21st. I would like to write you a long letter but cannot as I am about leaving. Ware we are going I cannot say. I will write to you though as soon as I reach my destination. Give my love to all Yours affectionately

W Makely

Lieutenant James Wentworth, who had been in the same group as Wesley when they left Johnson's Island, continued to record their travels. The prisoners left Point Lookout at midnight on April 25 and were put on the steamer *Weybosset*. They traveled for two days to Fort Delaware, arriving at 10:00 the morning of the April 27.

Fort Delaware
April 27th/65

Dear Kate

I arrived here this morning. I hope I may soon have the pleasure off taking a trip home. They have taken the names of all the officers here who wish to take the Oath of Allegiance. I think about two thirds are willing to take it. I gave them my name. I don't know though if we will be released soon or not. I wish Jack and you would try and have me released as soon as possible. I received the letter Lill and you wrote me just before I left Point Lookout. Tell her I am very much obliged to her for the money she sent me. I must try and answer her letter very shortly. I hope though to be with you all again before I may have an opportunity of writing more letters. Give my love to all. Write soon one page of letter paper.

    Yours affectionately

    W Makely

Fort Delaware is located on Pea Patch Island in the Delaware River at Delaware City. Original construction of the fort began in 1817. During the Civil War additional barracks were added to house Confederate prisoners. This prison achieved an unsavory reputation, with almost three thousand perishing during its use (Casstevens 2005:60–75).

James Wentworth notes that of the 317 prisoners brought to Fort Delaware, only fourteen took the oath when offered upon arrival. Wesley was one of the fourteen. Wentworth noted though that most of the officers already in the "pen" had taken the oath (Wentworth 1990). The discrepancy between Wesley's account and Wentworth's discussion of the oath takers is understandable. Wesley was probably referring to all the officers in the prison, and not just those arriving in his group, thus making his decision seem inevitable.

Taking the Oath of Allegiance was always an option for the prisoner-of-war in the North. The Rebels referred to this as "swallowing the eagle." Those prisoners taking the oath prior to the end of the war were considered "razor backs" and were often verbally if not physically abused. At Johnson's Island, a portion of Block 1 was separated off for the modest number taking the oath before the war ended (Wilds 2005:322–23).

Once the war ended the only way to be released from prison was through taking the oath. Following is the text of the oath:

The Oath of Allegiance

United States of America

I,_____, of the County of_____, State of_____,
do solemnly swear that I will support, protect, and defend the

Constitution and Government of the United States against all enemies, whether domestic or foreign; that I will bear true faith, allegiance, and loyalty to the same, any ordinance, resolution, or laws of any State, Convention, or Legislature, to the contrary not-withstanding; and further, that I will faithfully perform all the duties which may be required of me by the laws of the United States; and I take this oath freely and voluntarily, without any mental reservation or evasion whatever.

_____

[prisoner's signature]
Subscribed and sworn to before me, this _____day of_____
A.D. 1865.

_____

Col. Com'd'g

Fort Delaware April 29th/65

Dear Kate

I arrived here on the morning of the 27th. I wrote to you the same evening, and hope it has reached you before this, as I am very anxious to hear from you. Little did I think when I left Johnsons Island that I would be sent here. I left there in fine spirits, thinking I would be with you again soon, and when I thought of the great pleasure I was intoxicated with the idea. It is truly discouraging to be so disappointed. It really seems as if some malignant foredoom had determined that we should not meet, but I must not lament the disappointment of the great enjoyment I had promised myself, for it certainly will not be long before I will be with you again. I will try and console myself in my disappointment with the thought of the great enjoyment that is in store for me.

But dreary tho the moments fleet
Oh let me think we yet shall meet,
The only ray of solace sweet.

Kate I have expressed my willingness to take the Oath of Allegiance. I think about two thirds of the offices here have done the same. All have given the cause up as hopeless. I wish you would try and get a special order for my release, and come in here with it. I have no doubt but what we all will be released, but as there are so many who have made application for the Oath it may be sometime before it will get around. I am in hopes I may soon hear that you have succeeded, and find myself on my way home again. Tell Lill she must excuse me. I certainly thought I had done so. I was told that letters sent here must have the rank regt, and co, I have since learned that it is only necessary on money letters. You need only put my rank and division, (division 28). Give my love to all. Yours affectionately,

W. Makely

This is the last letter written by Wesley in The Library of Virginia's collection. On May 9, 1865, Wesley Makely took the Oath of Allegiance at Fort Delaware and was released. Many of his Johnson's Island companions remained there for at least another month. His offer to take the Oath of Allegiance upon arrival at Fort Delaware resulted in his being released much closer to his home and at least a month earlier.

Wesley returned to Alexandria, where he was listed in the 1870 census as a liquor dealer. The 1882 city directory of Alexandria recorded Wesley Makely as a north side grocer, and after 1888 Wesley was noted as a city measurer. He remained married to Catherine and they had a total of seven children: Mary Louise (Lillie) Makely, born in 1860 or 1861; Virginia L. Makely, 1867; David Albert Makely, 1868; Carrie G. Makely, December 6, 1875; Kate E. Makely, 1878; Weslina Makely, 1880; and Hallie Appich Makely, 1883. Carrie lived until December 6, 1951; Lillie until December 21, 1953; and Hallie until 1971. Most records point to Wesley being deceased by 1895, although the exact date of death is unknown.

Catherine Appich Makely, wife of Wesley, continued to live in Alexandria after Wesley's death. She died on August 27, 1927. Both Wesley and Catherine are buried at the Washington Street United Methodist Church Cemetery in Alexandria, Virginia.

It is unfortunate that we do not know more about the life of Wesley and Kate after the war. Extensive genealogical searching has

Fig. 49. Tombstone of Wesley and Catherine Makely, Union Cemetery of the Washington Street United Methodist Church, Alexandria, Virginia. (By permission of Daniel Janzegers, photographer.)

not uncovered additional diaries or letters among Wesley and Kate's descendants.

Reading the interaction between Wesley and Kate during his imprisonment allows some insight into their personalities. They were frustrated with an unreliable mail system, changing prisoner policies by both governments, and continual bouts of ill health. At times they were impatient and at other times more understanding. The letters provide not only a voice from the past but also a greater understanding of the materials left behind at the Johnson's Island Civil War Prison site. The real significance of this set of letters was how they expressed the prison experience during the American Civil War.

The Prisoner-of-War Experience

A man is not half a Soldier until he has been a prisoner. he don't know
anything until then. I thought I was a pretty good Soldier before but am
a much better one now.

Captain Charles E. Rhodes, 9th Alabama Cavalry, Co. G,
to his sister from Johnson's Island, September 1, 1864

Wesley and Kate's letters provide a true glimpse into the life of a Civil
War prisoner-of-war. As one of some ten thousand prisoners held at
Johnson's Island, he provides a story that was not one of fame or even
note by others at the prison. Of the choices that faced Wesley upon his
imprisonment—to attempt escape, assimilate through the Oath of Allegiance, or survive—he chose survival. He survived through his ability
to adapt and utilize the resources available, filtered by what the prison
allowed.

The multidisciplinary nature of this work is partially dependent
upon the multitude of primary accounts of the prison experience. Letters written by prisoners-of-war were brief encounters with their life.
The information contained in a prisoner-of-war letter was subject to
censorship by the prisoner and the guard. The audience influenced subjects addressed inside the envelope. And, of course, the perspective of
the prisoner had enormous effects on the letter's content. Examples of
other prisoners' writings have demonstrated how selective each individual was when engaged in the execution of a letter.

The multivocal nature of these primary sources provides a much
broader spectrum of accounts of prisoner survival. The daily choices
Wesley made while a prisoner were not the same choices all prisoners made. What Wesley brought to the prison in terms of his background and family history greatly influenced how he responded to the

"opportunities" presented within the prison walls. His experience would have been significantly different if he had been housed in Block 11, one of the blocks built for enlisted inmates. He would have had forty or fifty roommates instead of only five. The idea of "prisonization" discussed earlier affected all prisoners brought to Johnson's Island. Wherever they found themselves once in prison, the choices were affected by a combination of their housing, their roommates, their timing on arrival, and what they brought to the mix. Wesley's choice of survival is manifested through his focus on family and what assurances he provided.

The study of institutionalization provides a context upon which we consider the balance between "protection and human rights" (Casella 2007). Institutionalization encompasses many forms in which a segment of human society is marginalized or disenfranchised from the mainstream population. This form can range from being as benign as a seniors' day care center to being as restrictive as a maximum security prison. In either case, the institution has its own operating procedures arrived at through a combination of what society condones, the management's objectives, and the influences brought by those incarcerated. In the case of prisoners-of-war, those incarcerated are not society's deviants in need of rehabilitation. They are unfortunate soldiers now behind enemy lines, warehoused for indefinite periods. Free, these individuals would again pose a deadly threat in battle, but confined, they present no immediate risk. During the American Civil War governments needed to find workable solutions to housing thousands of prisoners-of-war.

Both the Union and Confederacy were ill-prepared to cope with the numbers of prisoners. The facilities chosen to house prisoners-of-war typify this lack of preparedness. Johnson's Island, as the only Union facility built as a stand-alone military prison, demonstrated the military's lack of a consistent approach to the treatment of prisoners-of-war. Although it was originally built to house both officers and enlisted men, within only a few days of its being placed in use, the Union government changed its role to house only Confederate officers (ORA, ser. 2, 3:448).

Casstevens (2005:5) identified six categories of Civil War prison types: civilian jails, coastal fortifications, converted warehouses, enclosed barracks (as at Johnson's Island), walled tent camps, and empty stockades. No single facility type was advocated above the others by either government. Open fields, easy to construct, offered little protection to the captive and were less humane than the barracks built at a facility like Johnson's Island. These varied types of prison facilities bring into question the intent of the commissary general of prisoners in the development of an adequate prison system for captives. What was at the core of the incarceration issue was defining adequate treatment.

Quartermaster General M. C. Meigs wrote to Lieutenant Colonel William Hoffman, commissary general of prisoners, on October 23, 1861, granting him authorization to construct the Johnson's Island prison depot. Meigs notes:

> As far as practicable they [the POWs] must be required to furnish their own clothing, and to provide themselves the means for this purpose, they may be permitted to engage in any occupation which they can make profitable and which will not interfere with their safe-keeping. . . . Trusting much to your discretion and knowledge, and believing that your appointment will alleviate the hardship of confinement to these erring men. (ORA, ser. 2, 3:122–23)

The regulations authorized one ration regardless of rank, adequate medical treatment, and respect of private property when captured. The directive from General Meigs was broad and thus would have to be interpreted by the individual commandant. In a sense, though, the message is clearly promoting humane treatment, identifying the sole purpose of incarceration as the prisoners' "safe-keeping." It was the interpretation of "safe-keeping" that resulted in many of the original hardships and adjustments the prisoners had to face. Incarceration inherently results in the imprisoned feeling a loss of freedom. Even if housed, fed, and clothed appropriately, inmates had to face the inequity of their newfound role, no matter what their previous position in society had demanded. As prisoners-of-war they had lost power over others and had lost property, the prestige of their military rank, and pleasures brought by family and friends. This was probably most evident among the South's finest.

At Johnson's Island, the housing of thousands of the most affluent and educated of the South brought an intellectual reserve where all they had was time. The composition of this prison population was eloquently described by Colonel Isaiah Steedman in a speech he gave in 1866:

> This was a prison expressly constricted and noted for the confinement of officers and, with a few exceptions, none others were ever kept here. These men were from the best classes of the southern people; they were men of education and property. The great majority of them were young and in the prime of life. Hence a better clan of men considered in any aspect, has never been, or never will be assembled again, in the same anomalous situation. (Steedman 1866)

Wesley's accounts document many pursuits of these enterprising minds in their attempts to regain lost freedoms: jewelry manufacture; pencil drawings of portraits; photographic images of portraits; composing of poetry; theatrical productions by the Rebellonians; playing chess; reading; remodeling rooms; and writing letters. Wesley was able to participate in many of these activities through his intellect and access to funds. Prisoners without money from the outside, if they wanted to improve their existence, needed to find means of earning money.

Domestic tasks such as preparing food, cleaning dishes, and mending, washing, and ironing clothes were necessities for the southern man but were viewed as tasks for servants rather than for gentlemen. Captain John H. Guy wrote in his diary, "Officers were not allowed to bring their servants with them to this prison. Some of us feel greatly the loss of them. There are luckily however some of the prisoners who are willing to cook and to wash clothes for pay and thus most of us are able to get rid of two very disagreeable necessities" (Guy 1862, entry for May 15, 1862). Throughout the time prisoners were incarcerated at Johnson's Island, those who could afford to have others perform these tasks did so for modest amounts per week or month. Some chose to perform the tasks themselves and save the money, while others executed these menial chores for pay. This may speak to the possibility of there being different classes of officers at the prison. At Johnson's Island there were subtle differences among subpopulations of Confederate officers, but the differences were noted more on a one-to-one basis than among larger classes of individuals. At Elmira Prison, with both Confederate officers and enlisted men incarcerated, larger class distinctions were recognized. Education, professional training, trade skills, and willingness to improve one's condition all contributed to the hierarchy at Elmira (Gray 2001:88).

Some services prisoners provided at Johnson's Island were more prestigious than others. Domestic chores were viewed as the least desirable to perform, and no one was mentioned in any diary or letter as being most proficient at this service. William B. Gowen sums up this attitude best: "This has been cook day for our room again. You would be interested if you could see me wiping the dishes and setting the Table etc. but I am getting very tired of it. I had much rather be where such things are done by Women" (Gowen 1865, entry for June 13, 1863). Wesley never mentioned to Kate how he was able to meet the demands of domestic chores. Whatever work a prisoner chose to pursue in the name of survival was not ridiculed by fellow prisoners. However, a prisoner would be subject to direct or behind the back berating should he expose a lack of education.

To achieve prestige at Johnson's Island required prowess in intellectual, artistic, or professional pursuits. Prisoners talk of the best chess or draughts player. Colonel Levin M. Lewis, 16th Missouri Infantry, was mentioned in numerous diaries as the finest preacher (Meissner and Meissner 2005:18; Wilds 2005:121). Wesley notes the talents of Lieutenant William Waesche in making fine jewelry. Lieutenant John Taylor, 7th South Carolina Cavalry, wrote of Waesche's talents as well as those of Captain Robert McCulloch of Company B, 18th Virginia Infantry (Meissner and Meissner 2005:21). Lieutenants Robert Smith, 61st Tennessee Infantry, and William Peel, 11th Mississippi Infantry, were both well known for their jewelry. Lieutenant Smith later became prominent as the clandestine photographer within the prison compound (Durkin 2005:166–67). Many achieved acclaim for various talents but none for their domestic excellence. Among the prisoners, the only action that universally drew derogatory opinion was taking the Oath of Allegiance; prisoners who did so were considered the lowest of class.

Primary accounts have provided great insight into how the prisoners at Johnson's Island coped with their loss of freedom. However, these individual writings do not provide all the data used to tell even this one story of Wesley's experience. The integrity of the archaeological resources from Johnson's Island allows both spatial and chronological segregation of the cultural materials. The ability to examine the remains that had fallen through the floorboards of the various blocks allows for spatial-use studies. The excavations of a general housing block (Block 4) and the prison hospital (Block 6) uncovered significantly different types of cultural materials. Block 4 contained hundreds of items related to prisoner craft activities. The prison hospital produced little craft material but many artifacts representing medical treatment. There were also significant differences in the amounts and types of bone remains, ceramics, and glass wares recovered from the two blocks.

Specific to this book are the cultural remains from the creation of jewelry. The archaeological investigations recovered more than 760 hard rubber artifacts. The majority of these are discarded waste products or pieces of jewelry abandoned during manufacture. These hundreds of provenienced items have enabled a reconstruction of how jewelry was made and what materials were used. The prisoners talked about working with gutta-percha, but other than a reference to "slab" gutta-percha and thin buttons, there was no clear description of the manner in which the rings, breast pins, and other items were made. Most prisoners' discussions related to jewelry manufacturing were cursory (as was Wesley's) and only described the finished products. Through careful study of the hard rubber objects left behind, a step by step recreation of this craft industry was achieved.

To the rear of each block were the latrines. Each latrine was used for a discrete period of time, typically four to six months. Excavation of the latrines behind Blocks 4, 6, and 8 provided a chronological view of prisoner-of-war treatment. No other prison within the Union or Confederate systems has the archaeological integrity necessary for this form of temporal study (Bush 2000).

The latrines from 1862 until July 1864 have provided evidence of tunnels being constructed as potential escape routes for the prisoner who was determined to rejoin the South. No primary accounts gave details about the construction or use of these tunnels. Their archaeological exploration has provided not only the tools used but also how the prisoners shielded the contents of the latrines from the tunnel excavation (Bush 2000:71). In the preparation of an escape tunnel, prisoners were taking back portions of their lost freedom in the dangerous task of escape. If successful, the prisoner regained everything.

The latrines have also provided comparative evidence of the living conditions within the prison compound throughout its use. The primary documents expose the harsh conditions to which prisoners were subjected in the later part of 1864 and 1865. The contents of the latrines show marked decreases in certain types of luxury items as well as general rations (Bush 2000:75–76).

The archaeological record speaks to the prisoners' attempts to regain aspects of their prestige and property through the acquisition of items that promoted their societal position. Activities that did not endanger their safekeeping—acquiring finer tableware, crystal glass, and utensils; making or purchasing hard rubber jewelry; and making gaming pieces—are all represented. The archaeological record is inclusive of all prisoners' attempts to create a balance of power where by design there is a gross imbalance.

The housing of the Union guards was destroyed when the island was quarried for limestone in the late 1800s. The archaeological expression of the life of the guard cannot be recovered. Imagine the comparative possibilities had these archaeological remains been preserved. There are prisoner accounts of the guards trading services for hard rubber jewelry items, but were the guards involved in its manufacture? If so, were the items they made different from what the prisoners created? These questions, along with many more, can never be archaeologically explored at Johnson's Island.

The prisoners-of-war at Johnson's Island realized they had the power to survive their imprisonment without being totally subjugated by the guard. Even in their somewhat limited subject matter, Wesley's letters illustrate the potential prisoners had to achieve some control over imprisonment. In Wesley's case, he first attempted to arrange for an exchange. Failing exchange, he manipulated his imprisonment to provide contact with and gifts for his family. His prewar social position allowed him access to funds that were used to purchase the goods and services required to sustain a tolerable existence reminiscent of his prior status. He alters his immediate physical surroundings to gain a more familiar appearance. Excavations within Block 4 (comparable to the block where Wesley was housed) produced a mixture of common and higher status ceramics and glassware associated with mid-nineteenth-century occupations. Most military sites reflect the temporary nature of occupation. Military units cannot be weighed down with fine tableware. The occurrence of stemmed drinking glasses, porcelain plates, and bone-handled utensils suggests that these prisoners-of-war tried to recreate their previous lifestyle. Prisoners had the opportunity to recapture some of their lost identity (with minor impact to the guards' overall goal of incarceration) through the purchase of such items from the sutler or by having them shipped to the prison by family and friends.

In earlier discussions about these letters, it was suggested that understanding treatment for prisoners-of-war requires examination from both historical and personal perspectives. Going back to the American Civil War to view the approach to prisoner-of-war treatment helps establish a context for the justifications of containment, censorship, and even torture. The reference here is to the context for treatment, not an argument for the appropriateness of treatment. At Johnson's Island the Union made decisions to cut rations, cut access to personal items previously allowed, and restrict various forms of communication with the outside. These changes were not out of necessity for "safe-keeping" but the result of retaliation to accusations of mistreatment. Humane treatment was certainly redefined if not abandoned once one side suspected the other was intentionally mistreating its prisoners.

The story of Wesley Makely's imprisonment was one of the hundreds of thousands from the American Civil War. With the failure of the exchange system, the governments were faced with insurmountable numbers of prisoners needing to be incarcerated for unknown periods of time. Going all the way to the personal level allows exploration into the plight of prisoners-of-war, regardless of their previous positions. The multivocal nature of this study helped to normalize some of the biases inherent in firsthand accounts.

Wesley struggled most with the isolation experienced from lack of communication with his family. He demonstrated his position of wealth and stature through the jewelry and images he sent home, but he could not control his own personal fate of exchange. Through his disappointment with the Confederate government over exchange, he began to question his commitment to their cause. Wesley finally suggested to his wife, because of the pain imprisonment brought, that he could no longer think of family. However dark those moments were, he continued to write, sent jewelry, and hoped to be with them again one day.

The prisoner-of-war experience at Johnson's Island was not typical for all prison camps during the American Civil War. However, some of the same personal experiences faced at Johnson's Island were encountered at other prisons. At times, the prisoner accounts from Johnson's Island as a prison depot were positive. These were typically from 1862 and 1863 and during the warmer months. With the loss of exchange in mid-1863 and the imposition of harsh regulations by mid-1864, prisoners suffered hardships for no other reason than the Union chose to change the policy of humane treatment.

The archaeological record at Johnson's Island gave voice to some of the thousands of prisoners for whom a written record was missing. The archaeological study also provided insight into prisoners' reactions as they attempted to regain portions of their lost freedoms.

Why did the Union government abandon its position of "safe-keeping" for a less humane stance? In April 1863 Colonel William Hoffman, commissary general of prisoners for the Union, was relating to Colonel R. Buchanan, commander at Fort Delaware, "that prisoners of war shall be treated with all the kindness which a proper humane feeling prompts and which is consistent with their position." In the same letter he described the treatment of Union soldiers taken to Richmond: "It has frequently happened that they have been stripped of all their outer garments and then crowded into prisons inconceivably filthy, so much so that it would be shocking to humanity to confine in such a place even the most abandoned criminals. Here too were confined men of all ranks, from generals to privates." Hoffman ends this letter to Buchanan with the following statement: "In conclusion say to the general that I trust the humane example which has been set by the Government of the United States in its care for the welfare of prisoners of war may be followed by the Government at Richmond, a course which cannot fail to greatly mitigate the hardships which must unavoidably be experienced by all who are so unfortunate as to be captured" (ORA, ser. 2, 5:487).

Hoffman's attitude on the issue of humane treatment began to change by February 1864, when he ordered Captain Frank Battle to be placed in irons in retaliation for Captain Shad Harris's confinement in Richmond. On April 20, 1864, Colonel Hoffman circulated orders to all prison commanders prohibiting prisoners from receiving undergarments or socks between April and October 1, 1864. In the same document he noted that prisoners should only have clothing of inferior quality and any excess of clothing was considered contraband. Finally, on April 29, 1864, he wrote:

> I respectfully suggest as a means of compelling the rebels to adopt a less barbarous policy toward the prisoners in their hands that the rebel officers at Johnson's Island be allowed only half-rations; that their clothing be reduced to what is only sufficient to cover their nakedness, and that they be denied the privilege of purchasing the articles allowed to other prisoners. (ORA, ser. 2, 7:81)

Not only was Hoffman advocating less than humane treatment; he suggested specifically that the treatment of officers, accustomed to superior conditions, be targeted for this retaliatory action. The question of humane treatment was difficult to endorse once public sentiment moved toward retaliation. By the end of 1864 there was little public support for treatment "with all the kindness which a proper humane feeling prompts" (ORA, ser. 2, 5:447). By November 1864 the prisoners at Johnson's Island recorded supplementing their diet with rats. On February 19, 1865, Lieutenant William B. Gowen wrote:

> Several months have passed since I have written a line in my Journal. . . . The sutler has been deprived of the privilege of selling us anything at all in the way of food and our rations at the same time were curtailed so that we are allowed barely enough to sustain life. I am hungry from one day's end to another. Many of the prisoners have resorted to catching and eating rats in order to help out their rations. I have never tried any rat yet myself, I choose rather to suffer while rather than resort to such food. I have seen other

prisoners licking up crumbs from the ditches and slop barrels and eating them. (Gowen 1865:106)

Wesley never wrote to Kate about suffering want of food or other comforts. He only noted his bouts with sickness during those difficult times. His last letter from Johnson's Island expressed a sentiment he had never previously shared with Kate. He began this letter with, "In a short time I will be on my way from this hated Island." Most of his letters were brief. He rarely expanded on his thoughts or expressed them with such vehemence. Further into this letter, he says, "Happiness I have found to be out of the question while I am separated from you." For Wesley, the separation from his family seemed to override all other forms of pain.

How did the changes in Union treatment of the prisoners affect Wesley? Did the restrictions in rations, clothing, or other items increase his loneliness? Did these retaliatory actions endear him to the Union's cause? In fact, what were the overall goals accomplished by the Union in the implementation of less than humane treatment of the prisoners-of-war under their charge? These actions affected individuals like Wesley not only during imprisonment but for the rest of their lives. The Union engaged in unnecessarily harsh treatment of these prisoners-of-war without a sincere exploration and consideration of the consequences. How does understanding Wesley's experience help formulate the prisoner-of-war approach today?

This brings us back to the very beginning of this book questioning the relationship of present governmental treatment of prisoners-of-war to what transpired during the American Civil War. Several have explored this question from various perspectives, mostly through the military's organizational and legal roles (Brown 1998; Fogarty 2005; Foucault 1977; Gebhardt 2005; Tucker, 1990). These studies have brought to light several operating factors that seem to influence how the United State government, and specifically its military arm, approaches the humane treatment of enemy prisoners-of-war (EPW). Most recently, the definition of prisoner-of-war has been manipulated carefully to exclude groups like "unlawful combatants," who become marginalized even further and do not have the same rights as those identified as EPW. During the American Civil War, President Lincoln struggled with identifying any captured

Confederate soldier as a prisoner-of-war, thus not only recognizing the rights of the captured but legitimizing their government. Therefore, one of the first hurdles confronting any government when faced with war is recognition of the status of those captured during its implementation.

Tucker (1990) makes the case that throughout the U.S. history of warfare, humane treatment guided the management of prisoners-of-war. She proposes that organizational structure, the quality of personnel, and a responsive government were key to providing successful prisoner-of-war treatment. She does note that the conclusions and recommendations made are not a vindication of United States treatment of all individuals captured and detained in war. General trends and statistics of past wars directed her analysis more than the individual accounts.

In times of warfare, maintaining a humane commitment to life, especially that of the enemy, is a difficult task. "The enemy of the United States is not the soldier, whether on the battlefield or in a prison camp, but is the state which that soldier represents; a fact obscured and misplaced too often in American military conflicts" (Tucker 1990:237). Fogarty's (2005) exploration of the impact of incidents reported from Guantanamo Bay also emphasizes the negative implications of less than humane treatment of those captured. He wrote that beyond these inhumane actions "undermining the rule of law, the consequence of the Administration's new system of military justice is to fuel global anti-Americanism, reduce cooperation and support for the GWOT [global war on terror] and to deny the US the moral high ground it needs to promote international human rights in the future" (Fogarty 2005:iii). The location of Abu Ghraib and Guantanamo Bay, outside the United States, speaks to the issues of the effect a prison's location can have on the incarcerated as well as on those in charge of their care. Even in the United States there seems to be a growing acceptance of this new classification of the ambiguously defined. Once someone is identified as a possible terrorist, deportation to some unknown location threatens many fictional characters on television crime shows. This repeating theme normalizes the inhumanity it implies.

During the American Civil War, the Union was ill prepared to cope with the large numbers of prisoners. The guard for the prisons were not trained military police, as are present at military prisons today. The organizational structure implemented to maintain order over the prison system occurred months after the war had started and thousands had been captured. Through the later nineteenth and twentieth centuries, the United States learned some lessons about managing prisoners-of-war, however defined. The impact of the guard to inflict inhumane treatment on the individual prisoner needs to be addressed further.

Ambiguously defined "noncitizens" describes soldiers captured in battle and confined in the makeshift prison system (Casella 2007:5). Political pressures eventually influenced their recognition as prisoners-of-war. The politicizing of these individuals resulted in their being pawns in the overall posturing of war rather than either the Confederacy or Union taking a strong humane position of treatment for the individual. Policies changed from the secretary of war (and the president) down through the individual prison depot. In the end, the prisoners suffered and reacted using whatever means were available. At Johnson's Island, prisoners who could acquire money bought their way to a less harsh survival. Others not so fortunate hunted rats, lost weight, and may eventually have succumbed to disease. At Andersonville, Georgia, treatment became so extreme that one group of prisoners pillaged their fellow prisoners for needed supplies. The inhumane treatment of the individual prisoner has played out repeatedly in subsequent wars and most recently has surfaced with the atrocities at Abu Ghraib and Guantanamo Bay.

One thing missing from all the explorations into United States policies toward the treatment of prisoners-of-war was the story of the individual incarcerated. The reactions of the prisoners at Johnson's Island, Ohio, or Andersonville, Georgia, manifest in their efforts for regaining freedoms lost. Understanding the dynamics of the prisoner-of-war's desires to regain any part of the power, property, prestige, and pleasure denied to the imprisoned could facilitate policies of humane treatment that meet the objectives of incarceration. The significance of the story of Wesley Makely's imprisonment lies in presenting this anthropological perspective of the individual prison experience and the implications for more humane management.

This story is one of thousands that come from the Johnson's Island Prison Depot and hundreds of thousands from the American Civil War. The combination of the letters, the artifacts, and the physical location provides the context for a meaningful appreciation of the experience. Personal stories like Wesley's offer a gateway for understanding the implications of—and changing—how the governmentally sanctioned incarcerated are treated.

Acknowledgments

Prisoners' letters and diary entries often begin with: "Nothing of importance has happened this week." Then they proceed to describe various events contradicting that first statement. This feels somewhat like the frustration in trying to thank all those who have been a part of my journey in completing this work on Johnson's Island—the longer I think about this the more I find to say. Conducting both archaeological and historical research over twenty years results in an acknowledgments list that will probably not be inclusive of all those who have provided insight and assistance to this work. I wish nothing more than to assure all who have had contact with the site how much I appreciate your influence.

I want to thank John Brown, whose introduction to Carl Zipfel of Baycliffs Development led to my working on Johnson's Island since 1988. Carl, as the landowner, was very supportive of my research work at the island. Case Western Reserve University and the University of Pittsburg were likewise supportive of my early work at Johnson's Island. Earthwatch and the Center for Field Research contributed to three summers of field research. More recently, my association with the Center for Historic and Military Archaeology at Heidelberg University has allowed me to continue my research at Johnson's Island. Heidelberg University provided a sabbatical allowing me finally to finish this manuscript.

For their support in those early years I wish to thank Al Tonetti, Jeff Reichwein, G. Michael Pratt (who helped in the later years as well), and Ray Luce. I want to acknowledge the staff assisting in the archaeological exploration of the site—Judy Thomas, Jim Bowers, Bob O'Deens, Mark Kollecker, and Frank Cantelas—and the hundreds of volunteers who faithfully came to excavate in the early 1990s. In later years I have had the help of Marcia George, Dave Fadley, Jeremy Freeman, Laurel Heyman, and many Heidelberg University students and volunteers assisting with the various archaeological programs at the site.

I would like to thank Mary Puffenberger, who served as the administrative assistant for the Center for Historic and Military Archaeology and the Department of Anthropology. She assists me year after year in helping to organize the Johnson's Island programs. I also wish to thank Marcia George, educational coordinator for the Experiential Learning Program in Historic Archaeology at Heidelberg University, for her role in utilizing the site for the benefit of younger students, for her assistance with the graduate teacher classes, and for continuing to update the Teacher's Manual used in these programs.

There are several people I wish to acknowledge who have inspired me in this quest for understanding the prisoner-of-war experience. Stella Eismann brought home to me the idea of how connected people are to the past. Russ Umbenhour exemplifies the idea of the lifelong student. Mike Woshner has continued in his journey to understand all that can be understood about hard rubber, and I have enjoyed trading thoughts with him over every detail.

I need to thank all the members of the Friends and Descendants of Johnson's Island Civil War Prison who have given of their time, money, and family history to ensure the preservation of this National Historic Landmark site. Without their constant encouragement, works like this could not be completed. I also want to thank the Friends for granting me permission to conduct these investigations on land under their ownership since 2002. Of special note is Roy Swartz, who has supported my work at the island since its inception. Over the years I have had the honor and pleasure of meeting hundreds of descendants of the prisoners and guard from Johnson's Island. I wish I could thank them all for their kindness in sharing a part of the island's history with us.

The historical research has been ongoing as well. For this work, I need to acknowledge The Library of Virginia for granting permission to publish the letters in the Makely Family Papers. Special thanks are extended to Archives Research Coordinator J. Christian Kolbe, Senior Research Archivist R. Thomas Crew Jr., and Archives Research Coordinator Jennifer Davis McDaid, all from The Library of Virginia, for their assistance in this project over many years. I wish to thank the many people who volunteered their time in the transcription of the Makely letters. They include Leslie Walter, Phyllis A. Watts, Cindy Meeker, Sarah Huffman, Mary Puffenberger, Marcia George, and Sue Umbenhour. However, any errors of transcription are mine. Early drafts of this manuscript were read by Theresa Lichko and her insight was most appreciated.

And finally, I wish to give special thanks to my family, who have been there throughout the struggles and success. I want to thank my brother Mike, who has shared the enthusiasm of discovery with me since we were college students. My sons, Jake and Adam, have literally grown up with Johnson's Island as part of their lives. Although they have their own paths to follow, I am fortunate that they always find time to come back to the site to help in any way they can. I wish to acknowledge particularly all the help and insight my partner Sue Umbenhour has given. I cannot imagine how difficult the completion of this work would have been without her help.

Notes

Chapter 1. Introduction

1. The captain's letter of December 27, 1864 is in the Makely Family Papers, personal papers collection 1859–1865, accession 27034, 25829, Library of Virginia, Richmond.

2. A lunette is an earthen fortification of secondary importance to other fortifications. Although typically crescent shaped, in this particular case the lunette was chevron shaped.

3. Wesley is called Nessa by Catherine, and Catherine is called Kate by Wesley.

4. Mourning jewelry was popularized by Queen Victoria's mourning of Prince Albert in 1861 (Bush, "Maintaining or Mixing Southern Culture"). It was also known as jet jewelry. The prisoners were able to replicate many fine examples of this jewelry through their craft work.

5. Mike Woshner (1999) describes the differences between hard rubber and gutta-percha. Almost all references the prisoners made to this hard black material were gutta-percha, when in fact the material was hard rubber.

Chapter 2. Johnson's Island Prison

1. Within the prison compound there was a separate structure built to house those sick with what were recognized as infectious and deadly diseases. At this time the pest house was used for those seriously infected with smallpox.

2. The archaeological discovery and establishment of the site design were first reported in an article in *Historic Archaeology* titled "Interpreting the Latrines of the Johnson's Island Civil War Military Prison" (Bush 2000).

3. In late 1864 a portion of Block 1 was set aside to house prisoners taking the Oath of Allegiance, protecting them from the loyal prisoners' retaliation.

4. Colonel Michael L. Woods, 46th Alabama Infantry, captured at Champion Hill, May 16, 1863.

Chapter 3. Where Is Your Letter? (August 16–December 13, 1863)

1. It did not take long for prisoners or their families to become impatient with not hearing from their loved ones. Letters were the only form of communication available to the families, and the mail system proved unreliable at times.

2. Sickness was the most common reason for death within prisoner-of-war camps (Bush 2007).

3. These two letters are not part of the collection at The Library of Virginia, thus I was unable to put them into this book.

4. Mrs. Fountain was the mother of Captain Nehemiah Fountain, 10th Virginia Infantry.

5. Kate was traveling from Stribling Springs, Virginia, to her home in Alexandria. There was no indication of how she traveled or why there were no letters for the month of November. Wesley gives us no indication of his lapse in letters.

6. The mail typically went out from the Island twice a week. Prisoners would try to get their letters written in time for the censors to review the mail and get it posted.

7. The ring Wesley mentioned was a hard rubber finger ring made by a prisoner. There are many references in the Johnson's Island letters to various types of jewelry being made by prisoners.

8. Block 1, Room 6 is where Wesley resided at Johnson's Island. Block 1 is on the bay side of the prison compound closest to the main gate.

Chapter 4. Thoughts of Exchange (December 24, 1863–May 8, 1864)

1. "The pen" meant those in the prison yard.

2. Another pejorative term used to describe someone who had taken the oath (Wilds 2005:323).

3. His note to Kate indicates that he would accept Judge Underwood's condition for help in getting released, which was his taking the oath, but he did not indicate in his letter what the condition was. Wesley also notes Kate's disapproval of this action.

4. At this time in his imprisonment, Wesley was still of the opinion that exchange was a real possibility. Although no formal wholesale exchanges had taken place for months, prisoners were too removed from the commands to realize exchange was no longer viable.

5. Dysentery, producing severe diarrhea, was the number one cause of death among prisoners at most Civil War prisons.

6. Lieutenant Henry C. Knicely of the 18th Virginia was captured at the same time as Captain Makely. He is mentioned several times in Wesley's letters. Wesley never mentions their being roommates, but letters written by Knicely also put Block 1, Mess 6 for his location at Johnson's Island. See figure 34. The Civil War Soldiers and Sailors System maintained by the National Park Service (http://www.civilwar.nps.gov/cwss/info.htm) is the official listing of all participants in the Civil War obtained from the National Archives. In this listing, Lieutenant Knicely's last name is recorded as Kniceley. His letter (figure 34) has his signature as Knicely, which is the spelling used here.

7. Wesley Makely's father died on November 1, 1861. His mother, Elizabeth Kels Makely, died in 1868.

8. Kate is referring to her mother and father, Gottlieb and Gertrude Appich.

9. General Henry Walton Wessells served as commissary of prisoners. Colonel Hoffman was the commissary-general of prisoners for the Union (Official Records, Armies, ser. 2, vol. 7, p. 1168; hereafter cited as ORA).

10. George L. Shell, Captain of 88th Pennsylvania Infantry (ORA, ser. 2, vol. 7, p. 117).

11. Ethan Allan Hitchcock, major general of volunteers, commissioner of the exchange of prisoners.

12. Also known to Confederates as "swallowing the eagle," the Oath of Allegiance would be taken by prisoners wishing to be released and assimilating to the Union.

13. Farina is flour made from cereal grain, corn, or potatoes.

14. The health of prisoners is a constant theme throughout all letters. It is worth noting that most prisoners complained of some illness much of the time. Only the very sick went to Block 6, the prison hospital.

15. She may be referring to Lieutenant Colonel Edward A. Scovill, who enlisted as a captain on January 3, 1862. He was promoted to major on August 25, 1863, and promoted to lieutenant colonel on August 6, 1864. Therefore at this time he would have been a major in Company B of the 128th OVI. Originally the guard was known as the Hoffman's Battalion, named after Lieutenant Colonel William Hoffman, who had been given the task of finding a suitable location for a prison in the western Lake Erie area. In January 1864 with an expansion of the number of companies composing the guard, the Hoffman's Battalion was renamed the 128th Ohio Volunteer Infantry (OVI; Frohman 1965:6–14).

16. Captain Frederick Richard Windsor, 5th Virginia Cavalry, was wounded and captured on June 17, 1863, in Aldie, Virginia. He arrived at Johnson's Island on September 15, 1863, and was transferred on February 24, 1865 (National Archives, General Registry of Prisoners, 1865; hereafter cited as NAGRP).

17. Probably referring to Brigadier General Henry D. Terry.

18. General Benjamin F. Butler, agent of exchange for the Union. It is impressive how much access family had to those at the highest levels of command.

19. Captain Mathias Ginevan, 18th Virginia Cavalry, was wounded and captured on July 2, 1863, at Chambersburg, Pennsylvania. He arrived at Johnson's Island on September 28, 1863. He remained there until March 23, 1865, when he was transferred to Point Lookout for exchange.

20. Lieutenant William B. Triplett, 18th Virginia Cavalry, was captured at Hancock, Maryland, on July 2, 1863. He was transferred from Fort Delaware to Johnson's Island on July 20, 1863, and escaped. The official rolls indicate his escape, but no date was given (NAGRP 1865).

21. Purdy Makely and Albert Makely were Wesley's older brothers. When Kate refers to Jack, I believe she means Wesley's brother Metrah (see Wesley's letter of April 2, 1864, later in chapter 4).

22. Thomas Benton Cochran, 7th Virginia Cavalry, was captured on February 6, 1864, at Fauquier County, Virginia. He was transferred to Fort Delaware in June 1864 and eventually paroled for exchange on February 7, 1865 (NAGRP 1865).

23. The permission slip upon which Catherine was granted access to the island on March 8, 1864, noted that her brother, M. Makely, was with her. As earlier indicated, this was probably Metrah Makely, Wesley's brother. From this letter, it may be inferred that Metrah Makely was called "Jack." This would make sense since there was no Jack noted in the family records.

24. Gentlemen's shirts had detachable collars that would be replaced more often than the shirt.

25. Point Lookout was located in Maryland where the Potomac River flows into Chesapeake Bay. Prisoners were housed in tents on a forty-acre tract of land with conditions worse than at Johnson's Island (Casstevens 2005:162–67). Capitol refers to the Old Capitol, in Washington, D.C. This building had originally served as a government building, then as a boarding house, and had then been converted into a prison for Confederates. Prisoners housed at the Old Capitol did not have the space or opportunities afforded those at Johnson's Island (Casstevens 2005:153–61).

26. Letters had to remain unsealed when they were given to the guard because the Union inspector had to examine the letter prior to it being officially mailed. Therefore it probably only meant that the guard did not seal the envelope prior to it being sent off the island.

27. There are no letters in the collection from Wesley Makely to Kate between March 13 and April 2.

28. Friday, April 8, 1864, was proclaimed by Jefferson Davis as Fast Day for the Confederate States, a day of humility, fasting, and prayer (Wilds 2005:157).

29. Mosby's Guerrillas were a band of citizens raiding Union supply routes in Virginia, causing much disruption (Anonymous 1863:567).

30. Lieutenant William Morton Simpson, 17th Virginia Infantry, was a prisoner at Johnson's Island from August 2, 1863, until June 1, 1865. He was captured at Manassas on July 21, 1863 (NAGRP 1865).

31. There is no one by this name listed in any Confederate unit numbered 18. There is a James W. Parker in Company D, 8th Confederate Cavalry (Wade's) (Anonymous, n.d). There is no way of knowing if this is the person requesting aid.

32. Negotiations were taking place between Robert Ould, agent of exchange for the Confederacy, and Major General Benjamin Butler, Union commissioner of exchange. This was the first real interchange between these two since the Confederacy refused to deal with Butler in December 1863. Many issues were presented, with a report finally going to General U. S. Grant via Major General Hitchcock. Grant ceased all negotiations, keeping Confederate prisoners from rejoining the ranks (Hesseltine 1930:219–32).

33. In late March General Terry, in command at Johnson's Island, replaced Mr. Johnson as the sutler, appointing his (Terry's) nephew. Johnson was replaced because he had been forcing prisoners to purchase a picture of the island and Sandusky Bay for three dollars before they could make another purchase; there

were indications that Colonel Pierson was in collusion with Mr. Johnson on this. The sutler was shut down for a short time, reopening with the reinstatement of Mr. Johnson (Frohman 1965:16).

34. Accusations of theft by the Union guard persisted throughout imprisonment. The guards were accused of taking stamps and money out of the envelopes and rifling through boxes shipped to the prisoners. Prisoners lodged complaints but achieved little resolution. Wesley Makely would never find out what happened to his Hostetter's Bitters.

35. Kate's original May 3 letter shows evidence of stamps having been attached to the top.

36. Wesley's "letter of the 24th" is not part of the historical record.

Chapter 5. Sending Images (May 11–September 15, 1864)

1. This is one of the few times Wesley actually noted to Kate his interactions with others at the prison. Typically, he discusses only matters directly related to Kate and Lillie.

2. The most common types of material used for sets discovered at Johnson's Island include shell, silver, bronze, and gold. Many designs were incorporated into the jewelry made at prison.

3. No doubt there was a fee involved in this service.

4. Most of the chess sets from Johnson's Island are made of wood. They appear to have been partly made on a lathe.

5. No one by this name was imprisoned at Johnson's Island at this time. However, a Lieutenant John W. Pence of the 18th Virginia Cavalry was captured and sent to Fort Delaware. He was described as 5 feet, 11 inches, with light complexion, hazel eyes, and dark hair (Delauter 1985). Wesley was described as 6 feet, 1 inch tall, with dark hair and gray eyes.

6. Lieutenant Thomas Branch Jackson, 3rd Virginia Infantry, was from Brunswick County, Virginia. He was captured at Gettysburg and remained at Johnson's Island until March 14, 1865 (NAGRP 1865).

7. Crosses were one of the common designs carved by prisoners recovered from the site.

8. This was a very specific reference by Wesley to creating familiar surroundings in his place of imprisonment. This was an attempt by Wesley to exert some power over his situation. This action by Wesley and his roommates demonstrates their wish to alter their immediate space to fit their perceived identity better. Kate commented on this later, wondering what type of paper he used. It was the only time he mentioned his roommates.

9. Captain John B. Withers of Mosby's Battalion arrived on Johnson's Island on November 14, 1863, after being captured on September 22, 1863, in Fauquier County, Virginia. The historical record is somewhat unclear about the actual rank Withers held. He was sent off Johnson's Island on March 21, 1865 to Point Lookout for exchange (NAGRP 1865).

10. The sets she was talking about were jewelry sets. It is unclear whether these were the settings for something to be placed into or the actual insets for jewelry made through Wesley's direction.

11. This set of letters was unusual in the amount of materials Kate sent to Wesley for jewelry making. Typically, materials were received from other sources and not directly from family. Unfortunately, there was no family record of exactly what items were sent to Wesley.

12. Even Kate's letters were not immune to the political commentary on how prisoners in the South were being treated so well. At this time there were many accusations about the mistreatment of prisoners, in both North and South.

13. This is a good example of how this prison jewelry was in demand in the South among the more affluent. Oval brooches were popular and had various types of sets placed in them.

14. There was a sentimentality associated with jewelry made by prisoners-of-war in addition to the jewelry being very fashionable. The Union guard appreciated the jewelry being made and traded items for services rendered to the prisoners. Although this is difficult to calculate, the majority of the items prisoners made were either kept or sent to family and friends. A few prisoners had connections with others who would sell their wares. William Peel, of the 11th Mississippi Infantry, captured at Gettysburg and housed in Block 8 of Johnson's Island, had two women in Baltimore to whom he sent jewelry and fans for sale (Wilds 2005). He arranged with them to sell his goods and then send him additional raw materials and/or cash.

15. He wrote on May 28 of papering his room. He did not mention where he would get the paper. Her suggestion of using old letters was either an endearing suggestion or sarcasm.

16. Her involvement with charitable causes was another indication of their social status in the community.

17. These two poems were transcribed from the book Wesley sent to Kate. They are found on pages 242–43 and 246–47 of that book. These and other poems of George McKnight's can be found in Frohman (1965:146–52).

18. Jewelry made of hard rubber was not exclusive to Johnson's Island. Here, Kate wishes to have Wesley find someone making chains from hard rubber.

19. Dental hygiene was only beginning to become a part of the daily routine. The use of toothbrushes was more prevalent among the educated and wealthy. At Johnson's Island there is evidence of some prisoners utilizing toothbrushes but certainly not all prisoners.

20. Kate was probably writing about the two pictures of Wesley he had sent her.

21. Wesley was writing about more prisoners arriving at Johnson's Island from the recent military actions.

22. Captain Francis Marion Imboden, 18th Virginia Cavalry, was captured on

June 5, 1864, and arrived at Johnson's Island on June 23, 1864. Lieutenant David Milton Ream, also of the 18th Virginia cavalry, was captured June 6 and arrived at Johnson's Island on June 22, 1864 (NAGRP 1865).

23. The Rebellonians performed minstrel shows within the prison compound. Shows were well attended by the prisoners and even some guards. This particular performance was on June 23, 1864.

24. The Old Capitol was by this time earning a reputation as one of the worst prisons in the Union system (Casstevens 2005:153).

25. Lieutenant William H. Waesche, 10th Virginia, captured at Gettysburg and arriving at Johnson's Island on July 20, 1863 (NAGRP 1865).

26. Engraving typically cost $.05 per letter.

27. *In hoc signo vinces.*

28. This was one of the letters in which Wesley discussed at greatest length the jewelry he was sending. The next chapter provides greater detail on how these items were crafted.

29. This was probably Annadale, Virginia, southwest of Alexandria.

30. Although they experienced periods of few letters, both continually thought they were being intentionally slighted. When one thinks of how little they could control the movement of information, it was no wonder they got frustrated.

31. "Pro" meant provost marshal.

Chapter 6. Hard Rubber and Hard Times (September 19, 1864–March 12, 1865)

1. Restrictions at this time included only one letter-sized page no more than twenty-eight lines long. This regulation had gone into effect in July 1862 (ORA, ser. 2, 4:153).

2. Lieutenant Colonel Edward A. Scovill, of the 128th OVI, was very fair to the prisoners at Johnson's Island and received much admiration from them. The Western Reserve Historical Society in Cleveland, Ohio, has a collection of letters from prisoners written to Scovill that reflect his kindness to them.

3. Wesley meant Union officials would not allow what he wished for to get through and not that Kate would never get around to sending things.

4. In early October 1864 Major Henry Eversman was telling his fiancée he had been selecting the sick prisoners for exchange (Eversman 1865, letter of October 2, 1864).

5. Kate had mastered the art of packing information into a very short letter. She touched on many topics and covered many things that affected Wesley.

6. She was talking about kissing Lillie and being unable to kiss herself.

7. "Pone" meant fried cornbread made without milk or eggs.

8. There is no one by this name listed as a prisoner on Johnson's Island.

9. Prisoners with money fared much better than those without, especially during harsh periods. Wesley was fortunate to have relatives who continued to send him money, which he drew upon for his needs.

10. Captain George L. Shell, 88th Pennsylvania, was confined at the Danville Prison, Virginia, which consisted of six tobacco warehouses adapted for the purpose. Conditions at Danville were crowded and dirty and provisions were slight. Overcrowding, malnutrition, and disease resulted in more than thirteen hundred deaths between 1863 and 1865 (Casstevens 2005:255–62).

11. Lillie's ring bore an M because her full name was Mary Louise Makely.

12. Lieutenant Elisha M. Stone, 7th Virginia Infantry, was captured at Gettysburg on July 3, 1863, and imprisoned at Johnson's Island on July 20, 1863. I wondered since Wesley was sending boxes from these individuals, and Knicely was one of his roommates, if possibly Lieutenant Stone was also one of his roommates.

13. Colonel Charles W. Hill was the commander at Johnson's Island.

14. The practice at the time was to send provisions like those in Kate's box to the prison hospital if there was no permission granted to the prisoner to whom the package was addressed. One can only assume this was the outcome for her box, but no official records were kept.

15. Wesley notes in his letter of December 15 Lillie's dilemma over the items being a Christmas gift or a present. Kate's letter of November 24, which was not part of the collection, apparently mentioned it, as did this one of December 9. It was not unusual for both of them to repeat requests in letters over the course of a week or two, never knowing which letters would make it through.

16. Lieutenant Jacob B. Rosenberger, Company D, 18th Virginia Cavalry, was captured with Wesley on July 9, 1863.

17. It is difficult to understand completely what upset Wesley most here; he had become disillusioned with the Confederate government and its handling of exchanges.

18. This is Lieutenant William Waesche, a prisoner making hard rubber jewelry pieces for Wesley. The reference was to the fifty dollars Kate told Wesley Jack had sent to the person of his asking (letter of January 17, 1865).

19. To give parole meant you would not rejoin your unit to fight, nor travel to certain locations, nor lend support to the enemy (Hesseltine 1962).

20. Lieutenant Rosenberger was sent to Point Lookout, where he was finally released on June 12, 1865.

Chapter 7. Going Home (March 21–April 29, 1865)

1. Wesley received this letter and the next prior to leaving Johnson's Island.

2. Captain Francis Imboden was released from Johnson's Island after taking the Oath of Allegiance on June 15, 1865.

3. Fort McHenry is in Baltimore and was Wesley's first stop.

4. When Lee surrendered to Grant, Confederates under Lee were paroled until they could be officially exchanged. The men who were paroled ended up having to take the Oath of Allegiance or face imprisonment.

Bibliography

Allen, Littlebury W. 1863–64. Diary Kept While a Prisoner: Nov. 1864–Mar. 1864. Original in Brock Collection, Huntington Library, San Marino, California.

Anonymous. 1863. "Moseby's Guerrillas." *Harper's Weekly*, September 5, 1863: 567.

———. N.d. "Soldiers Names and Records of Union and Confederate Troops." National Park Service: Civil War Soldiers and Sailors System. http://www.civilwar.nps.gov/cwss/soldiers.cfm (accessed September 27, 2010).

Beisaw, April M., and James G. Gibb, eds. 2009. *The Archaeology of Institutional Life*. Tuscaloosa: University of Alabama Press.

Boatner, Mark Mayo III. 1987. The *Civil War Dictionary: Revised Edition*. New York: David McKay Company.

Brown, M. G. 1998. "Prisoner of War Parole: Ancient Concept, Modern Utility." *Military Law Review* 156: 200–23.

Bukstel, Lee H., and Peter R. Kilmann. 1980. "Psychological Effects of Imprisonment on Confined Individuals." *Psychological Bulletin* 88(2): 469–93.

Bush, David R. 1992. "The Unknown Soldier: A Lost Confederate Ring Sheds New Light on Life in a Yankee Prison." *Gamut* 36 (June). Cleveland State University publication.

———. 2000. "Interpreting the Latrines of the Johnson's Island Civil War Military Prison." *Historical Archaeology* 34(1): 62–78.

———. 2007. "Understanding the Medical Treatment of Prisoners at the Johnson's Island Civil War Military Prison." Paper presented at the Annual Conference of the Society for Historic Archaeology.

———. 2009. "Maintaining or Mixing Southern Culture in a Northern Prison: Johnson's Island Military Prison." In *The Archaeology of Institutional Life*, ed. April M. Beisaw and James Gibb, 153–71. Tuscaloosa, Alabama: University of Alabama Press.

Casella, Eleanor Colin. 2007. *The Archaeology of Institutional Confinement*. Gainesville: University Press of Florida.

Casstevens, Frances H. 2005. *Out of the Mouth of Hell: Civil War Prisons and Escapes*. Jefferson, N.C.: McFarland and Company.

Clay, Ezekiel F. 1864. Family Collection of Ezekiel F. Clay's Prisoner Letters. Copy on file in the Collections of the Friends and Descendants of Johnson's Island Civil War Prison, Center for Historic and Military Archaeology, Heidelberg University, Tiffin, Ohio.

Crow, Mattie Lou Teague. 1977. *The Diary of a Confederate Soldier: John Washington Inzer 1834–1928*. Privately published.

Delauter, Roger U. 1985. *18th Virginia Cavalry*. Lynchburg, Va.: H. E. Howard.

Dietz, August. 1929. *The Postal Service of the Confederate States of America*. Richmond, Va.: Press of the Dietz Printing Company.

Doyle, Robert C. 1994. *Voices from Captivity: Interpreting the American POW Narrative*. Lawrence: University Press of Kansas.

Durkin, Joseph T., ed. 2005. *John Dooley, Confederate Soldier: His War Journal*. Alabama: University of Alabama Press.

Eversman, Henry R. 1865. Letters to his Fiance, 1864–1865. Unpublished, owned by Engbring Family. Copy on file in the Collections of the Friends and Descendants of Johnson's Island Civil War Prison, Center for Historic and Military Archaeology, Heidelberg University, Tiffin, Ohio.

Fike, Richard E. 1987. *The Bottle Book: A Comprehensive Guide to Historic, Embossed Medicine Bottles*. Salt Lake City: Gibbs M. Smith, Peregrine Smith Books.

Fogarty, G. P. 2005. "Guantanamo Bay: Undermining the Global War on Terror." Thesis, U.S. Army War College, Carlisle Barracks, Pennsylvania.

Foucault, Michel. 1977. *Discipline and Punish: The Birth of the Prison*. New York: Vintage Books.

Frohman, Charles E. 1965. *Rebels on Lake Erie*. Columbus: Ohio Historical Society.

Gebhardt, M. J. 2005. *The Road to Abu Ghraib: U.S. Army Detainee Doctrine and Experience*. Fort Leavenworth: Combat Studies Institute Press.

Gowen, William B. 1865. Diary of Lieutenant W. B. Gowen, C.S.A., 1863–1865. Copied by permission of Lister Gowen, grandson of Lieutenant Gowen. Original in Texas State Library, Austin.

Gray, Michael P. 2001. *The Business of Captivity: Elmira and Its Civil War Prison*. Kent, Ohio: Kent State University Press.

Guy, John H. 1862. Diary, 1862—April 5–September 17. Papers of John Henry Guy, 1833–1890. Virginia Historical Society, Richmond.

Hesseltine, William B. 1930. *Civil War Prisons: A Study in War Psychology*. Columbus: Ohio State University Press.

———. 1962. *Civil War Prisons*. Kent, Ohio: Kent State University Press.

Kovel, Ralph M., and Terry H. Kovel. 1986. *Kovel's New Dictionary of Marks*. New York: Crown Publishers.

Lessem, Harold I., and George C. Mackenzie. 1954. *Fort McHenry National Monument and Historic Shrine, Maryland*. Historical Handbook Series no. 5. Washington, D. C.: National Park Service.

Lindsey, Bill. 2010. Historic Glass Bottle Identification and Information website, housed by Society for Historical Archaeology. http://www.sha.org/bottle/Index.html.

Makely Family Papers. 1863–65. 1859–1865 Personal papers collection, Accession 27034, 25829. The Library of Virginia, Richmond.

Meissner, Francis Taylor, and Charles William Meissner, eds. 2005. *I'd Rather Lose a Limb & be Free: The Johnson's Island Experiences of John Taylor, 7th SC Cavalry*. Seaford, Va.: Privately published.

Murphy, James. 1864. Letter to Major Scovill, August 23, 1864. Scovill Papers, Western Reserve Historical Society, Cleveland, Ohio.

Murphy, Virgil S. 1865. Diary of Virgil S. Murphy: November 1864–February 1865.Original in Southern Historical Collection, Wilson Library, University of North Carolina at Chapel Hill.

National Archives, General Registry of Prisoners (NAGRP). 1865. General Registry of Prisoners (GRP), Johnson's Island 1862–1865. National Archives, Washington, D.C.

Official Records, Armies (ORA). 1880–1901. *The War of the Rebellion: A Compilation of the Official Records of the Union and Confederate Armies.* Series 2, vols. 2–8. Washington, D.C.

Patterson, Edmund B., and John G. Barrett, eds. 1966. *Yankee Rebel: The Civil War Journal of Edmund DeWitt Patterson.* Chapel Hill: University of North Carolina Press.

Ready, Moses C. 1864. Letters from Moses C. Ready to Wife Ellen. Family-provided copies in Collections of the Friends and Descendants of Johnson's Island Civil War Prison, Center for Historic and Military Archaeology, Heidelberg University, Tiffin, Ohio.

Reece, John H. 1865. Diary of Captain John H. Reece, 1st CSA GA Infantry. Collections of the Friends and Descendants of Johnson's Island Civil War Prison, Center for Historic and Military Archaeology, Heidelberg University, Tiffin, Ohio.

Rodgers, Bradley A. 1985. "The Iron Sentinel: U.S.S. Michigan, 1844–1949." Master's thesis, Department of History, East Carolina University, Greenville, N.C.

Russell, Mike. 1988. The *Collector's Guide to Civil War Period Bottles and Jars.*: Arlington, Va.: Russell Publications.

Smith, Robert M. 1863–65. Personal Collection of Smith's Activities conducted at Johnson's Island. Robert M. Smith Collection, Center for Historic and Military Archaeology, Heidelberg University, Tiffin, Ohio.

———. 1864. Robert M. Smith, 1864 Diary. Robert M. Smith Collection, Center for Historic and Military Archaeology, Heidelberg University, Tiffin, Ohio.

Stakes, Major E. T. 1864. Diary of Major E. T. Stakes, Johnson's Island, Ohio. Family Collection. Copy on file in the Johnson's Island Collections, Center for Historic and Military Archaeology, Heidelberg University, Tiffin, Ohio.

Steedman, Isaiah George Washington. 1866. A Medical History of the United States Military Prison on Johnson's Island, Lake Erie. Transcribed by David R. Bush. Manuscript on file at Hill Memorial Library, Louisiana State University, Baton Rouge, Louisiana.

Stockdale, Patricia Ann. 2010. *Diary of a Confederate: Johnson's Island.* Riverside: Americausa Publishing.

Swadley, Alan Franklin. 1864. Letter dated September 25, 1864 to George Swadley (brother), Denver City, Colorado Territory. Original in Collections of the Friends and Descendants of Johnson's Island Civil War Prison, Tiffin, Ohio.

Tucker, G. A., 1990. "Effects of Organizational Structure on American Enemy Prisoner of War Operations." Thesis, U.S. Army Command and General Staff College, Fort Leavenworth.

Van der Elst, Dirk. 1999. *Culture as Given, Culture as Choice*. Prospect Heights, Ill.: Waveland Press.

Walske, Steven C., and Scott R. Trepel. 2008. *Special Mail Routes of the American Civil War: A Guide to Across-the-Lines Postal History*. Confederate Stamp Alliance.

Wentworth, James H. 1990. "Letters, July 2, 1863 to June 23, 1865." *United Daughters of the Confederacy Magazine*, 53(1): 22–28.

Wilds, Ellen Sheffield. 2005. *Far from Home: The Diary of Lt. William H. Peel 1863–1865*. Carrollton, Miss.: Pioneer Publishing Company.

Woshner, Mike. 1999. *India-Rubber and Gutta-Percha in the Civil War Era*. Alexandria, Va.: O'Donnell Publications.

Index

Danville, Va., 200

Danville Prison, 160, 165, 248n10

Davis, Jefferson, 34, 43, 244n28

Delaware City, 221

Delaware River, 221

DeMoss, William E., *71*

Denelt, Dr., 104

Denver City, Colo., 133, 134

Dix-Hill cartel, 32

Dulaney, Col., 98, 117, 118, 145, 152

Elmira Prison, 228–29

Entarsel, Mary, 43

Entwisel, Mrs., 69, 81, 85, 87

Ervin, William, 22

Escapes and escape attempts: guards' reactions to rumors of, 84, 112; methods of, 33–34, 51, 119, 130, 175, 230–31; omission of, from Wesley Makely's letters, 143; as option for prisoners, 2, 16, 33, 159, 207, 225; prevalence of, 34; prisoners killed during, 33, 175; successful, 34, 51, 243n20; *USS Michigan* and, 84, 112, 130

Eversman, Henry: correspondence of, 134, 142, 185–86, 188, 211, 247n4; and gifts from prisoners, 142; and prisoner exchanges, 188, 195, 247n4; and prisoners' packages, 141–42, 148, 176; and prisoner transfers, 112; responsibilities of, 112, *141–42*, 185; and Thanksgiving 1864, 163–64; on tornado at Johnson's Island, 134

Exchanges of prisoners-of-war: agreements for, 23–24, 32, 33, 41; Confederacy and, 2, 23, 32, 41–43, 179, 188, 244n32; and contraband mail, 19; Fort McHenry as transfer point for, 211; general, 184, 189, 198; and Lee's surrender, 248n4; likelihood of, 24, 32, 33, 242n4; and military rank, 4, 24, 32, 33, 145; numbers of, 2, 41, 145,

187, 189, 195, 198, 199, 202, 211; and parole, 31, 32, 179; from Point Lookout, 83, 245n9; and prisoners' borrowing money for, 214; and prisoners' health, 60, 142, 150, 195, 247n4; resumption of, 196, 199; route traveled after, 211; special, 33, 145, 160, 179, 183, 184, 189, 195, 200; suspension of, 24, 32, 42–43, 233, 244n32; timing of, 4, 23, 24, 31, 32; Union and, 2, 23, 32, 33, 41–43, 179, 243n11, 243n18, 244n32; and Union Oath of Allegiance, 35, 219, 221, 243n12, 248n4; during War of 1812, 32. *See also* Makely, Wesley, exchange or parole

Fairal, Mr., 135

Fairal, Mrs., 135

Fairar, Mr., 135

Fairfax County, Va., 117

Fast days, 57, 244n28

Fauquier County, Va., 243n22, 245n9

Fogarty, G. P., 236

Foods and beverages: apple butter, 141; apple cider, 141; apples, 45, 141; bacon, 25; beans, 155; beef, 25, 45, 60, 149, 155, 167, 181; beets, 25; bologna, 45; bread, 25, 149, 155, 181; butter, 25, 45; cabbage, 25; cheese, 25, 45; chicory coffee, 25; coffee, 152; contraband, 39, 49; cornbread, 247n7; cornmeal, 45; cornmeal pudding, 182; costs of, 62; crackers, 25, 45; eggs, 25; farina, 243n13; fish, 45, 62, 155; fruit, dried, 25, 45; goose, 186; hominy, 25, 155; Irish potatoes, 25; lard, 45; lemons, 45; lettuce, 25; liquor, 39; liquors, 49, 103; meats, canned, 45; milk, 91; molasses, 25; mustard, 25, 45; nutmeg, 45; nuts, 45; onions, 25; pepper, 45; pickles, 25, 45; pies, 182; pork, 155; potatoes, 167; rabbits, 156; rats as, 146–47, 149, 152, 161, 167, 234, 237; regulations governing, 39;

rice, 25, 155; salt, 45; sauces, 25, 45; scarcity of in Alexandria, 57; snap beans, 25; squirrel, 146, 149; sugar, 25, 45; syrup, 45; turkeys, 185, 209; vegetables, 45; yeast, 45. *See also* Makely, Wesley, foods and beverages for; Prisoners-of-war, treatment of: reduced rations

Ford, Antonia, 50

Ford, William, 49–50, 168, 178

Fort Delaware: commander of, 233; construction and expansion of, 221; James W. Parker at, 58; John W. Pence at, 245n5; location of, 123, 221; Mathias Ginevan at, 243n19; paroled prisoners at, 220, 221; prisoner deaths at, 221; prisoner population at, 6; Thomas Benton Cochran at, 243n22; transfer of prisoners to, 106; Wesley Makely at, 35, 207, 220–21, 222; William B. Triplett at, 243n20

Fort Hill, 3, 9

Fort Johnson, 3, 9

Fort McHenry, 101, 207, 210–11, 248n3

Fortress Monroe, 18, 189

Fort Warren, 6, 172

Fosters (family), 157

Fosters, H., 131

Fountain, Mr., 26

Fountain, Mrs., 26, 65, 242n4

Fountain, Nehemiah: clothing for, 61, 65, 66; correspondence of, 29; items sent to, 114; mentioned by Kate Makely, 109; and money, 66, 78; mother of, 26, 29, 65, 242n4; release of, 65; and Wesley Makely, 29

Frazier, Gen., 152

Fred, Will, 57, 61

French, Mrs. M. E., 173

Frichell, Mr., 69

Friends and Descendants of Johnson's Island Civil War Prison, 30

Games: backgammon, 11; baseball, 60; cards, 11; chess, 11, 76, 91, 228, 229, 245n4; draughts, 11, 229; indoor and outdoor, 15

Gettysburg, battle of: aftermath, 17; Confederates captured at or near, 1, 2, 17, 21, 22, 33, 165, 193, 245n6, 246n14, 247n25, 248n12; Union soldiers wounded at, 214

Ginevan, C., 49

Ginevan, Mathias: capture of, 22, 243n19; exchange of, 243n19; and jewelry, 49, 52, 58, 66, 67, 83, 84

Ginevan, Mrs., 67

Goldsbourough, Mr., 23

Goochland [Va.] Light Artillery, 11

Goodyear, Nelson, 125, 170

Gould, Edward, 9

Gowen, William B., 229, 234

Grant, Ulysses S., 69, 219, 244n32, 248n4

Great Britain, 32

Green, L., 63

Gregg, Nathan, 13–14

Guantanamo Bay, 236, 237

Guards: 21st-century, 237; accusations of theft against, 245n34; and bribes, 19, 93; and escape attempts, 12, 33, 112; impact of job on, 10; and jewelry made by prisoners, 126, 246n14; lack of archaeological evidence for, 231; as mail inspectors, 12, 19, 225, 244n26; mentioned in inspection report, 167; and prisoner population, 42; and prisoners' purchases, 120; relationships of, with prisoners, 10; and shows put on by prisoners, 247n23; trade with, 231; training of, 237; treatment of prisoners by, 158

Gutta-percha, 125, 241n5. *See also* Rubber, hard

Guy, John H., 11, 228

stylishness of, 246n14; tools for making, *165*; value placed on, 168–69; watch chains and ornaments, 11, 127, 142. *See also* Crosses; Makely, Catherine Appich ("Kate"), and jewelry: rings

Johnson, Andrew, 218

Johnson, L. B., 15, 25, 36, 119, 244n33

Johnson's Island Civil War Military Prison: during 20th century, 3; 21st-century remains of, 3; class and status at, 228, 229; commanders of, 9–10, 41–42, 44, 47, 74, 147, 244n33, 248n13; conditions at, 145, 159, 167, 216; construction of, 8, 227; description of, 7–8; escapes from, 34, 51, 119, 175, 243n20; executions at, 27; expansion and renovation of, 8, 42, 77, 112, 119; guards at, 10, 243n15; historical evidence for, 6, 10, 11–12, 133, 229–30; illnesses and deaths at, 27; illustrations and photos of, *9, 76, 77, 80–81, 120*, 244n33; inspection report for, 167; lists of prisoners at, 76, 77, 79; location of, 7, 8, 243n15; mail schedule at, 15, 122, 242n6; prisoner population at, 7, 8, 9, 10, 11, 21, 32–33, 34, 40, 42, 60, 70, 72, 119, 150, 167, 225, 227–28, 246n21; prisoners' arrivals and intake at, 7–8, 10, 15–16, 22; purpose of, 3, 5–6, 8, 10, 226, 228; transportation to and from, 174–75, 181, 201, 202, 205; uniqueness of, 5–6, 10, 226; and *USS Michigan*, 130; and visitors and visitation policies, 28–29, 105; weather at, 67, 84, 92, 101, 132–33, 134, 142, 143, 144–45, 153, 155, 173, 174, 192, 193, 195, 201, 205, 233

—archaeological site: and Block 1 (housing block) excavations, 41, *162–63*; and Block 2 (housing block) excavations, *161*; and Block 4 (housing block) excavations, 12, 37, 126–27, 170, 171, 206, 226, 230; and Block 6 (hospital block)

excavations, 170, 171, 180–81, 230; and Block 8 (housing block) excavations, 230; and evidence of dental hygiene, 246n19; and evidence of deteriorating conditions for prisoners, 150, 231; and evidence of escape attempts, 230–31; and evidence of jewelry making, 5, 126–27, 206, 230; and evidence of prisoners' efforts to create balance of power, 231; integrity of, 230; and lack of evidence on guards, 231; and latrine excavations, 41, 52, 56, 150, *162–63*, 171, 180–81, 230–31; richness of, 3–4, 5, 6, 10, 11; scholarship on, 241n2; and site design, 241n2; and spatial-use studies, 230; and temporal study of prisoner experience, 230; unspecified location, 113. *See also* Artifacts, archaeological

—buildings and features at: barns, 9; barracks, 15, 119, 227; Block 1 (housing block), 1, 8, 15, 22, 81, 112, 138, 159, 221, 241n3, 242n8, 242n6; Block 2 (housing block), 8; Block 3 (housing block), 8; Block 4 (housing block), 8, 72, 190; Block 6 (hospital block), 8, 22, 81, 132–33, 243n14; Block 8 (housing block), 54, 59, 147, 246n14; Block 10 (housing block), 167; Block 11 (housing block), 226; Block 12 (housing block), 8; Block 13 (housing block), 8; condemned prisoner huts, 8, 81; dead house, 81; fences and walls, 8, 22, 81; forts, 9; guards' barracks, 9, 81; housing blocks, 80; illustrations of, 9, 80; kitchen, 167; latrines, 8, 62; lime kiln, 9; mess areas, 8, 9, 22, 77, 81, 119, 138, 167, 242n6; pest house, 8, 241n1; powder magazine, 9; prison yard, 112; stables, 9; stockade, 9; sutler's stand, 8, 81; Union officers' barracks, 9; water pumps, 81; wells, 8. *See also* Johnson's Island Civil War Military Prison, archaeological site

Johnston, Samuel, 219
Jones, Bill, 149
Jordan, J. B., 115

Kelly's Island, 193
Kennedy, John Pendleton, 192
Kingston, N.C., 52
Klubs, Duce. *See* McKnight, George
("Asa Hartz," "Duce Klubs")
Knicely, Henry C.: capture of, 22, 242n6;
correspondence of, *138*, 242n6; items
and money sent to, 35, 36, 136; items
sent by, 107, 173; messages for, 136;
messages from, 137; quarters of, 138;
and Wesley Makely, 137, 242n6

Lake Erie: bathing in, 104; Johnson's
Island in, 7, 8; transportation on, 7,
174, 201; *USS Michigan* on, 84, 130;
weather on, 7, 201, 205; western region of, 243n15; winters on, 144–45
Lee, James C., 196
Lee, Major, 186
Lee, Robert E., 69, 219, 248n4
Letters: censorship of, 19, 93, 122, 206,
225, 242n6, 244n26; contents of, 18,
19, 20, 21, 84, 126, 199, 225, 243n14;
contraband, 19, 69, 129, 143, 151; erratic delivery of, 198, 199; as historical
evidence, 2, 3–5, 12, 14, 15, 133, 225,
239; importance of, to prisoners and
families, 17, 18, 21, 51, 198–99, 241n1;
items stolen from, 245n34; length
of, 18, 19, 39, 40, 49, 92, 93, 129–30,
131, 135, 151, 192–93, 247n1; materials required for writing, 50; numbers
of, 40, 122, 130, 151, 166, 174, 193;
regulations governing, 96–97; seal-
ing of, 55, 244n26; sending of, from
Union to Confederacy, 18–19; stamps
for, 18, 44, 245n34; timeliness of, 18,
19–20, 95, 116, 119, 120, 167, 247n30;

transcription of, 14–15; and writers'
social status, 70. *See also* Packages
Lewis, Levin M., 229
Libby prison, 154
Library of Virginia, 88, 111, 144, 223
Life of Mahomet (Irving), 192
Lincoln, Abraham: and 1864 presidential
election, 154, 157; and 1865 inaugura-
tion, 202; assassination of, 208, 218,
219; and prisoners-of-war policies, 235,
237
Longport, England, 180, 181
Loring, General, 98
Lunettes, 3, 241n2

Makely, Albert: food sent by, 156, 185,
209; health of, 52; identification of,
243n21; and Mosby's Guerrillas, 57;
travels by, 83, 109, 136
Makely, Carrie G., 223
Makely, Catherine Appich ("Kate"): and
1864 presidential election, 152, 153, 157;
on 1865 presidential inauguration, 202;
activities of, 98, 199, 200; and April
fool's jokes, 52, 54; and black troops,
67, 93; children of, 1, 223; death of, 223;
and gaps in receiving letters, 247n30;
grave of, 223, 224; hair of, 156, 159;
health of, 24, 49, 60, 103, 104, 116, 121,
130, 135, 143, 187, 191, 216, 217, 224; and
husband's portraits and photos, 68–69,
70, 73, 74, 78, 81, 91, 191, 246n20; on
husband's wallpapering quarters, 97,
245n8, 246n15; and John Pence, 185;
and location of husband's imprisonment, 55, 106–7, 110–11; marriage of, 1;
nickname for, 23, 241n3; and permission to visit husband, 204–5, 208, 210,
213, 218; photos of, 60, 75, 78, 79, 83,
88, *89*; and servants, 111, 118; and status, 124, 246n16; travel by, 29, 49, 101,
103, 104, 105, 108–9, 112–13, 116, 117,

Prisoners-of-war: 21st-century, 6, 235;
blacks as, 33; and class and status, 72,
194, 228–29, 231; and communication
with outside world, 2, 4; Confederacy
and, 2, 3, 32, 226, 237; coping strategies
of, 119, 237; deaths of, 27, 65, 77, 241n2,
242n5, 248n10; definitions of, 235–36;
executions of, 27; health of, 27, 28, 33,
44, 54, 65, 112, 113, 167, 184, 237, 241n2,
242n5, 243n14; and Hostetter's Bitters,
49; and hygiene, 104, 246n19; items
permitted for purchase by, 44–45;
items sent to, 59, 143; and military
rank, 6, 70, 72, 227; and money, 22,
122, 214, 228, 237, 245n34, 247n9;
news sources for, 18; numbers of, 2, 8,
31–32, 44, 226, 237; options available
to, 2, 16, 33, 159, 207, 225; and return
home, 5; slang for, 242n1, 242n2; theft
from, 245n34; Union and, 2, 3, 8, 32,
226, 237; visits to, 28–29, 44; during
War of 1812, 32. *See also* Exchanges of
prisoners-of-war
—activities: acquiring luxury items, 231;
archaeological record of, 206, 231;
autograph collecting, 77; book lending,
194; book making and selling, 77; craft
industry, 15; domestic chores, 149, 228,
229; drawing and portraiture, 71, 72, 76,
77, 80, 228; escape tunnel construction,
34, 51, 230–31; fan making, 143; games
and gaming, 15, 79, 228, 229, 231; gar-
dening, 64, 112; jewelry making, 5, 11,
37–38, 72, 125, 126, 205–6, 228, 230, 231,
241n4, 242n7; language classes, 194;
law classes, 194; letter writing, 228;
medical classes, 194; money-making,
227, 228; photography, 228, 229; playing
April fool's jokes, 54; poetry writing,
72, 76, 77, 98, 228; prayer meetings, 15;
preaching, 229; purchasing jewelry, 231;
reading, 11, 194, 228; room remodeling,

228; shoemaking, 11; and status, 72,
194, 228, 229; tailoring, 11; theater and
music, 60, 72, 228, 247n23; walking, 54
—clothing and accessories: boots, 167;
caps, 45; coats, 74, 167; costs of, 94;
distribution of, 189; gloves, 61, 62, 65,
66, 78; handkerchiefs, 45; hats, 141;
jackets, 141, 144; Lt. Scovill on, 167;
provision of, 227; regulations governing, 39, 44–45, 234; seen in photos, 74;
sent via Wesley Makely, 79–80; shirts,
86, 141, 167; shoes, 35, 45, 86, 94, 141;
socks, 45, 86, 141, 142, 234; stockings,
167; suspenders, 45; underclothes, 45,
142, 167, 234; uniforms, 72, 74; vests, 74
—treatment of: during 21st century,
236, 237; archaeological record of, 231;
Confederacy and, 3, 5, 32, 33, 43–44,
233–34, 237, 246n12; guards' firing into
prison yard, 112; and hunger, 149, 152;
limitations placed on, 2, 31, 36, 44, 122,
143, 147, 152, 161, 227, 232; and military
rank, 227, 233, 234; and race, 33; reduced rations, 36, 44, 54, 122, 143, 146,
147, 155, 161, 167, 232, 234; scholarship
on, 236; Union and, 3, 5, 32, 43–44, 54,
93, 158, 161, 226, 227, 231, 233–34, 237,
246n12

Prisonization, 10–11, 226

Prisons, military, 44–45, 226–27, 230,
236–37, 248n10. *See also* Castle Thunder; Camp Chase; Elmira Prison; Fort
Delaware; Fort Warren; Johnson's
Island Civil War Military Prison; Libby
prison; Old Capitol; Point Lookout,
Md.

Rader, Lewis F., *190*
Railroads, 114, 153, 157, 200, 211
Rations. *See* Foods and beverages; Prisoners-of-war, treatment of: reduced
rations

Wendel, Mr., 135

Wentworth, James, 149, 211, 220, 221

Wessells, Henry Walton, 38, 176, 242n9

Western Reserve Historical Society, 247n2

Weybosset (ship), 220

Wheeling, Va. (now W. Va.), 58

White (Confederate officer), 63

Wickart, J., 66, 83

Williamsport, Md., 1

Williard, Major, 50

Windsor, Dave, 201

Windsor, Frederick Richard ("Capt. Winser," "Capt. Winsor," or "Doc"), 48, 51,
102, 201, 204, 243n16

Wisewell, Col., 186

Withers, John B., 91–92, 94, 245n9

Withers, Miss, 91

Withers, Mr., 89

Wood, L. M., 54

Woodbridge, Mrs., 186

Woods, Michael L., 16, 241n4

Woshner, Mike, 125, 241n5

Zanesville, Ohio, 211

David R. Bush is professor of anthropology at Heidelberg University and chair of the Friends and Descendants of Johnson's Island Civil War Prison. He has authored many articles and reports on the archaeology of Johnson's Island and Ohio Civil War sites.